Paul Dalziel • Caroline Saunders
Joe Saunders

# Wellbeing Economics

## The Capabilities Approach to Prosperity

Paul Dalziel
Agribusiness and Economics Research Unit
Lincoln University
Lincoln, New Zealand

Caroline Saunders
Agribusiness and Economics Research Unit
Lincoln University
Lincoln, New Zealand

Joe Saunders
Inter-Disciplinary Ethics Applied Centre
University of Leeds
Leeds, UK

https://doi.org/10.1007/978-3-319-93194-4

# Preface

Wellbeing is a word that has entered the vocabulary of almost everyone concerned with current economic and social trends, with good reason. Many families and communities struggle with issues of wellbeing (including various forms of depression, addiction and self-harm). Obtaining paid employment is no longer sufficient for a person to be confident of earning enough resources to support wellbeing; instead, the market economy is creating large numbers of jobs that pay less than the living wage, reinforced by new forms of work such as zero-hour contracts and the gig economy. Measures of objective and subjective wellbeing indicate that rising prosperity is not shared by everyone, and some groups of people are falling further behind.

Observations such as these have stimulated global attention to wellbeing. A major impulse was the 2009 *Report by the Commission on the Measurement of Economic Performance and Social Progress*, headed by Joseph Stiglitz, Amartya Sen and Jean-Paul Fitoussi. The report concluded as its main theme that "the time is ripe for our measurement system to shift emphasis from measuring economic production to measuring people's well-being". This shift is taking place around the world, including in the United Kingdom, where the Measuring National Wellbeing Programme was initiated in November 2010 by the then Prime Minister, David Cameron.

International organisations are implementing programmes to measure and promote wellbeing. Important examples include the wellbeing conceptual framework of the Organisation for Economic Co-operation and Development (OECD), the quality of life framework of the European Union, the indicators of global development maintained by the World Bank and the 2030 Agenda for Sustainable Development created by the United Nations.

Despite this renewed focus on wellbeing, the priority of regional and national decision-makers typically remains tied to economic growth. David Cameron, for example, emphasised this priority at the launch of the United Kingdom's Measuring National Wellbeing Programme: "Now, let me be very, very clear," he said, "growth is the essential foundation of all our aspirations." Even as scientific evidence shows with increasing clarity that current patterns of economic production are causing dangerous climate change, the political impetus for higher growth in gross domestic product remains unabated.

There have been counter voices. A courageous example was Tim Jackson's report for the UK Sustainable Development Commission, published in March 2009. Entitled *Prosperity without Growth*, it set out in a compelling manner how a genuine focus on wellbeing will require a different approach to economics.

This book responds to Jackson's challenge. It does not claim to develop a *new* economics; rather it seeks to recover insights from the economics tradition on how persons can create wellbeing through personal effort and through collaboration with others at different levels of choice-making. Thus, the reader will find the text is peppered with references to scholars recognised as giants in the field, from Adam Smith writing in the eighteenth century to recent recipients of the Nobel Prize in Economics. We draw on key elements in their work, supplemented by the published findings of other researchers, to create a synthesis that we call *the wellbeing economics framework*.

The framework is developed in this book as a series of 24 propositions, beginning with the proposition that the primary purpose of economics is to contribute to enhanced wellbeing of persons. Subsequent analysis then explains how this purpose can be achieved. Public policy is important in this analysis, but it is not the sole, or even the first, focus of the book. Instead, the framework recognises that wellbeing is supported by capabilities at several different levels of choice-making, with successive chapters focusing on persons, households and families, civil society, the market economy, local government, the Nation State and the global community.

We received considerable assistance as we prepared this book. Our thanks begin with colleagues, students, clients and partners of the Agribusiness and Economics Research Unit at Lincoln University and of the Inter-Disciplinary Ethics Applied Centre at the University of Leeds. The strong collegiality and engagement at both institutes contributed to the development of our ideas and analysis expressed in this book.

This book builds on an earlier text on wellbeing economics, published for a general audience in New Zealand by Bridget Williams Books. The new book goes well beyond that text, but we remain grateful to Bridget Williams and to Tom Rennie for supporting our initial efforts to synthesise a wellbeing economics framework.

In April 2016, we were approached by Laura Pacey at Palgrave Macmillan. Laura introduced us to the *Wellbeing in Politics and Policy* series, edited by Ian Bache, Karen Scott and Paul Allin, and invited us to submit a formal proposal for the series. Our plans for this book were further developed after two insightful reviews by anonymous referees. We are grateful to Laura, to the two referees and to the three editors, for their support for this project.

Parts of the book were written while Paul Dalziel was a Visitor at the Leeds University Business School and at the Victoria University of Wellington School of Government. We are grateful to Giuseppe Fontana and to Girol Karacaoglu for their hospitality in arranging these visits. We also gratefully acknowledge insightful comments from participants in seminars Paul presented during both visits, as well as from participants in conference sessions hosted by the Regional Studies Association, the Australia and New Zealand Regional Science Association International and the New Zealand Association of Economists.

Paul Dalziel enjoyed an opportunity to talk about the book with Tim Jackson, during the latter's visit to New Zealand as the 2016 Hillary Laureate. This preface has already acknowledged the importance of Jackson's book *Prosperity without Growth* for our research; all three authors are grateful to him for his encouragement of this project.

Early drafts of the manuscript for the book were read by Paul Allin, Allan Brent, Arthur Grimes and Karen Scott, each of whom provided written feedback. We are grateful to all four readers for their generosity, their clarity and their insightfulness, which greatly improved the final analysis and presentation. Of course, responsibility for the final text lies with us.

Finally, we thank the team at Palgrave Macmillan for translating our manuscript into its published form. We particularly thank Laura Pacey and Clara Heathcock, who worked hard to produce the book to Palgrave Macmillan's high standards.

Lincoln, New Zealand — Paul Dalziel
Lincoln, New Zealand — Caroline Saunders
Leeds, UK — Joe Saunders
April 2018

# Contents

# About the Authors

**Paul Dalziel** has been Professor of Economics at Lincoln University since 2002. His research concentrates on regional and national economic policies, particularly the way in which they affect the wellbeing of persons. He has served on the Council of the Regional Science Association International, 2011–2013, and is Executive Officer of its Australia and New Zealand branch. He is Ambassador in New Zealand for the Regional Studies Association.

**Caroline Saunders** has been Director of the Agribusiness and Economics Research Unit at Lincoln University since 2002. Her research focuses on sustainable wellbeing. She received the NZIER Economics Award in 2007 and was made an Officer of the New Zealand Order of Merit in 2009 for contributions to agricultural research. She is the 2019–2020 President of the Agricultural Economic Society.

**Joe Saunders** was a teaching fellow in the Inter-Disciplinary Ethics Applied Centre at the University of Leeds during the writing of this book, and is now Assistant Professor in Post-Kantian Philosophy at the University of Durham. In 2015, he was awarded the Robert Papazian Annual Essay Prize on Themes from Ethics and Political Philosophy.

# List of Figures

# List of Tables

# 1

# From Economic Growth to Wellbeing Economics

**Abstract** The primary purpose of economics is to contribute to enhanced wellbeing of persons. Economists have often assumed this is best achieved through high economic growth. Nevertheless, experience shows that the pursuit of growth for its own sake can result in policies that harm the wellbeing of large numbers of people. Threats of global climate change, as well as other environmental and social damage caused by current patterns of economic growth, intensify this concern. This first chapter argues for a new framework—wellbeing economics—to guide private and public sector efforts for expanding the capabilities of persons to lead the kinds of lives they value and have reason to value. The wellbeing economics framework focuses on seven types of capital investment at seven levels of human choice. This typology provides the structure for the book's remaining chapters.

**Keywords** Wellbeing • Austerity • Economic growth • Climate change • Capabilities

On 25 November 2010, then Prime Minister David Cameron launched the United Kingdom's Measuring National Wellbeing Programme: "From April next year," he said, "we'll start measuring our progress as a country, not just by


P. Dalziel et al., *Wellbeing Economics*, Wellbeing in Politics and Policy,
https://doi.org/10.1007/978-3-319-93194-4_1

how our economy is growing, but by how our lives are improving; not just by our standard of living, but by our quality of life" (Cameron 2010, par. 1; see Allin and Hand 2017, for an explanation of the programme and its background). That initiative reflected a wider global trend. Six years earlier, the Australian Treasury had published a wellbeing framework for analysis and policy advice (Treasury 2004; Gorecki and Kelly 2012). In 2008, French President Nicholas Sarkozy had set up the Commission on the Measurement of Economic Performance and Social Progress, headed by Joseph Stiglitz, Amartya Sen and Jean Paul Fitoussi. The unifying theme of its report was: "the time is ripe for our measurement system to shift emphasis from measuring economic production to measuring people's well-being" (Stiglitz et al. 2009, p. 12). In 2010, Italy similarly launched BES (*benessere equo e sostenibile*), involving multi-dimensional measures of equitable and sustainable wellbeing (CNEL and ISTAT 2010).

At the supranational level, the Organisation for Economic Co-operation and Development has created a wellbeing framework with three pillars: quality of life, material living conditions and sustainability (OECD 2011, 2013, 2015, 2017a). The statistical system of the European Union similarly offers a quality of life framework organised into eight themes of objective wellbeing indicators plus a ninth theme for subjective or self-evaluated measures (Eurostat 2015). The World Bank (2016) has compiled 1300 data series as indicators of global development and the quality of people's lives in more than 200 countries. The 2030 Agenda for Sustainable Development includes a vision of a world where physical, mental and social wellbeing are assured (United Nations 2015, par. 7).

These developments are consistent with a long tradition in economics that aims to promote the wellbeing of people. Consider, for example, the critique of mercantilism in Adam Smith's *Wealth of Nations*, the book that founded modern economics (Smith 1776, Volume 2, p. 179):

> Consumption is the sole end and purpose of all production; and the interest of the producer ought to be attended to, only so far as it may be necessary for promoting that of the consumer. The maxim is so perfectly self-evident, that it would be absurd to attempt to prove it. But in the mercantile system the interest of the consumer is almost constantly sacrificed to that of the producer; and it seems to consider production, and not consumption, as the ultimate end and object of all industry and commerce.

Another prominent example was the Cambridge professor, Alfred Marshall, who removed economics from the Moral Sciences and History Tripos to make it an independent discipline (Groenewegen 1995, Chap. 15). As quoted by Keynes

(1924, p. 319), Marshall chose economics as his lifetime study because he wanted to address systematic causes of poverty:

> "From Metaphysics I went to Ethics, and thought that the justification of the existing condition of society was not easy. A friend, who had read a great deal of what are now called the Moral Sciences, constantly said: 'Ah! if you understood Political Economy you would not say that.' So I read Mill's Political Economy and got much excited about it. I had doubts as to the propriety of inequalities of opportunity, rather than of material comfort. Then, in my vacations I visited the poorest quarters of several cities and walked through one street after another, looking at the faces of the poorest people. Next, I resolved to make as thorough a study as I could of Political Economy."

Other examples could be provided, but the point is made: economists have long understood that the primary purpose of the discipline is to contribute to enhanced wellbeing of persons.[1] The wellbeing economics framework is founded on this understanding, expressed as the first of 24 propositions set out in this book to describe key points in the framework (the propositions can be read together in the first section of Chap. 9):

**Proposition 1** The primary purpose of economics is to contribute to enhanced wellbeing of persons.

In the same year that the Measuring National Wellbeing Programme was launched, the British government imposed austerity measures that included cutbacks in annual social welfare spending of £11 billion, reductions in other areas of government spending of £21 billion, an increase in value added tax and a two-year freeze in public sector pay for those earning more than £21,000 per annum (HM Treasury 2010). These austerity measures were expanded in subsequent years. The 2014 Budget included a welfare cap to limit total welfare spending, for example, while the 2015 Budget announced further reductions in government spending of £30 billion over 2 years (HM Treasury 2014, 2015).

There was a sharp rise in the number of charity food banks after these policies, among other indicators of increased social distress (Jackson 2015; Loopstra et al. 2015; O'Hara 2015, Chap. 1; Purdam et al. 2015; Garthwaite 2016). This leads to an obvious question: if the primary purpose of economics is to contribute to enhanced wellbeing of persons, and if the government's stated intention is to measure progress by how our lives are improving, how can policymakers justify austerity and other economic policies that result in such high levels of increased suffering?

## Wellbeing and Economic Growth

Economists typically answer this question in three steps. First, it is argued that wellbeing is enhanced when individuals can satisfy more of their personal preferences, perhaps because they can afford a wider range of choices (Dolan and Peasgood 2008; Hausman and McPherson 2009). Hence, wellbeing is improved if a policy allows some people to increase preference satisfaction without anyone facing reduced choices (Pareto 1906; Hicks 1939). Such a policy is said to increase Pareto efficiency.

This seldom occurs in practice, since policies typically create losers as well as winners. The analysis may suggest, however, that the winners could fully compensate the losers and still be better off. Even if the compensation is not paid in practice, such a policy is likely to be considered reasonable. This is because wins and losses experienced by an individual from all policy changes over a lifetime, if randomly distributed, might be expected to produce an overall gain when all policy changes meet this criterion (Hicks 1941).

The second step argues that economic growth is a dominant example of what provides the general population with a greater range of choices and allows more preferences to be satisfied. A famous observation by Nobel laureate Robert Lucas illustrates the significance attributed to growth as a source of wellbeing. After noting that there is a large spread between the growth rates of countries, Lucas (1988, p. 5) commented:

> Is there some action a government of India could take that would lead the Indian economy to grow like Indonesia's or Egypt's? If so, *what*, exactly? If not, what is it about the 'nature of India' that makes it so? The consequences for human welfare involved in questions like these are simply staggering: Once one starts to think about them, it is hard to think about anything else.

Thus, although wellbeing may be the ultimate objective, policy priorities typically focus on achieving higher economic growth as the best means for expanding wellbeing in the long-term. Indeed, this was emphasised at the launch of the United Kingdom's Measuring National Wellbeing Programme, when the Prime Minister addressed concerns that it sidelined economic growth (Cameron 2010, par. 4, emphasis added):

> Now, let me be very, very clear: *growth is the essential foundation of all our aspirations*. Without a job that pays a decent wage, it is hard for people to look after their families in the way they want, whether that's taking the children on holiday or

> making your home a more comfortable place. Without money in your pocket it is difficult to do so many of the things we enjoy, from going out in the evening to shopping at the weekend. So, at this time I am absolutely clear that our most urgent priority is to get the economy moving, to create jobs, to spread opportunity for everyone.

The third step argues that economic growth requires specific policies to be implemented. The austerity measures, for example, were justified in precisely these terms (HM Treasury 2010, p. 1):

> The most urgent task facing this country is to implement an accelerated plan to reduce the deficit. Reducing the deficit is a necessary precondition for sustained economic growth.

Economists devote considerable effort to exploring how to foster economic growth (Jones and Vollrath 2013). A major advance was Robert Solow's (1956) *neoclassical growth model*, which demonstrated how countries tend to achieve higher levels of output per person if they have a higher rate of investment in physical capital such as factories, plant and machinery.[2] Solow's model also shows how output per person tends to grow more quickly with higher growth in labour productivity (that is, faster increases in the average value of output per hour of work, which indicates a country's rate of technological progress).

Important extensions have been made to the neoclassical growth model. Mankiw et al. (1992) demonstrated that education levels of the workforce are an important factor influencing labour productivity, while Knowles and Owen (1995) demonstrated the importance of good health. More profoundly, Romer (1986, 1990) incorporated the idea that technological progress is influenced by the amount of effort devoted to producing new knowledge. His insight led to a new class of *endogenous growth* models, which will be discussed in this book's Chap. 7.

Economists also explore the role of social institutions and norms in supporting economic growth (North 1987; Rodrik et al. 2004). In his Nobel Prize lecture, Douglass North (1994) pointed out that the neoclassical growth model does not apply in countries lacking the necessary institutions for markets to operate. An important example is that effective legal protections for property rights are essential for strong economic growth (La Porta et al. 2008; Xu 2011). Some studies emphasise social values such as trust (Fukuyama 1995; Quddus et al. 2000; McCloskey 2010), while others focus on good government and good governance (Krueger 1990; Kaufmann et al. 1999; Hulme et al. 2015) including strict requirements for macroeconomic stability (Fischer 1991; Fatás and Mihov 2013).

This research has created a consensus among economists about what constitutes good economic policy, represented for example by the contents of the *Going for Growth* report published annually by the OECD (2017b). Taking these arguments together, the promise is that orthodox economic policies will increase growth of per capita real gross domestic product (GDP), which will allow individuals to increase the range of their choices, which will promote wellbeing. This is the vision behind statements such as the one cited above from David Cameron that growth is the essential foundation of all our aspirations.

Experience shows, however, that economic growth cannot always be relied upon to improve wellbeing. Referring to Cameron's examples, it is possible to have economic growth *without* new jobs paying a decent wage, *without* people finding it easier to look after their families in the way they want and *without* opportunity for everyone. Indeed, a country can experience economic growth at the same time that large groups in the population find they are unable to maintain their material living standards.

## The Limits to Growth

The title of this section comes from a famous report prepared in the early 1970s by researchers at the Massachusetts Institute of Technology. Building on a tradition going back at least to Ricardo (1817, Chap. 2), the report examined interconnections between accelerating industrialisation, rapid population growth, widespread malnutrition, depletion of non-renewable resources and a deteriorating environment (Meadows et al. 1972). Its analysis of prevailing trends led the research team to conclude that "the limits to growth on this planet will be reached sometime within the next one hundred years" (idem, p. 23).[3]

Modern studies continue to find evidence that persistent production growth is inconsistent with finite resources (Meadows et al. 2005; Hall and Day 2009; Rockström et al. 2009a, b; Nørgård et al. 2010; Bardi 2011; Turner 2012; Jackson and Webster 2016). Not only does increasing material consumption put pressure on the planet's non-renewable resources, but also natural ecosystems have limited capacities to absorb higher pollution associated with economic growth, including accumulating greenhouse gas emissions. The Intergovernmental Panel on Climate Change makes the following key observation (IPCC 2015, p. 4, emphasis added):

> Anthropogenic greenhouse gas emissions have increased since the pre-industrial era, *driven largely by economic and population growth*, and are now higher than ever. This has led to atmospheric concentrations of carbon dioxide, methane and nitrous oxide that are unprecedented in at least the last 800,000 years. Their effects, together with those of other anthropogenic drivers, have been detected throughout the climate system and are extremely likely to have been the dominant cause of the observed warming since the mid-20th century.

The lesson from this research is that *how* economies grow is vital for wellbeing. Indeed, if current patterns of economic production continue, the planet's surface is likely to be in the order of 3° C to 5° C warmer by 2050, creating considerable risks such as damage to unique ecosystems and more frequent extreme weather events (IPCC 2015, p. 18). Thus, the claim that "growth is the essential foundation of all our aspirations" is false.

Tim Jackson (2009, 2017) argues that policy needs to consider prosperity without growth. He defines prosperity as an ability to flourish as human beings, which certainly involves material dimensions, but much more (Jackson 2017, p. 212):

> To do well is in part about the ability to give and receive love, to enjoy the respect of our peers, to contribute usefully to society, to have a sense of belonging and trust in the community, to help create the social world and find a credible place in it. In short, an important component of prosperity is the ability to participate meaningfully in the life of society.

Jackson therefore advocates policies that target flourishing directly, rather than aiming for economic growth as an intermediate step. Since flourishing depends on our natural environment, this must include respect for the planet's ecological limits. Current economic growth trajectories are imposing ecological costs on future generations that will threaten wellbeing on a global scale. Jackson therefore appeals for a new macroeconomics in which economic activity is constrained to stay within sustainable limits (idem, p. 160).[4]

These concerns are amplified by the way in which growth is currently measured; that is, as percentage increases in GDP. The rules for calculating GDP are set out in the United Nations System of National Accounts (United Nations 2009), which sets boundaries on what categories of economic activity are included in the measure. Certain forms of unpaid work are excluded, such as care for children by parents within their own households. Also excluded is most environmental damage caused by economic production.

An early critique of these rules was made by Marilyn Waring (1988).[5] As a member of the New Zealand Parliament between 1975 and 1984, Waring saw the results of policy being based on claims such as "growth is the essential foundation of all our aspirations", when growth is defined narrowly by GDP. Policies focus on activities included within the GDP boundaries, and so other dimensions of wellbeing, including the natural environment, are sacrificed in the pursuit of measured growth.

Herman Daly and John Cobb (1989) similarly argued that GDP cannot measure genuine economic progress. They created an *index of sustainable economic welfare* (ISEW) to include considerations such as distributional inequality, household production for own consumption and degraded natural environments. Daly and Cobb showed that the average growth in the ISEW for the United States is substantially below the growth rate of GDP (idem, p. 453). Similar conclusions have been reached for other countries using either the ISEW or variants such as the genuine progress indicator and the sustainable net benefit index.[6]

An important example of how a focus on GDP growth can overlook deteriorating trends in aspects of wellbeing, highlighted in Daly and Cobb's original analysis, is widening income inequality. This remains an urgent concern three decades later, with numerous recent studies presenting evidence on rising inequality and associated losses of wellbeing (Wilkinson and Pickett 2009; Stiglitz 2012; Piketty 2013; Atkinson 2015; Marmot 2015). This phenomenon is not visible to policy advisors if the dominant measure of policy success is growth in GDP.

In short, it is not reasonable to presume that GDP growth, regardless of the nature of that growth, will increase wellbeing. Indeed, certain patterns of growth can cause harm to wellbeing, and so economics must recover a deeper understanding of how wellbeing is enhanced.[7] A good starting point is the capabilities approach developed by Amartya Sen.

## Wellbeing and Capabilities

Consistent with the focus of economists on growth, Walt Rostow (1960) famously defined development as a process of countries moving through five stages of rising economic growth: (1) living in traditional society; (2) creating the pre-conditions for take-off; (3) achieving take-off; (4) driving to maturity; and (5) enjoying high mass consumption. Reacting to that theory, Amartya Sen offered an alternative understanding based on what people are able to do in their lives (Sen 1983, p. 754):

> Ultimately, the process of economic development has to be concerned with what people can or cannot do, e.g. whether they can live long, escape avoidable morbidity, be well nourished, be able to read and write and communicate, take part in literary and scientific pursuits, and so forth.

Sen's conceptualisation of development is known as the "capabilities approach" (Nussbaum 2000, 2011; Alkire 2002; Robeyns 2006; Schischka et al. 2008). The core idea is captured in the following short extract from Sen's influential book, *Development as Freedom* (Sen 1999a, p. 18):

> The analysis of development presented in this book treats the freedoms of individuals as the basic building blocks. Attention is thus paid particularly to the expansion of the 'capabilities' of persons to lead the kinds of lives they value – and have reason to value.

Note how Sen refers to *persons*, rather than *people* (which can indicate a mass of indistinguishable humans) or *individuals* (which can suggest an actor in isolation from all others). We follow that usage throughout this book, to convey that persons are simultaneously social beings and unique personalities. The capabilities approach is reflected in our second proposition.

**Proposition 2** Wellbeing can be enhanced by expanding the capabilities of persons to lead the kinds of lives they value, and have reason to value.

Presented originally in the context of development studies, this approach has been adopted in more general studies of wellbeing (Sen 1993; Clark 2005). Sen was a member of the Commission on the Measurement of Economic Performance and Social Progress (Stiglitz et al. 2009), where his research was highly influential. The capabilities approach was applied in the design of the Australian Treasury's wellbeing framework (Henry 2006, pp. 6–7) and the design of the New Zealand Treasury's higher living standards framework (Gleisner et al. 2011, pp. 11–13). Jackson (2009, pp. 43–47) recognises that Sen's approach resonates with his own vision of prosperity, emphasising that development of human capabilities must also respect ecological limits.

A feature of Sen's approach, reflected in his quote above, is that persons make their own judgements about what constitutes a valued kind of life, but judgements must be supported by reason. Thus, Sen does not identify wellbeing with satisfying individual preferences, or with the unreflective preferences of groups of individuals. Instead, his formulation highlights the value of contested and dynamic processes of communal reasoning, particularly in determining how public policy can contribute to enhanced wellbeing (see also Sen 1999b; White 2017, pp. 124–125).

Proposition 2 invites policies that aim to expand capabilities, rather than to increase economic growth for its own sake. This mirrors Adam Smith's point at the beginning of this chapter: it is not production that is important, but the wellbeing of consumers. The approach taken in this book is inspired by Solow's (1956) neoclassical growth model, but expanded to address a wider range of capabilities and wellbeing outcomes. Solow demonstrated that investment in physical capital can increase a country's material living standards. That result is consistent with Sen's theory, since construction of new assets such as buildings, machinery and roads can be conceptualised as expanding the capabilities of persons who use those assets.

Similarly, investment in other types of enduring assets—non-material as well as material—can improve wellbeing outcomes by expanding the capabilities of persons to lead valued lives. Each of these asset types can be described using "capital" as a metaphor (see, for example, Flora and Flora 2007; Arrow et al. 2012; IIRC 2013; Gleeson-White 2014). The wellbeing economics framework focuses on seven types of capital stock, listed in Table 1.1. Details will be explained in later chapters of the book, but are introduced briefly here.

Mincer (1958), Shultz (1960, 1961) and Becker (1962, 1964) coined the term "human capital" to describe participation in formal education, which has similar characteristics to investment in physical capital by requiring the sacrifice of current consumption to increase future income. Cultural capital refers to a

**Table 1.1** Types of capital in the wellbeing economics framework

| Capital | Examples of the Associated Capital Investment |
|---|---|
| Human | Developing personal skills through participation in education, through experience and through better health. |
| Cultural | Inheriting, practicing, transforming and passing on values from generation to generation. |
| Social | Strengthening diverse networks, voluntary organisations and bonds of trust within and between communities. |
| Economic | Constructing and owning enduring human-made physical and financial assets. |
| Natural | Conserving wilderness and managed natural areas to maintain or improve the environment's ecosystem services. |
| Knowledge | Researching and developing advances in technology and other intellectual property products. |
| Diplomatic | Cultivating institutions and norms that foster international collaboration for the common good. |

community's values and practices that are transformed and passed down from generation to generation (Bourdieu 1983; Throsby 1999). Social capital describes diverse networks, voluntary organisations and bonds of trust that exist within and between communities (Coleman 1986; Putnam 1995).

Economic capital encompasses the stock of physical capital and its ownership in the form of stocks, shares, debentures and other forms of financial capital (OECD 2015, pp. 129–137). Natural capital recognises that ecological environments are the setting for much human activity, which needs ongoing investment to be maintained (Helm 2015). Knowledge capital refers to technological discoveries and other forms of intellectual property, some of which may be recorded as assets in balance sheets (Nahapiet and Ghoshal 1998; Guthrie et al. 2012). Diplomatic capital is a term used in this book to describe organisations and norms needed for international collaboration to promote the global common good.

For each capital type in Table 1.1, the stock of capital provides flows of services important for *wellbeing*. Human capital provides the person who possesses it with skills that can be displayed in employment or other contributions to wellbeing. Cultural capital and social capital help give meaning to life and make social transactions easier. Economic capital increases labour productivity and offers financial returns to savers. Natural capital provides ecosystem services that are often irreplaceable for wellbeing. Drawing on knowledge capital allows people to do more with less, and the use of diplomatic capital helps the global community address some of the most pressing issues facing humanity.

A second dimension of the wellbeing economics framework recognises that choices affecting wellbeing are made at different levels of social interaction. Figure 1.1 provides a structure for considering these different scales. It shows levels of human choice that involve larger and larger numbers of people as the choices move outwards from the individual to the global community.

The diagram begins in the innermost oval with persons making choices about activities that contribute to the kind of life they value and have reason to value. Persons come together to form households and families, which gives rise to a second level of choices. Outside the home, people form community organisations to advance cultural, sporting, political, economic and other purposes; these organisations make up civil society. As market participants, people make choices as producers and as consumers of goods and services.

A household's place of residence typically has local government providing public services for the diverse individuals and communities living in that locality. The Nation State exercises authority on behalf of, but also over, citizens,

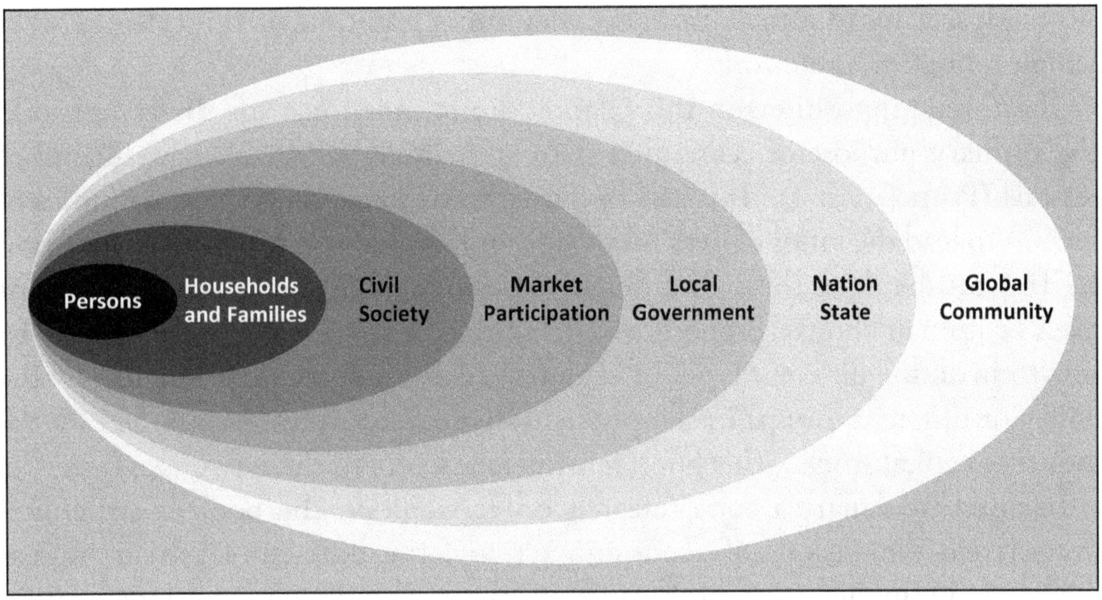


**Fig. 1.1** Levels of human choice in the wellbeing economics framework

producing potential tensions in how choices at the national policy level support or interfere with choices at other levels. Finally, some of the biggest issues affecting wellbeing (such as the threats of global climate change) require negotiated choices among international partners, including governmental and non-governmental organisations, acting globally.

A key task of wellbeing economics is to integrate the different levels of human choice represented in Fig. 1.1 with the different types of capital investment listed in Table 1.1. Investment in human capital, for example, may be made by an individual person, whereas growth in diplomatic capital requires global collaboration. The two dimensions of the framework are therefore brought together in the final proposition of this chapter.

**Proposition 3** The capabilities of persons can be expanded by different types of capital investment at different levels of human choices.

## Conclusion

Despite greater attention to measuring wellbeing, it is still common for the current wellbeing of some citizens to be sacrificed by policies intended to promote GDP growth. This practice ignores wider social issues important for wellbeing and is inconsistent with environmental limits to economic growth. Consequently, this book sets out to recover from the economics tradition what it calls the wellbeing economics framework.

The three propositions in this chapter are foundational for the framework. The primary purpose of economics is to contribute to enhanced wellbeing of persons (Proposition 1). This can be achieved by expanding the capabilities of persons to lead the kinds of lives they value and have reason to value (Proposition 2). This can be done through different types of capital investment at different levels of human choice (Proposition 3). Thus, wellbeing is affected not only by growth in all the different types of capital available in a country, but also by the ability of different groups in the population to access services provided by the country's capital stocks. This book returns repeatedly to these two issues.

Inspired by Amartya Sen's research on capabilities, the book is structured around two dimensions of economic activity: the different levels of human choice set out in Fig. 1.1; and the different types of capital investment set out in Table 1.1. Each of the following seven chapters focuses on one level of human choice and on one type of capital investment, guided by natural associations between these classifications.

Decisions about the number of years devoted to investing in human capital, for example, can be sensibly discussed in the context of persons making time-use choices; this is done in Chap. 2. Transmission of cultural capital across generations fits comfortably with choices made by persons living in families and households; this is addressed in Chap. 3. Social capital and the institutions of civil society are almost synonymous; see Chap. 4. A large literature on economic capital investment in the context of market participation is summarised in Chap. 5.

The book then turns to political institutions in the public sphere. Local government is typically required to maintain and enhance a locality's natural capital, considered in Chap. 6. There is considerable research on the role of a Nation State to support the development of intellectual property, which is explored in Chap. 7. Diplomatic capital is essential for cultivating collaboration by intergovernmental and non-governmental organisations in the global community; this topic is approached in Chap. 8.

In each case, the chapter draws insights from the economics literature to analyse how wellbeing can be enhanced, not just by public policy, but at all levels of human choice. Chapter 9 then integrates these different elements to introduce a wellbeing fabric for policy analysis. It demonstrates how wellbeing economics can contribute to expanding human capabilities for living the kinds of lives we value and have reason to value.

## Notes

1. This tradition continues: welfare economics is an established field, for example, and students majoring in economics are routinely required to demonstrate they can use mathematics to prove the Fundamental Theorems of Welfare Economics (Blaug 2007, p. 198).
2. Trevor Swan (1956) independently published a model of economic growth with similar results to Solow's more influential version.
3. There was an immediate reaction from economists, including from Solow (1974a, b) who argued this can be avoided by investment in physical capital to replace the depleted natural resources. Hartwick (1977) calculated the exact rate of physical capital investment that would allow sustainable growth. That response continues to be developed in research programmes on genuine savings and comprehensive wealth (World Bank 2011; Arrow et al. 2012; Hanley et al. 2015).
4. Macroeconomics deals with country-level outcomes such as economic growth. An interesting example of research on macroeconomics that respects ecological limits is Fontana and Sawyer (2016). An influential analysis of planetary boundaries can be found in Rockström et al. (2009a, b).
5. Recent reviews are provided by Bjørnholt and McKay (2014) and by Saunders and Dalziel (2017). Coyle (2014) presents a sympathetic account of GDP.
6. Lawn (2003) offers an overview of these measures.
7. This is recognised by others, of course. In the United Kingdom, mention should be made of initiatives such as the All-Party Parliamentary Group on Wellbeing Economics formed in March 2009 and legislation such as the Well-being of Future Generations (Wales) Act 2015.

## References

Alkire, Sabina. 2002. *Valuing Freedoms: Sen's Capability Approach and Poverty Reduction.* Oxford: Oxford University Press.

Allin, Paul, and David J. Hand. 2017. New Statistics for Old? – Measuring the Wellbeing of the UK. *Journal of Royal Statistical Society A* 180 (Part 1): 3–43.

Arrow, Kenneth J., Partha Dasgupta, Lawrence H. Goulder, Kevin J. Mumford, and Kirsten Oleson. 2012. Sustainability and the Measurement of Wealth. *Environment and Development Economics* 17 (3): 317–353.

Atkinson, Anthony B. 2015. *Inequality: What Can Be Done?* Cambridge, MA: Harvard University Press.

Bardi, Ugo. 2011. *The Limits to Growth Revisited.* New York: Springer.

Becker, Gary. 1962. Investment in Human Capital: A Theoretical Analysis. *Journal of Political Economy* 70 (5, Part 2): 9–49.

———. 1964. *Human Capital: A Theoretical and Empirical Analysis, with Special Reference to Education*. New York: Columbia University Press.

Bjørnholt, Margunn, and Ailsa McKay, eds. 2014. *Counting on Marilyn Waring: New Advances in Feminist Economics*. Bradford, Ontario: Demeter Press.

Blaug, Mark. 2007. The Fundamental Theorems of Modern Welfare Economics, Historically Contemplated. *History of Political Economy* 39 (2): 185–207.

Bourdieu, Pierre. 1983. Ökonomisches Kapital, Kulturelles Kapital, Soziales Kapital. In *Soziale Ungleichheiten* (Soziale Welt, Sonderheft 2), ed. Reinhard Kreckel, 183–198. Goettingen: Otto Schartz. Trans. Richard Nice and republished as The Forms of Capital in *Handbook of Theory and Research for the Sociology of Education*, ed. John C. Richardson, 241–258. Westport: Greenwood Publishing Group, 1986.

Cameron, Rt. Hon. David. 2010. PM Speech on Wellbeing. A transcript of a speech given by the Prime Minister on 25 November 2010. https://www.gov.uk/government/speeches/pm-speech-on-wellbeing.

Clark, David A. 2005. Sen's Capability Approach and the Many Spaces of Human Well-being. *Journal of Development Studies* 41 (8): 1339–1368.

CNEL and ISTAT. 2010. CNEL and ISTAT Measure Well-being: Set of Indicators to be Identified by 2011. Press Release. http://www.istat.it/en/archive/10128.

Coleman, James S. 1986. Social Capital in the Creation of Human Capital. *American Journal of Sociology* 94 (Supplement): S95–S120.

Coyle, Diane. 2014. *GDP: A Brief but Affectionate History*. Princeton and Oxford: Princeton University Press.

Daly, Herman E., and John B. Cobb Jr. 1989. *For the Common Good: Redirecting the Economic toward Community, the Environment, and a Sustainable Future*. Boston: Beacon Press.

Dolan, Paul, and Tessa Peasgood. 2008. Measuring Well-being for Public Policy: Preferences or Experiences? *Journal of Legal Studies* 37 (S2): S5–S31.

Eurostat. 2015. *Quality of Life: Facts and Figures*. Eurostat Statistical Books.

Fatás, Antonio, and Ilian Mihov. 2013. Policy Volatility, Institutions, and Economic Growth. *Review of Economics and Statistics* 95 (2): 362–376.

Fischer, Stanley. 1991. Growth, Macroeconomics, and Development. In *NBER Macroeconomics Annual*, ed. Olivier Jean Blanchard and Stanley Fischer, vol. 6, 329–379. Cambridge, MA: MIT Press.

Flora, Cornelia Butler, and Jan L. Flora. 2007. *Rural Communities: Legacy and Change*. 3rd ed. Boulder, CO: Westview Press.

Fontana, Giuseppe, and Malcolm Sawyer. 2016. Towards Post-Keynesian Ecological Economics. *Ecological Economics* 121: 186–195.

Fukuyama, Francis. 1995. *Trust: The Social Virtues and the Creation of Prosperity*. New York: Free Press.

Garthwaite, Kayleigh. 2016. *Hunger Pains: Life inside Foodbank Britain*. Bristol: Policy Press.

Gleeson-White, Jane. 2014. *Six Capital: The Revolution Capitalism Has to Have – Or Can Accountants Save the Planet*. Sydney: Allen & Unwin.
Gleisner, Ben, Mary Llewellyn-Fowler, and Fiona McAlister. 2011. Working Towards Higher Living Standards for New Zealanders. New Zealand Treasury Paper 11/02. Wellington: Treasury.
Gorecki, Stephanie, and James Kelly. 2012. Treasury's Wellbeing Framework. *Economic Roundup* 3: 27–64.
Groenewegen, Peter. 1995. *A Soaring Eagle: Alfred Marshall 1842–1924*. Cheltenham: Edward Elgar.
Guthrie, James, Federica Ricceri, and John Dumay. 2012. Reflections and Projections: A Decade of Intellectual Capital Accounting Research. *The British Accounting Review* 44 (2): 68–82.
Hall, Charles A.S., and John W. Day Jr. 2009. Revisiting the Limits to Growth After Peak Oil. *American Scientist* 97 (May–June): 230–237.
Hanley, Nick, Louis Dupuy, and Eoin McLaughlin. 2015. Genuine Savings and Sustainability. *Journal of Economic Surveys* 29 (4): 779–806.
Hartwick, John M. 1977. Intergenerational Equity and the Investing of Rents from Exhaustible Resources. *American Economic Review* 67 (5): 972–974.
Hausman, Daniel M., and Michael S. McPherson. 2009. Preference Satisfaction and Welfare Economics. *Economics and Philosophy* 25 (1): 1–25.
Helm, Dieter. 2015. *Natural Capital: Valuing the Planet*. New Haven and London: Yale University Press.
Henry, Ken. 2006. Wellbeing and Public Policy. Presentation to the Population Wellbeing Data Gaps Workshop, Australian Bureau of Statistics, Canberra, 8 June.
Hicks, John R. 1939. The Foundations of Welfare Economics. *Economic Journal* 49 (196): 696–712.
———. 1941. The Rehabilitation of Consumer' Surplus. *Review of Economic Studies* 8 (2): 108–116.
HM Treasury. 2010. *Budget 2010*. House of Commons document HC61. London: The Stationery Office.
———. 2014. *Budget 2014*. House of Commons document HC1104. London: The Stationery Office.
———. 2015. *Budget 2015*. House of Commons document HC1093. London: The Stationery Office.
Hulme, David, Antonio Savoia, and Kunal Sen. 2015. Governance as a Global Development Goal? Setting, Measuring and Monitoring the Post-2015 Development Agenda. *Global Policy* 6 (2): 85–96.
IIRC. 2013. *The International <IR> Framework*. London: The International Integrated Reporting Council.
IPCC. 2015. *Climate Change 2014: Synthesis Report*. Contribution of Working Groups I, II and III to the Fifth Assessment Report of the Intergovernmental Panel on Climate Change. Geneva: Intergovernmental Panel on Climate Change.

Jackson, Tim. 2009. *Prosperity without Growth: Economics for a Finite Planet*. London: Earthscan.

Jackson, Trevor. 2015. Austerity and the Rise of Food Banks. *BMJ* 350. https://doi.org/10.1136/bmj.h1880.

Jackson, Tim. 2017. *Prosperity without Growth: Foundations for the Economy of Tomorrow*. 2nd ed. Abingdon/New York: Routledge.

Jackson, Tim, and Robin Webster. 2016. *Limits Revisited: A Review of the Limits to Growth Debate*. Report prepared for the All-Party Parliamentary Group on Limits to Growth. http://limits2growth.org.uk/revisited/. Accessed 15 Aug 2016.

Jones, Charles I., and Dietrich Vollrath. 2013. *Introduction to Economic Growth*. 3rd ed. New York: W. W. Norton.

Kaufmann, Daniel, Aart Kraay, and Pablo Zoido-Lobatón. 1999. *Governance Matters*. Policy Research Working Paper 2196. Washington, DC: World Bank.

Keynes, John Maynard. 1924. Alfred Marshall, 1842–1924. *Economic Journal* 34 (135): 311–372.

Knowles, Stephen, and P. Dorian Owen. 1995. Health Capital and Cross-country Variation in Income per Capita in the Mankiw-Romer-Weil Model. *Economics Letters* 48 (1): 99–106.

Krueger, Anne O. 1990. Government Failures in Development. *Journal of Economic Perspectives* 4 (3): 9–23.

La Porta, Rafael, Florencio Lopez-de-Silanes, and Andrei Shleifer. 2008. The Economic Consequences of Legal Origins. *Journal of Economic Literature* 46 (2): 285–332.

Lawn, Philip A. 2003. A Theoretical Foundation to Support the Index of Sustainable Economic Welfare (ISEW), Genuine Progress Indicator (GPI), and Other Related Indexes. *Ecological Economics* 44 (1): 105–118.

Loopstra, Rachel, Aaron Reeves, David Taylor-Robinson, Ben Barr, Martin McKee, and David Stuckler. 2015. Austerity, Sanctions, and the Rise of Food Banks in the UK. *BMJ* 350. https://doi.org/10.1136/bmj.h1775.

Lucas, Robert E., Jr. 1988. On the Mechanics of Economic Development. *Journal of Monetary Economics* 22 (1): 3–42.

Mankiw, N. Gregory, David Romer, and David N. Weil. 1992. A Contribution to the Empirics of Economic Growth. *Quarterly Journal of Economics* 107 (2): 407–437.

Marmot, Michael. 2015. *The Health Gap: The Challenge of an Unequal World*. London: Bloomsbury Publishing.

McCloskey, Deirdre. 2010. *Bourgeois Dignity: Why Economics Can't Explain the Modern World*. Chicago: Chicago University Press.

Meadows, Donella H., Dennis L. Meadows, Jørgen Randers, and William W. Behrens III. 1972. *The Limits to Growth*. New York: Universe Books.

Meadows, Donella, Jørgen Randers, and Dennis Meadows. 2005. *The Limits to Growth: The 30-Year Update*. London: Earthscan.

Mincer, Jacob. 1958. Investment in Human Capital and Personal Income Distribution. *Journal of Political Economy* 66 (4): 281–302.

Nahapiet, Janine, and Sumantra Ghoshal. 1998. Social Capital, Intellectual Capital, and the Organizational Advantage. *Academy of Management Review* 23 (2): 242–266.

Nørgård, Jørgen Stig, John Peet, and Kristín Vala Ragnarsdóttir. 2010. The History of *The Limits to Growth*. *Solutions* 1 (2): 59–63.

North, Douglass C. 1987. Institutions, Transaction Costs and Economic Growth. *Economic Inquiry* 25 (3): 419–428.

———. 1994. Economic Performance through Time. *American Economic Review* 84 (3): 359–368.

Nussbaum, Martha C. 2000. *Women and Human Development: The Capabilities Approach*. Cambridge: Cambridge University Press.

———. 2011. *Creating Capabilities: The Human Development Approach*. Cambridge, MA: Belknap Press.

O'Hara, Mary. 2015. *Austerity Bites: A Journey to the Sharp End of Cuts in the UK*. Bristol: Policy Press.

OECD. 2011. *How's Life? Measuring Well-being*. Paris: OECD Publishing. https://doi.org/10.1787/9789264121164-en.

———. 2013. *How's Life? 2013: Measuring Well-being*. Paris: OECD Publishing. https://doi.org/10.1787/9789264201392-en.

———. 2015. *How's Life? 2015: Measuring Well-being*. Paris: OECD Publishing. https://doi.org/10.1787/how_life-2015-en.

———. 2017a. *How's Life? 2017: Measuring Well-being*. Paris: OECD Publishing. https://doi.org/10.1787/how_life-2017-en.

———. 2017b. *Economic Policy Reforms: Going for Growth 2017*. Paris: OECD Publishing. https://doi.org/10.1787/growth-2017-en.

Pareto, Vilfredo. 1906. *Manuale di Economia Politica*. Milan: Societa Editrice Libraria.

Piketty, Thomas. 2013. *Capital in the Twenty-First Century*. Trans. Arthur Goldhammer. Cambridge, MA: Harvard University Press.

Purdam, Kingsley, Elizabeth A. Garratt, and Aneez Esmail. 2015. Hungry? Food Insecurity, Social Stigma and Embarrassment in the UK. *Sociology*, published online. https://doi.org/10.1177/0038038515594092.

Putnam, Robert D. 1995. Bowling Alone: America's Declining Social Capital. *Journal of Democracy* 6 (1): 65–78.

Quddus, Munir, Michael Goldsby, and Mahmud Farooque. 2000. Trust: The Social Virtues and the Creation of Prosperity–A Review Article. *Eastern Economic Journal* 26 (1): 87–98.

Ricardo, David. 1817. *On the Principles of Political Economy and Taxation*. London: John Murray.

Robeyns, Ingrid. 2006. The Capability Approach in Practice. *Journal of Political Philosophy* 14 (3): 351–376.

Rockström, Johan, Will Steffen, Kevin Noone, Åsa Persson, F. Stuart Chapin III, Eric Lambin, Timothy M. Lenton, Marten Scheffer, Carl Folke, Hans Joachim Schellnhuber, Björn Nykvist, Cynthia A. de Wit, Terry Hughes, Sander van der Leeuw, Henning Rodhe, Sverker Sörlin, Peter K. Snyder, Robert Costanza, Uno

Svedin, Malin Falkenmark, Louise Karlberg, Robert W. Corell, Victoria J. Fabry, James Hansen, Brian Walker, Diana Liverman, Katherine Richardson, Paul Crutzen, and Jonathan Foley. 2009a. Planetary Boundaries: Exploring the Safe Operating Space for Humanity. *Ecology and Society* 14 (2): 32 [online] URL: http://www.ecologyandsociety.org/vol14/iss2/art32/.

———. 2009b. A Safe Operating Space for Humanity. *Nature* 461: 472–475.

Rodrik, Dani, Arvind Subramanian, and Francesco Trebbi. 2004. Institutions Rule: The Primacy of Institutions over Geography and Integration in Economic Development. *Journal of Economic Growth* 9 (2): 131–165.

Romer, Paul M. 1986. Increasing Returns and Long-Run Growth. *Journal of Political Economy* 94 (5): 1002–1037.

———. 1990. Endogenous Technological Change. *Journal of Political Economy* 98 (5 Part 2): S71–S102.

Rostow, Walt Whitman. 1960. *The Stages of Economic Growth: A Non-Communist Manifesto*. Cambridge: Cambridge University Press.

Saunders, Caroline, and Paul Dalziel. 2017. 25 Years of *Counting for Nothing*: Waring's Critique of National Accounts. *Feminist Economics* 23 (2): 200–218.

Schischka, John, Paul Dalziel, and Caroline Saunders. 2008. Applying Sen's Capability Approach to Poverty Alleviation Programmes: Two Case Studies. *Journal of Human Development and Capabilities* 9 (2): 229–246.

Sen, Amartya. 1983. Development: Which Way Now? Presidential Address of the Development Studies Association. *Economic Journal* 93 (December): 745–762.

———. 1993. Capability and Well-Being. In *The Quality of Life*, ed. Martha Nussbaum and Amartya Sen, 30–53. London/New York: Routledge.

———. 1999a. *Development as Freedom*. Oxford: Oxford University Press.

———. 1999b. *Reason Before Identity: The Romanes Lectures*. Oxford: Oxford University Press.

Shultz, Theodore W. 1961. Investment in Human Capital. *American Economic Review* 51 (1): 1–17.

———. 1961. Investment in Human Capital. *American Economic Review* 51 (1): 1–17.

Smith, Adam. 1776. *An Enquiry into the Nature and Causes of the Wealth of Nations*, 2 vols., University Paperbacks edition, ed. by Edwin Cannan. London: Methuen.

Solow, Robert M. 1956. A Contribution to the Theory of Economic Growth. *Quarterly Journal of Economics* 70 (1): 65–94.

———. 1974a. Intergenerational Equity and Exhaustible Resources. *The Review of Economic Studies* 40 (Symposium): 29–45.

———. 1974b. The Economics of Resources or the Resources of Economics. *American Economic Review* 64 (2): 1–14.

Stiglitz, Joseph. 2012. *The Price of Inequality: How Today's Divided Society Endangers Our Future*. New York: Norton.

Stiglitz, Joseph, Amartya Sen, and Jean-Paul Fitoussi. 2009. *Report by the Commission on the Measurement of Economic Performance and Social Progress*. https://www.insee.fr/en/information/2662494. Accessed 16 July 2017.

Swan, Trevor W. 1956. Economic Growth and Capital Accumulation. *Economic Record* 32 (2): 334–361.

Throsby, David. 1999. Cultural Capital. *Journal of Cultural Economics* 23 (1): 3–12.

Treasury. 2004. Policy Advice and Treasury's Wellbeing Framework. *Economic Roundup* (Winter): 1–20.

Turner, Graham M. 2012. On the Cusp of Global Collapse? Updated Comparison of the *Limits to Growth* with Historical Data. *GAIA – Ecological Perspectives for Science and Society* 21 (2): 116–124.

United Nations. 2009. *System of National Accounts 2008*. Published by the European Commission, the International Monetary Fund, the Organisation for Economic Co-operation and Development, the United Nations and the World Bank.

———. 2015. *Transforming Our World: The 2030 Agenda for Sustainable Development*. New York: United Nations.

Waring, Marilyn. 1988. *If Women Counted: A New Feminist Economics*. San Francisco: Harper & Row. Also published as *Counting for Nothing: What Men Value and What Women Are Worth*. Wellington: Allen & Unwin in Association with the Port Nicholson Press.

White, Sarah C. 2017. Relational Wellbeing: Re-centring the Politics of Happiness, Policy and the Self. *Policy & Politics* 45 (2): 121–136.

Wilkinson, Richard G., and Kate Pickett. 2009. *The Spirit Level: Why More Equal Societies Almost Always Do Better*. London: Allen Lane.

World Bank. 2011. *The Changing Wealth of Nations: Measuring Sustainable Development in the New Millennium*. Washington, DC: World Bank Group.

———. 2016. *World Development Indicators 2016*. Washington, DC: World Bank Group.

Xu, Guangdong. 2011. The Role of Law in Economic Growth: A Literature Review. *Journal of Economic Surveys* 25 (5): 833–871.

# 2

# Persons and Human Capital

**Abstract** The wellbeing economics framework begins with individual persons seeking to create the kinds of lives they value, and have reason to value. These persons are able to make time-use choices they reason will promote wellbeing, influenced by cultural values, personal abilities and social capabilities. The attention to choices about time-use is because persons have equal time to allocate each day, and because time-use choices influence monetary values recorded in market transactions. Persons can expand capabilities through formal education and through relevant experience, which are time-use choices that economists describe as investment in human capital. Progress in wellbeing can be monitored using measures of subjective and objective wellbeing, exemplified in the Organisation for Economic Co-operation and Development's *Better Life Initiative*.

**Keywords** Human capital • Wellbeing measures • Time-use choices • Skills • Sustainability

Our analysis begins with an individual person striving to live a valued kind of life. This person is presumed able to exercise relational autonomy, meaning that at key moments in life, we humans expect to be able to make reasoned choices within the context of our own cultural and social environments. This chapter



P. Dalziel et al., *Wellbeing Economics*, Wellbeing in Politics and Policy,
https://doi.org/10.1007/978-3-319-93194-4_2

pays attention to time-use choices, for two reasons. First, all persons have the same amount of time to spend each day, so that this fundamental equality is a useful starting point for inquiries into persistent inequalities in personal wellbeing over a lifetime. Second, time-use choices influence economic values recorded in the market economy. The first two sections of this chapter explore these aspects of time-use choices.

The chapter then introduces the first of the seven capitals in our wellbeing economics framework. Individuals can improve capabilities for wellbeing through formal education, relevant experience and better health. These are time-use choices that economists have long described as investment in human capital. The final section before the chapter's brief conclusion explains how a mixture of subjective and objective wellbeing measures can be used to monitor changes in wellbeing levels of a community or country.

## Living Life

Among the many ways for promoting wellbeing, this book focuses on private and public initiatives to expand the capabilities of persons for leading lives they value, and have reason to value. On a day-to-day basis, human lives are constructed by persons, living in communities, making choices about how to spend their time (see also Kahneman et al. 2006, p. 1910). Our approach to these choices is expressed in Proposition 4.

**Proposition 4** Persons can make time-use choices they reason will promote wellbeing, influenced by their cultural values, personal abilities and social capabilities.

This introduces concepts prominent throughout this book. First, the focus is on choices about time-use. As Waring (1996, p. 88) observes, "time is the one unit of exchange we all have in equal amounts, the one investment we all have to make" (see also Gershuny 2000; Stiglitz et al. 2009, pp. 126–128 and the Canadian Index of Wellbeing 2012, pp. 49–53). All humans in this respect have the same entitlement each day. Hence, persistent inequality in wellbeing can be explored by researching constraints on the range of time-use choices available to different segments of the population, as well as the different consequences of different time-use choices made by persons.

Further, time-use choices made at key moments in life can have profound impacts on wellbeing that are qualitatively greater than other types of choices. Examples include the number of years spent in formal education, patterns of behaviour within a household, volunteered commitments to community groups, participation in hours of market employment, and involvement in recreational and cultural activities, all of which have stronger and more enduring impacts on personal wellbeing than, say, choices between different brands of consumption goods.

Second, Proposition 4 states that persons can make choices they *reason* will promote wellbeing. There are important exceptions (young children lack this capacity, for example, as can people suffering certain illnesses), but at moments of big decisions in a lifetime, persons can expect they will be able to exercise personal agency, in the sense of using their "capacity to deliberate and to act on the basis of reason" (Mackenzie 2007, p. 105). At these moments, choice-making is not a matter of simply applying pre-determined preferences or tastes, but involves reasoned deliberation within a person's cultural and social contexts. This understanding of human agency has been termed *relational autonomy* (Mackenzie and Stoljar 2000; Stoljar 2015), with the resulting conceptualisation of wellbeing sometimes termed *relational wellbeing* (White 2015, 2017).

The claims in Proposition 4 are not strong or normative. The proposition does not say, for example, that promotion of wellbeing is the *only* motivation affecting time-use choices, nor does it say that *all* choices are, or should be, motivated in this way. There is no presumption that a person's reasoning is correct, immune from external criticism or unable to be influenced by policy nudges that recognise the limits of human cognitive capacities (Thaler and Sunstein 2008; Halpern 2015).

The proposition does not expect universal agreement on what constitutes wellbeing; indeed, this is not possible since wellbeing is influenced by the choice-maker's own cultural values. The values are "cultural" because they are developed within specific cultural settings and because social values are continuously being transformed as part of the wider community's cultural vitality (see Chap. 3).

Finally, Proposition 4 recognises that time-use choices are influenced by personal abilities and by social capabilities. To illustrate the difference, consider a boy and a girl with the same aptitude for learning. If custom or law permits boys to advance to higher education, but not girls, then the two children have equal personal abilities but unequal social capabilities for developing skills.[1] Similarly, a woman and a man may have equal personal abilities for paid employment in an occupation, but if women are routinely paid less than men in that occupation, then the social capabilities of the two persons are again unequal.[2]

Another important example concerns persons who are living with physical impairments compared to social peers. A physical impairment may affect personal abilities, but this is accentuated if accompanied by a loss of social capability (creating *social disability*; see, e.g., Oliver 1996) when public policy fails to account for the abilities of this population.

Proposition 1 states that economics is *to contribute to* enhanced wellbeing. The language is deliberate. Since persons are able to make reasoned time-use choices, policy advisors must engage with what persons are already doing to enhance the wellbeing of themselves, their families, their households and their communities, before designing policies that might build on those efforts to allow greater wellbeing to be achieved.

## Time-Use Choices and Market Values

To introduce links between time-use choices and market values, consider the time-use choice made by some persons to participate in sport. Sport England (2013) estimates that in the year ending 14 October 2012, 7.4 million adults in England engaged in at least 30 minutes of moderate intensity sport three times a week. Another 8.1 million did so weekly, and a further 5.5 million did so monthly. This was a substantial investment of time, amounting to more than 820.8 million hours in total over the year.

This is a practical example of persons making time-use choices as part of a kind of life they value. These choices are clearly influenced by cultural values, personal abilities and social capabilities, dependent on sporting associations catering for diverse interests and skills. The participants can reasonably expect this time-use choice to promote wellbeing, since the benefits of physical activity for good physical and mental health are well documented (see, e.g., Government Office for Science 2008; World Health Organization 2010; Institute of Medicine 2013).

This activity also requires significant amount of market transactions, including purchases of specialist goods and services such as sports clothing, sports equipment, club membership fees, facility fees, medical expenses and travel costs. Sport England (2013) reports that spending for active participation in sport contributed an estimated £11.8 billion to the English economy in 2010, which was 1.1 per cent of the country's gross value added that year.[3]

A great deal of attention is paid to the value of market purchases such as these, but note that the market value exists only because people have made time-use choices (in this case, to participate in sport). Without the time-use choices, there would be no demand to purchase sports equipment or to pay club membership fees, and hence no opportunity for the suppliers of sports goods and services to create market value.

The time allocated to sport has a cost, since it represents time that cannot be spent in other valued activities (see Gratton and Taylor 2000, pp. 50–51). The sacrifice is called the *opportunity cost* of time (Shaw 1992). Becker (1965) demonstrated how to measure this cost, by estimating the income that might have been earned if the time had been spent in market employment. The idea is that paid work is an alternative time-use choice. Thus, if the 820.8 million hours of participation in active sport had been spent in employment at the statutory adult minimum wage (which was £6.08 in October 2011), this would have created an income of £5.0 billion. That sacrificed income is a measure of the opportunity cost of participation in active sport.[4]

These ideas mean economists can estimate how much value participants obtain from active sports. It is reasonable to presume that participation creates value that outweighs all associated costs; otherwise, a person would choose an alternative activity that is more highly valued (Samuelson 1938, 1948). Thus, the personal value of active sport participation in England must have been at least £17 billion in 2011–2012 to cover £12 billion spent in the market economy on goods and services for sport participation and £5 billion to compensate for the opportunity cost of the participants' time.

The spending on market goods and services creates another connection between time-use choices and market values, since the income needed to finance these purchases comes through market employment.[5] Hence, a time-use choice to participate in sport is connected to a person's time-use choice to participate in paid work. This leads to the obvious point that the wage or salary that a person is capable of earning through an hour of paid employment is a crucial element of wellbeing, as will be analysed further in Chap. 5.

Figure 2.1 generalises from this example to highlight connections among wellbeing values, market values and time-use choices. The column on the right depicts the time allocated to earning market income to pay for the market goods and services needed for the valued activities (shown as the horizontal arrow to the lighter-shaded area of the left column). The darker shaded area of the left column shows time allocated to the valued activities themselves, using the purchased goods and services (shown as the vertical arrow). The personal wellbeing created from these choices is the value created by the person's time engaged in the valued activities (presumed to be greater than his or her opportunity cost of

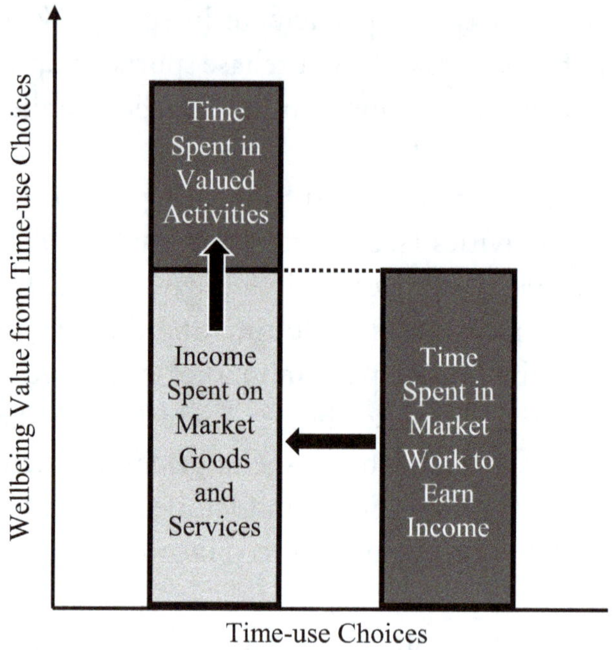


**Fig. 2.1** The wellbeing value from time-use choices

time) plus the value of the person's time spent earning the income need to purchase the relevant goods and services.

In summary, personal wellbeing and market values are both built on time-use choices. These choices take place within social and cultural contexts and are therefore influenced by personal abilities and social capabilities. Given Propositions 1 and 2, the analysis must explain how individual and collaborative actions can expand capabilities. Proposition 3 draws attention to capital investment and so the following section introduces the first of the seven capitals considered in this book—*human capital.*

## Human Capital

The term *human capital* to describe expanded capabilities through formal education, or through relevant experience, has been prominent in economics since its introduction by Mincer (1958), Shultz (1960, 1961) and Becker (1962, 1964); see, for example, reviews by Harmon et al. (2003), Sianesi and Van Reenen (2003) and Tobias and Li (2004). Education generates a range of personal and social benefits, including a reasonable expectation that greater skills will increase a person's labour productivity. An employee with more education, or with greater experience, can produce a greater value of output per hour of work compared to employees with basic skills only. This is analogous to how a greater amount of physical capital (a tractor rather than a spade, for example) can increase productivity. Because skills are embodied in persons—in contrast to the spade or tractor—this concept is called human capital.

Like physical capital, human capital requires sacrifices of current consumption in return for the prospect of future rewards. Consider a student choosing from two options: (1) enrolling for a further year of education; and (2) leaving formal education to accept paid employment. Option 1 means sacrificing income that could be earned in option 2, but new skills learned in the first option will result in higher income in future employment. Economic reasoning therefore advises the student to remain in education for as long as expected increases in future income are sufficiently high to compensate for sacrificed current income.

The purpose of education and experience is to develop *skills*. The Organisation for Economic Co-operation and Development (OECD) describes skills as "the global currency of the 21st century", warning that "without proper investment in skills, people languish on the margins of society, technological progress does not translate into economic growth, and countries can no longer compete in an increasingly knowledge-based global society" (OECD 2012, p. 3). In a wellbeing economics framework, this idea applies to skills that contribute to any aspect of wellbeing (such as cultural vitality, as well as economic wellbeing).

Since skills are embodied in persons, education begins with the individual learner (Cornelius-White 2007), who must be provided with opportunities to discover personal abilities, an idea going back at least to Rousseau (1762). The important role of self-discovery through education has been incorporated in economic models of human capital investment; see, for example, Altonji (1993), Weiler (1994) and Arcidiacono (2004). As Manski (1989) argues, an implication is that failure in education is not always a poor outcome, since it may be a necessary part of discovering genuine interests and abilities. Indeed, a society that encourages creativity and innovation should support learners to try new activities and explore potential skills.

Education then allows learners to discipline their discovered abilities through study and practice, which may be certified through qualifications trusted by potential employers or clients (Spence 1973; Riley 2001). These disciplined abilities may then be displayed as personal skills when the learner uses them to *contribute* to wellbeing, perhaps through employment, but also in any dimension of human flourishing (see Fig. 2.2).

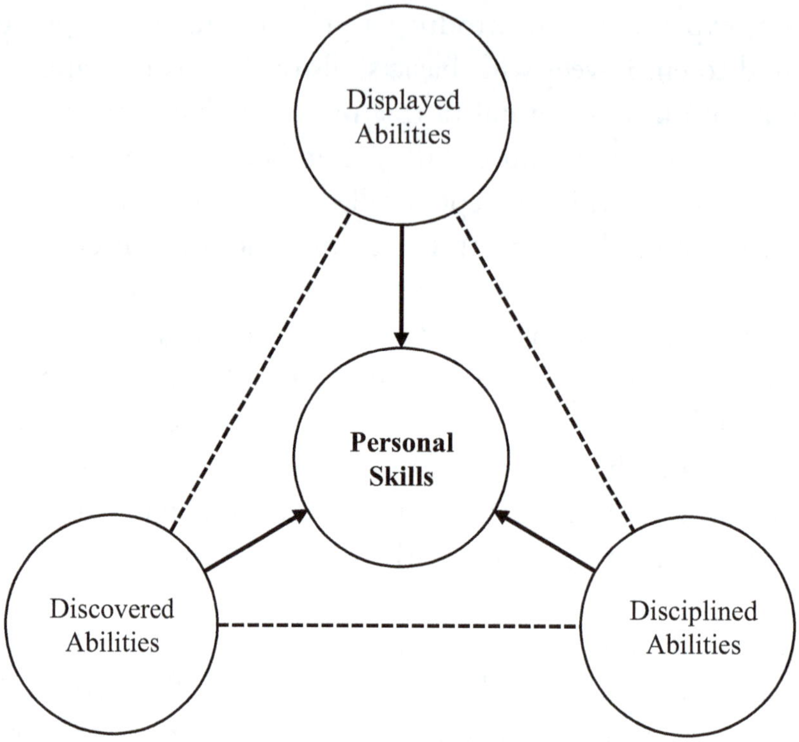


**Fig. 2.2** Personal skills as the integration of discovered, disciplined and displayed abilities. (Source: Adapted from Dalziel (2015, 2017))

Recall from Fig. 2.1 that adult lives are constructed around time spent in market work and time spent in other chosen activities. Both types of time-use choice can be expanded when a person has higher levels of relevant skills. Beginning with time spent in employment, there is strong evidence that education offers high market returns. Harmon et al. (2003) reviewed more than a thousand studies of the financial rewards to persons undertaking a further year of schooling. They found consistent reports of a return of around 6.5 per cent, which is well above the recommended return of 3.5 per cent for public sector investment projects in the United Kingdom (HM Treasury 2011, p. 26). Consequently, it is almost universal for government policy to aim for greater levels of human capital investment across the whole population (Buchanan et al. 2017).

As well as opening up the possibility of higher market incomes, higher skills across a range of recreational and cultural activities can expand the capabilities of persons to create lives they have reason to value. An education system with an exclusive focus on market-oriented skills would therefore result in impoverished lives if students do not have opportunities to discover, discipline and display other important life-skills (see, e.g., Connell 2000).

The discussion of this section is summarised in Proposition 5.

**Proposition 5** Investment in human capital through education can provide persons, in all their diversity, with opportunities to discover, discipline and display skills that contribute to wellbeing.

## Monitoring Wellbeing

Proposition 1 states that the primary purpose of economics is to contribute to enhanced wellbeing of persons. This section therefore examines how trends in personal wellbeing can be monitored, beginning with self-evaluations by persons of their own sense of wellbeing. Indicators based on self-assessments are termed measures of *subjective* wellbeing (Veenhoven 1996; Frey and Stutzer 2002; Peasgood 2008; Blanchflower and Oswald 2011). Indicators of this type are constructed from population surveys that ask participants to assess their wellbeing on a numerical scale, perhaps from zero to ten.

The question can be posed in different ways to focus on diverse aspects of subjective wellbeing, as shown in Table 2.1 (Dolan et al. 2011; see also Cabinet Office 2016, Fig. 17, p. 10). The first way invites participants to rate their current state of mind, both positively (their level of happiness) and negatively (their level of anxiety). These are typically asked as separate questions and result in *experience* measures of subjective wellbeing. The second type of question asks people to rate their life satisfaction, producing *evaluation* measures. The third approach requests participants to rate the extent to which they feel that what they do is worthwhile, resulting in a *eudemonic* measure of subjective wellbeing (see also Bruni 2010). The word comes from Aristotle's vision of eudemonia as living well, consistent with the objective of "human flourishing" emphasised by Tim Jackson (2017) and others. It is the measure emphasised in Sen's capabilities approach and reflected in our Proposition 2.

Survey questions such as those in Table 2.1 can be used to identify groups with lower self-assessed wellbeing than the general population (Krueger and Schkade 2008). An authoritative review by Dolan et al. (2008), for example, suggests that poor health, marital separation, unemployment and lack of social contact are strongly associated with low levels of subjective wellbeing (see also Helliwell and Putnam 2002). That review cautioned against drawing firm conclusions about *causes* of wellbeing until more data are available, and there are other concerns about whether self-assessed measures are sufficient for monitoring wellbeing. Amartya Sen (1987, p. 8), for example, has offered the following hypothetical case to illustrate a deeper problem:

**Table 2.1** Examples of survey questions to elicit three different types of subjective assessments of wellbeing

| Assessment Type | Example of Survey Question |
|---|---|
| Experience | Overall, on a rising scale from 0 to 10, how happy did you feel yesterday?<br>Overall, on a rising scale from 0 to 10, how anxious did you feel yesterday? |
| Evaluation | Overall, on a rising scale from 0 to 10, how satisfied are you with your life nowadays? |
| Eudemonic | Overall, on a rising scale from 0 to 10, to what extent do you feel that the things you do in your life are worthwhile? |

Source: Adapted from Dolan et al. (2011, Table 1, p. 14)

> Consider a very deprived person who is poor, exploited, overworked and ill, but who has been made satisfied with his lot by social conditioning (through, say, religion, political propaganda, or cultural pressure). Can we possibly believe that he is doing well just because he is happy and satisfied?

Consider also the limitations on social opportunities of women compared to men in most societies (Boserup 1970; Nussbaum and Glover 1995; Nussbaum 2001; Mackenzie 2007; Khader 2011). Betty Friedan, for example, analysed the post-war ideology that pressured women in the United States, and elsewhere, to accept "their own nature, which can find fulfilment only in sexual passivity, male domination, and nurturing maternal love" so that "lives were confined, by necessity, to cooking, cleaning, washing, bearing children" (Friedan 1963, p. 38).[6] The feminine mystique was widely accepted following World War II, but reason meant it had to be rejected: "Self-esteem in woman, as well as in man, can only be based on real capacity, competence, and achievement" (idem, p. 273).

The phenomenon of individual expectations adjusting to social experience is termed *adaptive preferences* (Nussbaum 2001). It is not unusual; indeed, Wilson and Gilbert (2003, p. 401) comment that "people are consummate sense makers who transform novel, emotion-producing events into ones that seem ordinary and mundane, through the processes of assimilation, accommodation, and explanation". Examples include Easterlin's (2001, p. 481) conclusion that over a person's life cycle, income growth does not cause reported happiness to rise "because it generates equivalent growth in material aspirations, and the negative effect of the latter on subjective well-being undercuts the positive effect of the former".[7] Graham (2008, p. 79) observes a similar effect in the relationship between health and happiness: "people no doubt adapt to better health conditions and, in turn, expect them".

Aspirations may also rest on ill-informed or limited knowledge (Somin 2004; Schnellenbach 2008). This is a wider policy issue than the measure of subjective wellbeing, but its relevance can be illustrated with the finding from the British Household Panel Survey that the level of environmental awareness affects a person's subjective wellbeing (Ferrer-i-Carbonell and Gowdy 2007). Thus, widespread underestimation of realistic climate change threats could result in inflated measures of subjective wellbeing compared to a situation where all survey participants understood the scientific consensus presented in authoritative documents such as IPCC (2015).

Consequently, indicators of subjective wellbeing are not sufficient for monitoring purposes. Recall from Proposition 2 that wellbeing can be enhanced by expanding the *capabilities* of persons to lead the kinds of lives they value and have reason to value. Thus, relevant influences on personal wellbeing (such as quality of available housing, levels of material living standards and state of the natural environment) can be identified and then monitored (Tomlinson and Kelly 2013; Scott 2015). Because they rely on externally observable data, these indicators are termed measures of *objective* wellbeing.

There is an important debate in the literature about how the influences on wellbeing should be identified (Nussbaum 2003; Sen 2004). Sen argues that the process should be undertaken by members of each community exercising their own agency, since outsiders should not presume to impose their own choices on a community (Sen 1999, p. 11):

> …with adequate social opportunities, individuals can effectively shape their own destiny and help each other. They need not be seen primarily as passive recipients of the benefits of cunning development programs. There is indeed a strong rationale for recognising the positive role of free and sustainable agency.

Nussbaum (2003) observes that adequate social opportunities are not universally available, and so Sen's opening proviso is not always realised. Nussbaum argues that a list of "central human capabilities" can be designed to reflect the fundamental dignity of the human person, while being sensitive to cultural difference and open to change. It can record essential entitlements for social justice, overlapping with the human rights literature (see also Nussbaum 1997). Nussbaum proposes an initial set of central capabilities, organised under ten themes (Nussbaum 2003, pp. 41–42; 2011, pp. 33–34):

1. Life
2. Bodily health

3. Bodily integrity
4. Senses, imagination and thought
5. Emotions
6. Practical reason
7. Affiliation
8. Other species
9. Play
10. Control over one's environment

Measures of subjective and objective wellbeing can be combined in a suite of indicators. An exemplar is the OECD's *Better Life Initiative* (OECD 2011, 2013, 2015; 2017), which has created the conceptual framework reproduced in Fig. 2.3.

The OECD framework has three domains. The first, *material conditions*, covers three headings: income and wealth; jobs and earning; and housing. Gross domestic product (GDP) is recognised as contributing to these material conditions, but is

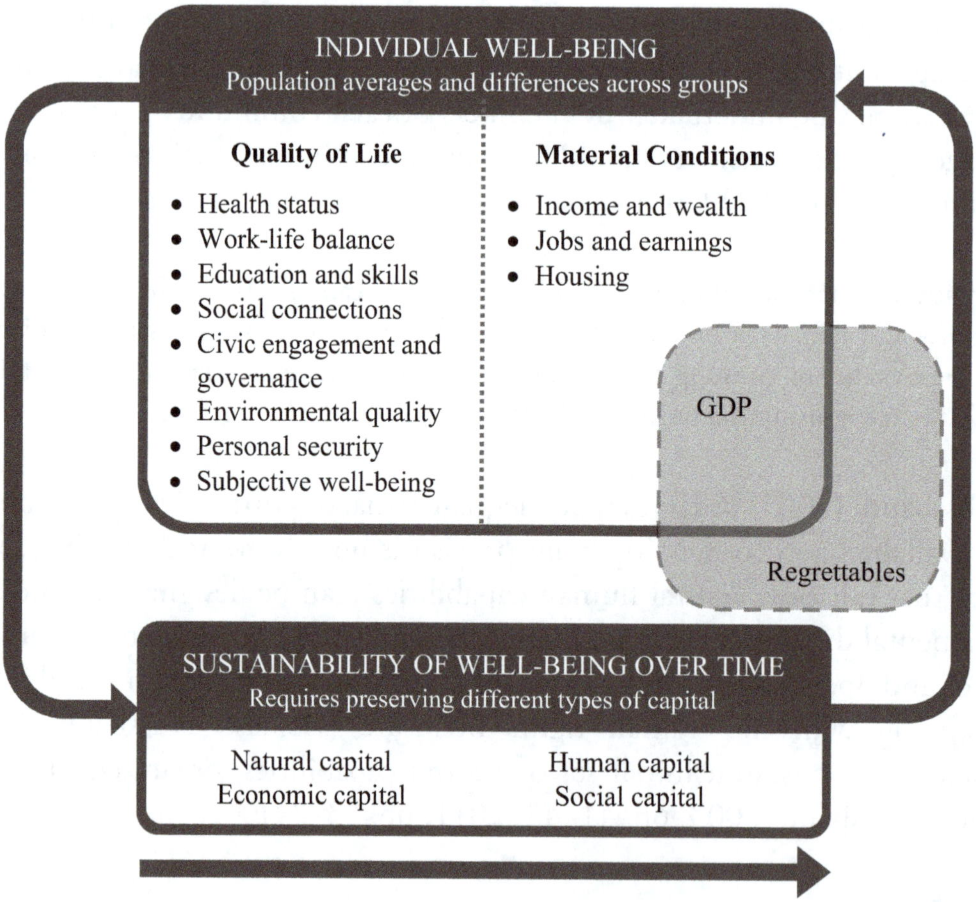


**Fig. 2.3** The OECD wellbeing conceptual framework. (Source: OECD (2013, Fig. 1.2, p. 21))

also associated with certain "regrettables" (such as damage to the natural environment) that detract from wellbeing.[8]

The second domain, *quality of life*, records other relevant measures. It includes seven groups of objective wellbeing indicators: health status; work-life balance; education and skills; social connections; civic engagement and governance; environmental quality; and personal security. An eighth set incorporates indicators of subjective wellbeing into the framework.

The third domain is *sustainability*. It draws attention to the preservation of four different types of capital stock: natural capital; human capital; economic capital and social capital. This recognises that wellbeing is likely to fall if the services provided by these assets decline over time, which is consistent with the capitals approach taken in this book.[9]

In this context of services provided by different types of capital stock, there is an important debate in the literature about strong sustainability versus weak sustainability (see, e.g., Hediger 2006). The issue is whether the economic system can be described as sustainable if the stock of one capital type is declining over time (especially reduced natural capital as a result of resource extraction or environmental degradation) but stocks of other capital types (such as economic or human capital) are increasing.

Proponents of weak sustainability argue that it is possible for investment in economic and human capital to compensate for degraded natural capital. Consequently, economists are attempting to measure comprehensive wealth for countries, defined as the aggregated value of all capital stocks measured at prices reflecting the marginal contribution of each capital type to wellbeing (see, e.g., World Bank 2011; Arrow et al. 2012; Hanley et al. 2015). The system is said to be sustainable if comprehensive wealth on a per capita basis does not decline over time, even if natural capital deteriorates.

Proponents of strong sustainability argue instead that at least some aspects of natural capital are not substitutable by other types of capital, especially once degradation moves beyond certain limits. This is the approach taken by Jackson (2017) discussed in Chap. 1. It also underlies the finding of the Stern Review in the United Kingdom that "climate change will have serious impacts on world output, on human life and on the environment" (Stern 2007, p. xvi). In this approach, the system is not sustainable unless key aspects of natural capital are preserved. Chapter 6 will return to this debate, but this section finishes by recording the feasibility of monitoring personal wellbeing trends.

**Proposition 6** Personal wellbeing can be monitored using a set of indicators that include measures of subjective and objective wellbeing, supplemented by measured trends in different types of capital.

## Conclusion

This chapter has introduced individual persons seeking to create lives they value, and have reason to value. These persons are able to make time-use choices they reason will promote wellbeing, influenced by their own cultural values, personal abilities and social capabilities. These time-use choices influence monetary values recorded in market transactions.

Because the choices are influenced by social capabilities, the wellbeing economics framework explores how capabilities can be expanded. An important example is education that helps learners in all their diversity to discover, discipline and display their full range of abilities. This is termed investment in human capital. The final section of the chapter finished with the OECD's wellbeing conceptual framework, presented as an exemplar of how to monitor trends across a range of personal wellbeing indicators.

The following chapter turns to how collaborative actions among different persons can enhance wellbeing, focusing in the first instance on the choices made by persons living in households and families.

## Notes

1. Duflo (2012) summarises evidence for the benefits of a policy commitment to equality in the education of children, both for its own sake and as a contribution to stronger economic development. See also Nussbaum (2000).
2. In the United States, an Equal Pay Act prohibiting this form of discrimination was passed only in 1963, and not until 1970 in the United Kingdom. Nevertheless, female-male wage gaps remain in these and other countries (National Equal Pay Task Force 2013; Rubery and Grimshaw 2015; European Union 2014).
3. Gross value added is the difference between the value of a sector's output and the value of goods and services purchased from other sectors as inputs into production. It is the core measure used in calculating a country's GDP. Of course, if the participants' income had not been spent on these goods and services, it could have been spent elsewhere; hence, this analysis is not claiming that the economy would have been smaller without this participation in sport.

4. Only people aged 21 and over are entitled to the statutory adult minimum wage, but this overestimate is more than offset by: not considering that most adults can earn more than the living wage; using the minimum 30 minutes as the time spent in each session of sport; and not including the opportunity cost of volunteered hours in the sector.
5. The analysis is made more complicated, but not fundamentally changed, if it incorporates the possibility of some earned income being saved for investment in financial assets that then generate future income for the saver.
6. Folbre and Hartmann (1988) and Folbre and Nelson (2000) analysed similar gender dualisms in the economics literature.
7. Easterlin's theory is not universally accepted; see Stevenson and Wolfers (2008) and the review by Clark et al. (2008). Wilkinson and Pickett (2009) hypothesise that expectations adapting to social relativities is a major mechanism through which greater inequality in a society diminishes wellbeing, by making people anxious about not being able to achieve, or maintain, a kind of life that is judged reasonable by their peers.
8. This feature of the figure has been removed in later publications; see, for example, OECD (2015, Fig. 1.1, p. 23).
9. This book's wellbeing economics framework expands the list of capital to include cultural capital, knowledge capital and diplomatic capital. These additional capitals are not currently as easily measured as the four highlighted by the OECD, but later chapters argue that their services are essential for wellbeing.

## References

Altonji, Joseph G. 1993. The Demand for and Return to Education When Education Outcomes Are Uncertain. *Journal of Labor Economics* 11 (1): 48–83.

Arcidiacono, Peter. 2004. Ability Sorting and the Returns to College Major. *Journal of Econometrics* 121 (1–2): 343–375.

Arrow, Kenneth J., Partha Dasgupta, Lawrence H. Goulder, Kevin J. Mumford, and Kirsten Oleson. 2012. Sustainability and the Measurement of Wealth. *Environment and Development Economics* 17 (3): 317–353.

Becker, Gary. 1962. Investment in Human Capital: A Theoretical Analysis. *Journal of Political Economy* 70 (5, Part 2): 9–49.

———. 1964. *Human Capital: A Theoretical and Empirical Analysis, with Special Reference to Education*. New York: Columbia University Press.

———. 1965. A Theory of the Allocation of Time. *Economic Journal* 75 (299): 493–517.

Blanchflower, David G., and Andrew J. Oswald. 2011. International Happiness: A New View on the Measure of Performance. *Academy of Management Perspectives* 25 (1): 6–22.

Boserup, Ester. 1970. *Woman's Role in Economic Development*. New York: St. Martin's Press.

Bruni, Luigino. 2010. The Happiness of Sociality. Economics and Eudaimonia: A Necessary Encounter. *Rationality and Society* 22 (4): 383–406.

Buchanan, John, David Finegold, Ken Mayhew, and Chris Warhurst, eds. 2017. *The Oxford Handbook of Skills and Training*. Oxford: Oxford University Press.

Cabinet Office. 2016. *Community Life Survey 2015–16 Statistical Bulletin*. London: Cabinet Office Official Statistics.

Canadian Index of Wellbeing. 2012. *How are Canadians Really Doing? The 2012 CIW Report*. Waterloo, ON: Canadian Index of Wellbeing and University of Waterloo.

Clark, Andrew E., Paul Frijters, and Michael A. Shields. 2008. Relative Income, Happiness, and Utility: An Explanation for the Easterlin Paradox and Other Puzzles. *Journal of Economic Literature* 46 (1): 95–144.

Connell, Jeanne M. 2000. Aesthetic Experiences in the School Curriculum: Assessing the Value of Rosenblatt's Transactional Theory. *Journal of Aesthetic Education* 34 (1): 27–35.

Cornelius-White, Jeffrey. 2007. Learner-centered Teacher-Student Relationships are Effective: A Meta-analysis. *Review of Educational Research* 77 (1): 113–143.

Dalziel, Paul. 2015. Regional Skill Ecosystems to Assist Young People Making Education Employment Linkages in Transition from School to Work. *Local Economy* 30 (1): 53–66.

———. 2017. Education and Qualifications as Skills. In *The Oxford Handbook of Skills and Training*, ed. John Buchanan, David Finegold, Ken Mayhew, and Chris Warhurst, 143–160. Oxford: Oxford University Press.

Dolan, Paul, Tessa Peasgood, and Mathew White. 2008. Do We Really Know What Makes Us Happy? A Review of the Economic Literature on the Factors Associated with Subjective Well-being. *Journal of Economic Psychology* 29 (1): 94–122.

Dolan, Paul, Richard Layard and Robert Metcalfe. 2011. Measuring Subjective Wellbeing for Public Policy: Recommendations on Measures. Special Paper No. 23, Centre for Economic Performance, London School of Economics. Retrieved September 20, 2016, from http://eprints.lse.ac.uk/47518/1/CEPSP23.pdf.

Duflo, Esther. 2012. Women Empowerment and Economic Development. *Journal of Economic Literature* 50 (4): 1051–1079.

Easterlin, Richard A. 2001. Income and Happiness: Towards a Unified Theory. *Economic Journal* 111 (July): 465–484.

European Union. 2014. *Tackling the Gender Pay Gap in the European Union*. Luxembourg: Publications Office of the European Union.

Ferrer-i-Carbonell, Ada, and John M. Gowdy. 2007. Environmental Degradation and Happiness. *Ecological Economics* 60: 509–516.

Folbre, Nancy, and Heidi Hartmann. 1988. The Rhetoric of Self-interest: Ideology and Gender in Economic Theory. In *The Consequences of Economic Rhetoric*, ed. Arjo

Klamer, Deirdre N. McCloskey, and Robert M. Solow, 184–203. Cambridge: Cambridge University Press.

Folbre, Nancy, and Julie A. Nelson. 2000. For Love or Money–Or Both? *Journal of Economic Perspectives* 14 (4): 123–140.

Frey, Bruno S., and Alois Stutzer. 2002. What Can Economists Learn from Happiness Research. *Journal of Economic Literature* 40 (2): 402–435.

Friedan, Betty. 1963. *The Feminine Mystique*. New York: W.W. Norton. Citations are from the Penguin edition. Harmondsworth: Penguin, 1965.

Gershuny, Jonathan. 2000. *Changing Times: Work and Leisure in Postindustrial Society*. Oxford: Oxford University Press.

Government Office for Science. 2008. *Mental Capital and Wellbeing: Making the Most of Ourselves in the 21st Century*. Foresight Mental Capital and Wellbeing Project, Final Project Report. London: Government Office for Science.

Graham, Carol. 2008. Happiness and Health: Lessons – and Questions – for Public Policy. *Health Affairs* 27 (1): 72–87.

Gratton, Chris, and Peter Taylor. 2000. *Economics of Sport and Recreation*. London: Spon Press.

Halpern, David. 2015. *Inside the Nudge Unit: How Small Changes Can Make a Big Difference*. London: WH Allen.

Hanley, Nick, Louis Dupuy, and Eoin McLaughlin. 2015. Genuine Savings and Sustainability. *Journal of Economic Surveys* 29 (4): 779–806.

Harmon, Colm, Hessel Oosterbeek, and Ian Walker. 2003. The Returns to Education: Microeconomics. *Journal of Economic Surveys* 17 (2): 115–155.

Hediger, Werner. 2006. Weak and Strong Sustainability, Environmental Conservation and Economic Growth. *Natural Resource Modelling* 19 (3): 359–394.

Helliwell, John F., and Robert D. Putnam. 2002. The Social Context of Well-being. *Philosophical Transactions – Royal Society of London Series B Biological Sciences* 359: 1435–1446.

HM Treasury. 2011. *The Green Book: Appraisal and Evaluation in Central Government*. London: The Stationery Office.

Institute of Medicine. 2013. *Educating the Student Body: Taking Physical Activity and Physical Education to School*, ed. Harold W. Kohl III and Heather D. Cook. Washington, DC: National Academies Press.

IPCC. 2015. *Climate Change 2014: Synthesis Report*. Contribution of Working Groups I, II and III to the Fifth Assessment Report of the Intergovernmental Panel on Climate Change. Geneva: Intergovernmental Panel on Climate Change.

Jackson, Tim. 2017. *Prosperity without Growth: Foundations for the Economy of Tomorrow*. 2nd ed. Abingdon/New York: Routledge.

Kahneman, Daniel, Alan B. Krueger, David Schkade, Norbert Schwarz, and Arthur A. Stone. 2006. Would You Be Happier If You Were Richer? A Focusing Illusion. *Science* 312 (5782): 1908–1910.

Khader, Serene J. 2011. *Adaptive Preferences and Women's Empowerment*. Oxford: Oxford University Press.

Krueger, Alan B., and David A. Schkade. 2008. The Reliability of Subjective Well-being Measures. *Journal of Public Economics* 92 (8–9): 1833–1845.

Mackenzie, Catriona. 2007. Relational Autonomy, Sexual Justice and Cultural Pluralism. In *Sexual Justice/Cultural Justice: Critical Perspectives on Political Theory and Practice*, ed. Barbara Arneil, Monique Deveaux, Rita Dhamoon, and Avigail Eisenberg, 103–121. London/New York: Routledge.

Mackenzie, Catriona, and Natalie Stoljar, eds. 2000. *Relational Autonomy: Feminist Perspectives on Autonomy, Agency, and the Social Self.* New York/Oxford: Oxford University Press.

Manski, Charles F. 1989. Schooling as Experimentation: A Reappraisal of the Postsecondary Dropout Phenomenon. *Economics of Education Review* 8 (4): 305–312.

Mincer, Jacob. 1958. Investment in Human Capital and Personal Income Distribution. *Journal of Political Economy* 66 (4): 281–302.

National Equal Pay Task Force. 2013. *Fifty Years after the Equal Pay Act*. Washington, DC: The White House.

Nussbaum, Martha C. 1997. Capabilities and Human Rights. *Fordham Law Review* 66 (2): 273–300.

———. 2000. *Women and Human Development: The Capabilities Approach*. Cambridge: Cambridge University Press.

———. 2001. Symposium on Amartya Sen's Philosophy: 5 Adaptive Preferences and Women's Options. *Economics & Philosophy* 17 (1): 67–88.

———. 2003. Capabilities as Fundamental Entitlements: Sen and Social Justice. *Feminist Economics* 9 (2–3): 33–59.

———. 2011. *Creating Capabilities: The Human Development Approach*. Cambridge, MA: Belknap Press.

Nussbaum, Martha, and Jonathan Glover, eds. 1995. *Women, Culture and Development: A Study of Human Capabilities*. Oxford: Clarendon Press.

OECD. 2011. *How's Life? Measuring Well-being*. Paris: OECD Publishing https://doi.org/10.1787/9789264121164-en.

———. 2012. *Better Skills, Better Jobs, Better Lives: A Strategic Approach to Skills Policies*. Paris: OECD Publishing https://doi.org/10.1787/9789264177338-en.

———. 2013. *How's Life? 2013: Measuring Well-being*. Paris: OECD Publishing https://doi.org/10.1787/9789264201392-en.

———. 2015. *How's Life? 2015: Measuring Well-being*. Paris: OECD Publishing https://doi.org/10.1787/how_life-2015-en.

———. 2017. *How's Life? 2017: Measuring Well-being*. Paris: OECD Publishing https://doi.org/10.1787/how_life-2017-en.

Oliver, Michael. 1996. *Understanding Disability: From Theory to Practice*. New York: St. Martin's Press.

Peasgood, Tessa. 2008. *Measuring Well-Being for Public Policy*. Unpublished Ph.D. Thesis, Imperial College London. http://hdl.handle.net/10044/1/5475. Accessed 3 Jan 2016

Riley, John G. 2001. Silver Signals: Twenty-Five Years of Screening and Signaling. *Journal of Economic Literature* 39 (2): 432–478.

Rousseau, Jean-Jacques. 1762. *Émile, or On Education*. Translated and annotated by Allan Bloom. Harmondsworth: Penguin, 1979.

Rubery, Jill, and Damian Grimshaw. 2015. The 40-year Pursuit of Equal Pay: A Case of Constantly Moving Goalposts. *Cambridge Journal of Economics* 39 (2): 319–343.

Samuelson, Paul A. 1938. A Note on the Pure Theory of Consumer's Behavior. *Economica* 5 (17): 61–71.

———. 1948. Consumption Theory in Terms of Revealed Preference. *Economica* 15 (60): 243–253.

Schnellenbach, Jan. 2008. Rational Ignorance is Not Bliss: When do Lazy Voters Learn from Decentralised Policy Experiments? *Jahrbücher für Nationalökonomie und Statistik* 228 (4): 372–393.

Scott, Karen. 2015. Happiness on Your Doorstep: Disputing the Boundaries of Wellbeing and Localism. *Geographical Journal* 181 (2): 129–137.

Sen, Amartya. 1987. *The Standard of Living*. The Tanner Lectures, Clare Hall, Cambridge, 1985, ed. Geoffrey Hawthorn. Cambridge: Cambridge University Press.

———. 1999. *Development as Freedom*. Oxford: Oxford University Press.

———. 2004. Capabilities, Lists, and Public Reason: Continuing the Conversation. *Feminist Economics* 10 (3): 77–80.

Shaw, W. Douglass. 1992. Searching for the Opportunity Cost of an Individual's Time. *Land Economics* 68 (1): 107–115.

Shultz, Theodore W. 1960. Capital Formation by Education. *Journal of Political Economy* 68 (6): 571–583.

———. 1961. Investment in Human Capital. *American Economic Review* 51 (1): 1–17.

Sianesi, Barbara, and John Van Reenen. 2003. The Returns to Education: Macroeconomics. *Journal of Economic Surveys* 17 (2): 157–200.

Somin, Ilya. 2004. When Ignorance Isn't Bliss: How Political Ignorance Threatens Democracy. *Policy Analysis* No. 525. https://object.cato.org/sites/cato.org/files/pubs/pdf/pa525.pdf. Accessed 4 Jan 2016.

Spence, Michael. 1973. Job Market Signaling. *Quarterly Journal of Economics* 87 (3): 355–374.

Sport England. 2013. *Economic Value of Sport in England*. London: Sport England.

Stern, Nicholas. 2007. *The Economics of Climate Change: The Stern Review*. Cambridge: Cambridge University Press.

Stevenson, Betsey, and Justin Wolfers. 2008. Economic Growth and Subjective Well-Being: Reassessing the Easterlin Paradox. *Brookings Papers on Economic Activity 2008* (Spring): 1–87.

Stiglitz, Joseph, Amartya Sen, and Jean-Paul Fitoussi. 2009. *Report by the Commission on the Measurement of Economic Performance and Social Progress*. https://www.insee.fr/en/information/2662494. Accessed 16 July 2017.

Stoljar, Natalie. 2015. Feminist Perspectives on Autonomy. In *The Stanford Encyclopedia of Philosophy*. Fall 2015 ed., ed. Edward N. Zalta. https://plato.stanford.edu/archives/fall2015/entries/feminism-autonomy/. Accessed 2 Jan 2016.

Thaler, Richard H., and Cass R. Sunstein. 2008. *Nudge: Improving Decisions about Health, Wealth, and Happiness*. New Haven: Yale University Press.

Tobias, Justin L., and Mingliang Li. 2004. Returns to Schooling and Bayesian Model Averaging: A Union of Two Literatures. *Journal of Economic Surveys* 18 (2): 153–180.

Tomlinson, Michael W., and Grace P. Kelly. 2013. Is Everybody Happy? The Politics and Measurement of National Wellbeing. *Policy & Politics* 41 (2): 139–157.

Veenhoven, Ruut. 1996. Developments in Satisfaction-Research. *Social Indicators Research* 37 (1): 1–46.

Waring, Marilyn. 1996. *Three Masquerades: Essays on Equality, Work and Human Rights*. Auckland: Auckland University Press with Bridget Williams Books.

Weiler, William C. 1994. Expectations, Undergraduate Debt and the Decision to Attend Graduate School: A Simultaneous Model of Student Choice. *Economics of Education Review* 13 (1): 29–41.

White, Sarah C. 2015. Introduction. The Many Faces of Wellbeing. In *Cultures of Wellbeing: Method, Place, Policy*, ed. Sarah C. White and Chloe Blackmore, 1–44. Basingstoke: Palgrave Macmillan.

———. 2017. Relational Wellbeing: Re-centring the Politics of Happiness, Policy and the Self. *Policy & Politics* 45 (2): 121–136.

Wilkinson, Richard G., and Kate Pickett. 2009. *The Spirit Level: Why More Equal Societies Almost Always Do Better*. London: Allen Lane.

Wilson, Timothy D., and Daniel T. Gilbert. 2003. Affective Forecasting. *Advances in Experimental Social Psychology* 35: 345–411.

World Bank. 2011. *The Changing Wealth of Nations: Measuring Sustainable Development in the New Millennium*. Washington, DC: World Bank Group.

World Health Organization. 2010. *Global Recommendations on Physical Activity for Health*. Geneva: World Health Organization Press.

# 3

# Households, Families and Cultural Capital

**Abstract** This chapter focuses on wellbeing within households and families, paying careful attention to child development. This is important from the perspective of the child, of the child's parents, of wider society and globally. Investment in cultural capital enhances wellbeing by creating opportunities for persons to express, develop, transform and pass on to the next generation their cultural inheritance. Men and women can have equal capabilities for wellbeing; yet studies show that significant sacrifices of time and financial costs for parents are carried disproportionately by women, who are also more vulnerable to intimate violence. After accounting for housing costs, nearly one in three children in the United Kingdom are growing up in households with income below 60 per cent of the country's median equivalised income. Thus, the chapter reveals serious problems that can be overlooked when policy advice focuses on economic growth rather than on wellbeing.

**Keywords** Cultural capital • Child care • Motherhood penalty • Intimate violence • Child poverty

A feature of human experience is that throughout childhood almost everyone grows up in family households of one form or another. Upon becoming adults, a large majority spend significant amounts of time in committed relationships that involve the care and development of children. Figure 3.1 presents data



P. Dalziel et al., *Wellbeing Economics*, Wellbeing in Politics and Policy,
https://doi.org/10.1007/978-3-319-93194-4_3

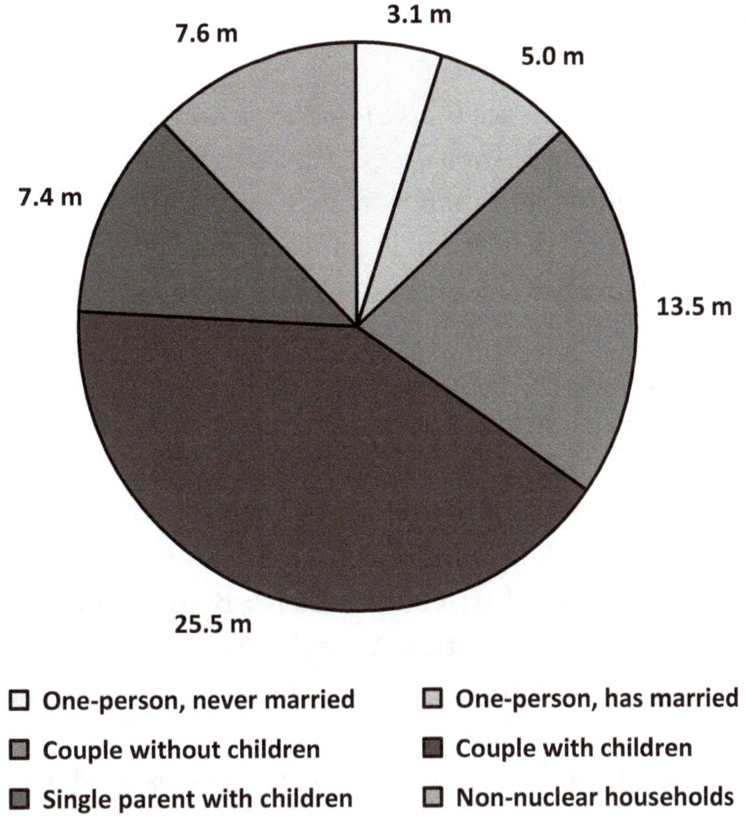


**Fig. 3.1** Number of people usually resident in the United Kingdom by household type, 27 March 2011. (Source: ONS (2015, Tables 53a and 57a))

on the living arrangements of 62 million adults and children normally resident in the United Kingdom on 27 March 2011. Only 5 per cent of the population (3.1 million people) were living in a one-person household, having never married. Another 5 million were living alone, but had been married. The remaining 54 million were in multi-person households, with the largest categories being couples with children (41 per cent of the population) and couples without children (22 per cent). Data such as these suggest that forming households and families is an important aspect of leading valued lives.

This chapter begins with definitions of households and families. This is followed by a discussion of the second type of capital in our wellbeing economics framework: cultural capital, which is deeply connected with household and family life. The chapter then examines gender divisions of labour within households and their implications for the wellbeing experiences of men and women, particularly when they are parents. This leads to an analysis of child poverty (including the role played by housing costs), using the wellbeing lens to focus on the capabilities of parents to co-create with their children lives that they all have reason to value. The chapter finishes with a brief conclusion.

## Households and Families

The Office for National Statistics (ONS) defines a household as "one person living alone, or a group of people (not necessarily related) living at the same address who share cooking facilities and share a living room, sitting room or dining area" (ONS 2016a, p. 2). This definition is adopted throughout this chapter. The Household Labour Force survey estimates there were 27.1 million UK households in 2016 (idem, p. 10).

The ONS then defines a family as "a married, civil partnered or cohabiting couple with or without children, or a lone parent, with at least one child, who live at the same address" (idem, p. 2). This is a restricted definition, conceptualising a family as a special type of household. Children, however, have vital experiences of family that go well beyond one household, one family (Morrow 1998; Dunn and Deater-Deckard 2001; Haugen 2010; Bjarnason et al. 2012; Davies 2015). Indeed, "even children within a single household can live in different 'families' and experience different levels of complexity and change" (Sligo et al. 2017, p. 53).

To illustrate, a child's biological parents may have separated, with one or both parents living with a partner who brings new family relationships into the child's life. Some children have bedrooms they call their own in two or more households. Families stretch back in time through remembered ancestors, while among those still living, grandparents, aunts, uncles, siblings and cousins may contribute to a child's upbringing, including on special family occasions or during holidays. Wellbeing economics is particularly concerned with child development, and so this chapter conceptualises a child's family as including all those who share responsibility for the child's care and development within the child's household or households.

The focus on child development can be justified for at least four reasons. First, there is substantial evidence that a child's wellbeing is badly affected by poverty (Griggs and Walker 2008; McCall 2016), and that lifelong wellbeing is strongly influenced by family circumstances during infancy and childhood (Blanden et al. 2008). Gaviria (2002, p. 331) expresses this succinctly: "If one were to summarize the main message of the massive scientific literature dealing with family influences, a single line would suffice: it pays to choose one's parents." A representative example is the analysis of young men in the United States by Keane and Wolpin (1997), which highlighted how differences in personal abilities by the age of 16 years are a dominating influence on lifetime inequalities.[1]

Second, close conjugal relationships and a good family life are important for the wellbeing of parents (Bok 2010, p. 17). As summarised in a recent authoritative review, "parenthood and parenting experiences have significant effects on well-being over the life course, potentially contributing to cumulative advantage for some and to disadvantage for others" (Umberson et al. 2010, p. 625). The success children enjoy in their own adult lives can affect the ongoing wellbeing of their parents (Greenfield and Marks 2006).

Third, the wider community has an interest in children, if only to avoid future costs associated with poor child development (Bramley and Watkins 2008; Hirsch 2008, 2013). A 40-year study of 1037 children born in New Zealand (see Poulton et al. 2015) found that nearly 80 per cent of the burden to central government finances attributable to survey participants by the age of 38 was due to just 20 per cent of those participants (Caspi et al. 2016). This burden involved disproportionate use of costly services in healthcare, criminal justice and social welfare. Members of the high-cost group could be predicted reasonably well by four indicators of disadvantage during their first decade: lower family household socioeconomic status; greater experience of childhood maltreatment; poorer scores on tests of childhood IQ; and lower scores on measures of childhood self-control.

Finally, the global community has recognised the importance of protecting children's innate rights to health, education, protection and equal opportunity (Lake 2014, p. 1). The Convention on the Rights of the Child, for example, was adopted by the United Nations in 1989. There were 194 state signatories 25 years later, making it the most widely ratified human rights treaty in history (Sandberg 2014, p. 60). The signatories record their conviction "that the family, as the fundamental group of society and the natural environment for the growth and well-being of all its members and particularly children, should be afforded the necessary protection and assistance so that it can fully assume its responsibilities within the community" (Convention on the Rights of the Child 1990, Preamble).

## Cultural Capital

The Convention on the Rights of the Child refers at several points to a child's culture. Article 29 states that a child's education shall be directed, among other things, to the development of respect for their own cultural identity, language and values. Article 30 states that a child belonging to an ethnic, religious or linguistic minority, or who is indigenous, shall not be denied the right, in community with other members of their group, to enjoy their own culture, to profess and practise their own religion or to use their own language. Article 31 recognises the right of the child to participate freely and fully in cultural and artistic life.

In the early 1960s, Pierre Bourdieu and Jean-Claude Passeron (1964) sought to understand why school children from wealthy households achieved better educational results in the French education system than those from households with fewer economic resources. Drawing on that research, Bourdieu (1973, 1983) later introduced the concept of *cultural capital*, intended as a deliberate counter to "human capital" theory. He argued that the latter's emphasis on differences in innate aptitude ignores that children arrive at their first day of school with different levels of "cultural capital previously invested by the family" (Bourdieu 1983, p. 244).[2]

The key idea is that a young person inherits from previous generations diverse cultural values and accepted norms for practising those values. Culture in this context can be defined as "the set of distinctive spiritual, material, intellectual and emotional features of society or a social group" that "encompasses, in addition to art and literature, lifestyles, ways of living together, value systems, traditions and beliefs" (UNESCO Universal Declaration on Cultural Diversity 2001, Preamble).[3] Cultural values and accepted norms are not set in stone; each generation transforms aspects of its cultural heritage to reflect, or perhaps to create, new social conditions. This understanding is reflected in Proposition 7.

**Proposition** 7 Investment in cultural capital can enhance the wellbeing of households and families by expanding opportunities to express, develop, transform and pass on to the next generation their cultural inheritance.

Describing cultural heritage using the metaphor of capital can be applied at two levels (Bourdieu 1983; Throsby 1995). Primarily, persons develop *embodied cultural capital* through investing their time in acquiring cultural values and norms. A young person may learn skills for a particular sport, or how to play a particular musical instrument, or how to appreciate the beauty of a wilderness area, or how the family engages in certain spiritual or religious practices and so on. This also refers to learning cultural norms concerning daily activities such as eating a meal or greeting a stranger. Investment in embodied cultural capital begins at birth and depends not only on the young person's time, but also on the time available for this task in the family (Bourdieu 1983, p. 253).

Young persons are not passive in this process; adolescence, in particular, can be a turbulent time as the next generation of emerging adults constructs cultural fits with their own developing self-identities and world views (Hammack and Toolis 2015; Trommsdorff 2015).

On the secondary level, the metaphor is used to describe how communities invest in conserving and creating *cultural capital assets* such as historical sites, environmental parks, heritage buildings, sport venues, museums and archives, art works, written literature and traditions of artistic performance. This too can be a turbulent process, particularly when artistic works challenge previously accepted values and norms.

Cultural capital assets may be irreplaceable in some cases, but their contribution to wellbeing depends on the ongoing cultural services they provide to people living valued cultural lives. Thus, a social group's cultural vitality depends primarily on the embodied cultural capital being expressed in the group's households and families (Bourdieu 1983, pp. 246–247).

Interaction between the two levels of cultural capital can be measured using indicators such as the number of visitors to heritage sites, the value of tickets sold for arts events, hours of participation in sport activities and the number of visits to museums and libraries. The Culture and Sport Evidence Programme (CASE) in the United Kingdom labels this as *engagement* (Cooper 2012). Echoing a major theme of this section, CASE (2010, Fig. 1, p. 16) has documented how engagement during childhood strongly influences engagement as an adult.

The programme also collates evidence on the economic value of engagement (CASE 2010, pp. 33–41; Marsh and Bertranou 2012; Fujiwara et al., 2014, provide further evidence). Although insightful for tracking trends, it is important to recognise that the value to a social group of its lived culture cannot be captured by economic measures (Walmsley 2012; Taylor 2016). Klamer (2002, p. 467), for example, argues that "cultural capital appears to generate the most important values of all, values that can give meaning to our life", while others have emphasised the cultural value that is enjoyed in "the lived experience of everyday life" (Highmore 2002; Back 2015; Ebrey 2016; Miles 2016).

Cultural capital is also associated with some of the worst crimes recorded against humanity, reflected in the horrors behind words such as genocide, the Holocaust, ethnic cleansing, terrorism, racial hatred, colonial dispossession, female genital mutilation and homophobic violence. The UNESCO Universal

Declaration on Cultural Diversity (2001, Article 2) affirms that "in our increasingly diverse societies, it is essential to ensure harmonious interaction among people and groups with plural, varied and dynamic cultural identities as well as their willingness to live together", but adds in Article 4 that cultural diversity cannot be invoked to infringe upon human rights. Consistent with that principle, Mackenzie (2007) has argued persuasively, among others, that "if the cultural or religious practices of particular communities can only be sustained by perpetuating women's subordination and stunting their capacities for autonomous agency, then liberals and democratic theorists cannot consistently accommodate the demands made by such communities" (idem, p. 105).

## Cultural Capital and Gender

The previous section described how developing cultural capital in children requires investment of time. Bourdieu identified this as the major reason why children growing up in families with more economic resources arrive at school with higher levels of cultural capital; wealthier families have greater amounts of usable time, "particularly in the form of the mother's free time" (Bourdieu 1983, p. 253). The description of a mother's time as "free" obviously reflects Bourdieu's own cultural norms. As Reay (1998, p. 94) has noted, "once mothers' time is harnessed to the acquisition of cultural capital, it is no longer free time." Time caring for children sacrifices opportunities for other time-choices, including earning income from paid employment.

There is no dispute that sacrifices associated with the arrival of a child into a household can be significant for both parents at the time (Genesoni and Tallandini 2009; Dew and Wilcox 2011, p. 1). Musick et al. (2016, p. 1070) report that "a substantial body of work shows lower levels of subjective well-being among parents compared to men and women without children" (see, e.g., Hansen 2012, and Deaton and Stone 2014).

It is not the presence of children per se producing this outcome (Pollmann-Schult 2014). An analysis of American Time Use Survey data by Connelly and Kimmel (2015, p. 1) found that "mothers and fathers engaged in child caregiving enjoy their time spent in child caregiving; fathers as much, or even more so, than mothers as evidenced by their average values for happiness, meaningfulness, tiredness, and stress and an aggregated statistic, the unpleasantness index". Instead, both studies suggest that lower parental wellbeing is due to the sacrifices imposed by high financial and time costs of parenthood (see also Fawcett 1988).

The sacrifices are disproportionately made by women. This begins with women carrying a greater responsibility for childcare than men (Pettit and Hook 2009; Hook 2010). This can be illustrated using time-use surveys (Gershuny 2011). The two most recent surveys in the United Kingdom took place in 2000 and 2015 (ONS 2003; Gershuny and Sullivan 2017). Figure 3.2 presents the average daily minutes recorded for parents spending time in the active care of children, distinguishing by the age band of the youngest child. Active care includes items such as feeding a child, but excludes time when the parent is primarily engaged in another activity while also being present as the responsible person on call if the child needs attention (ONS 2016b, p. 4).

In both survey years, and for both age bands of the youngest child, female parents spent more than twice as much time engaged in active child care as male parents. Over the 15 years between the two surveys, the gender gap narrowed for households where the youngest child was of preschool age, but increased for the older age group.

Further, objective wellbeing indicators show lower wages and lifetime losses of personal wealth for women with children, compared to men with children or to women without children. The gap is so clear that it is commonly termed the

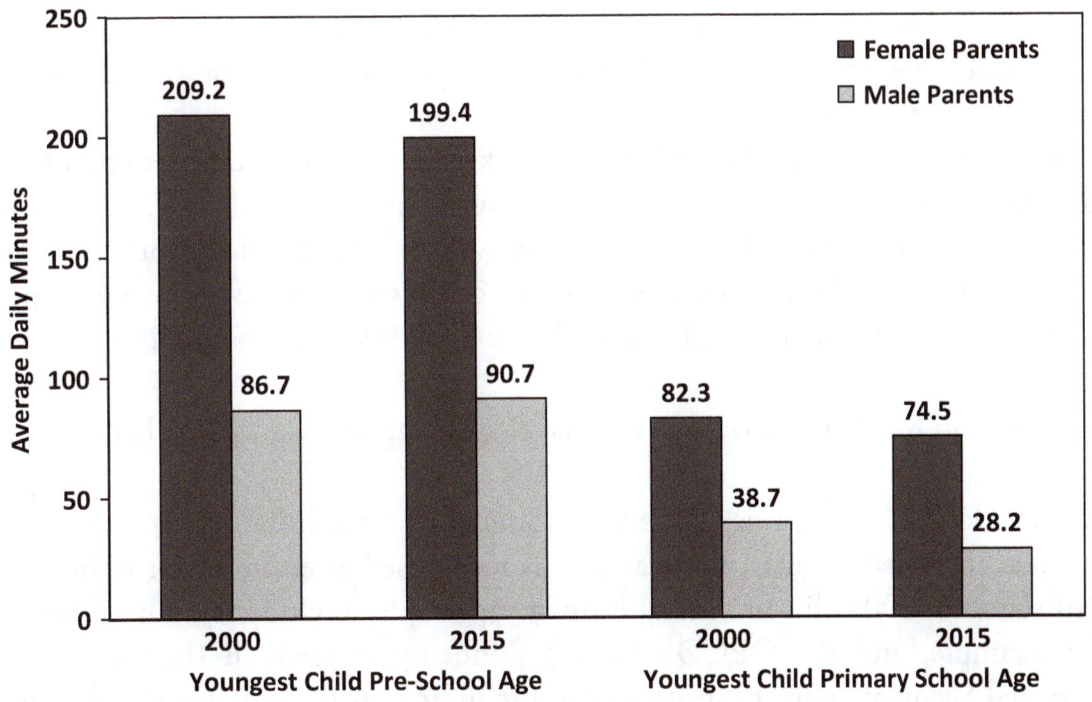


**Fig. 3.2** Average daily minutes of total active childcare provided while youngest child living in same household is preschool age or primary school age, by gender of parent, United Kingdom, 2000 and 2015. (Source: Adapted from ONS (2016b, Fig. 2, p. 6))

*motherhood penalty* (Gangl and Ziefle 2009; Gash 2009; Budig et al. 2012; Harkness 2016; Lersch et al. 2017), which may be driven by cultural values.

Gary Becker, for example, applied economic analysis to family issues in his *Treatise on the Family*, first published in 1981. In his Nobel Prize lecture, he expressed one of his key research questions in the following terms: "Why in almost all societies have married women specialized in bearing and rearing children" (Becker 1992, p. 47). His answer focused on biological differences and on cultural values reflected in labour market discrimination. His analysis suggested how economic forces, unchecked by public policy, are able to amplify small biological and cultural differences between men and women into a sharp division of childcare between mothers and fathers (Becker 1991, pp. 30–79; see more recently Ermisch 2003, pp. 6–7, and Browning et al. 2014, pp. 67–69).

Budig et al. (2012) have researched the influence of cultural attitudes on the impact of work and family policies in 22 industrialised countries. They measured cultural attitudes using survey questions on how strongly respondents agreed with the following statements: family life suffers if woman works full-time; preschool children suffer if mother works; and a man's job is to earn money, while a woman's job is to look after home and family. They found significant differences in outcomes where cultural attitudes supported the male breadwinner/female caregiver model compared to support for maternal employment, concluding that "culture amplifies the relationships between parental leave and maternal earnings, and of childcare policies with maternal earnings" (idem, p. 185).

Given these findings, the critique of Mackenzie (2007) cited at the end of the previous section applies. It is not legitimate to sustain social institutions and practices that perpetuate large penalties for women who become mothers, compared to men who become fathers. Instead, reason suggests the following proposition (see also Nussbaum and Glover 1995; Sen 1995; Nussbaum 2000).

**Proposition 8** Men and women can have equal capabilities for wellbeing.

The United Kingdom is a long way from equal capabilities between men and women. Personal security, for example, is recognised as essential for wellbeing. Nussbaum's (2003) list of central human capabilities includes Bodily Integrity, for example, and the OECD's (2017) wellbeing conceptual framework has Personal Security as one of its quality of life indicators for individual wellbeing. Article 3 of the Universal Declaration of Human Rights states everyone has the right to life, liberty and security of person. In that context, consider the prevalence of intimate violence in England and Wales, represented in Fig. 3.3.

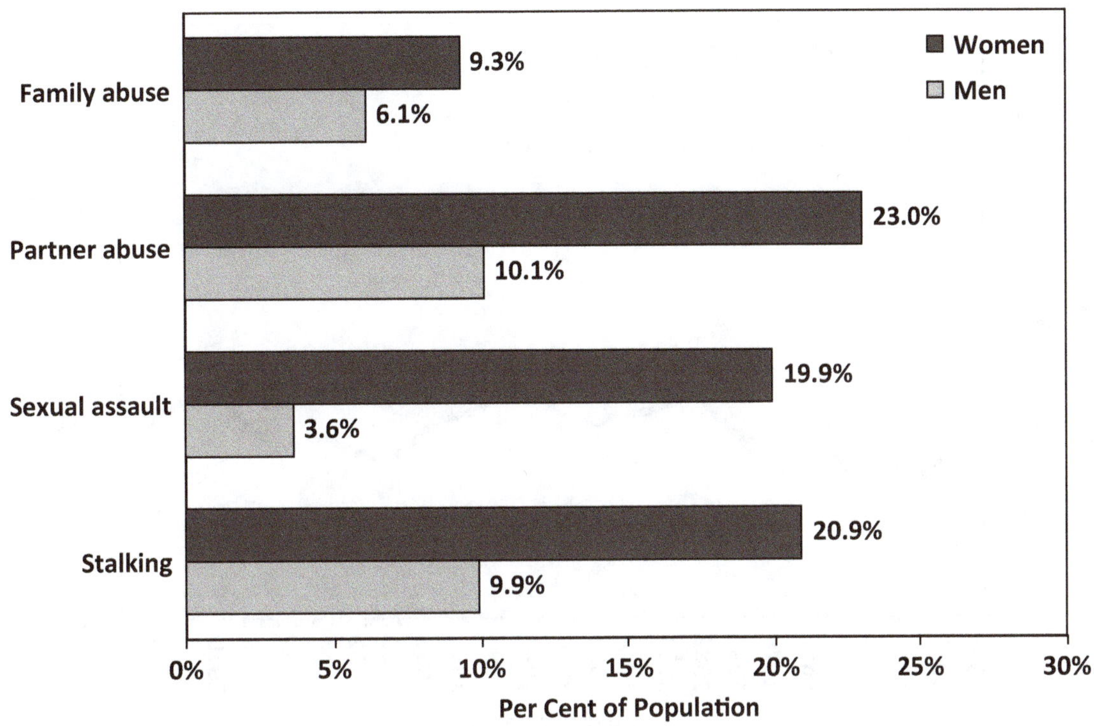


**Fig. 3.3** Prevalence of intimate violence since the age of 16 among adults aged 16 to 59, by category, England and Wales, year ending March 2016. (Source: ONS (2017, Appendix Table 4.01), reporting data from the Crime Survey for England and Wales)

The data come from the UK Crime Survey, which defines intimate violence as family abuse, partner abuse, sexual assault or stalking (ONS 2017, p. 74). The Survey offers self-reported data for each of these items, reproduced in Fig. 3.3. Women are much more likely than men to report having suffered intimate violence since the age of 16. The likelihood ratio is greater than two to one for partner abuse and for stalking, and is greater than five to one for sexual assault. These are very large differences in such an important item of wellbeing.

## The Blight of Child Poverty

The major focus of this chapter is the development of embodied cultural capital in children through the investment of time and financial resources by their families. This is critical for current and lifelong wellbeing of each child and for the wellbeing of the child's parents. Successful child development also produces benefits for wider society. Consequently, if a large number of children grow up in households without adequate economic resources, the ramifications persist through time and go well beyond the immediate families. This reflected in Proposition 9.

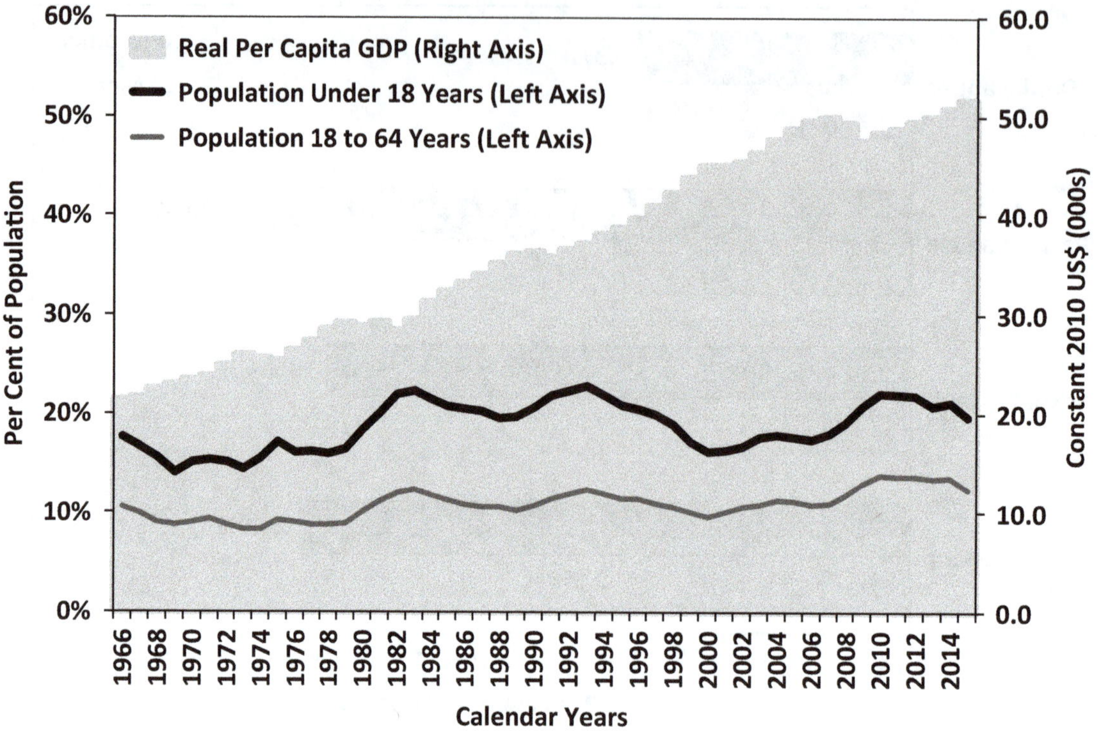


**Fig. 3.4** Real per capita gross domestic product and absolute poverty status of population by age group, United States, 1966 to 2015. (Source: World Bank (2017, Indicator NY.GDP.PCAP.KD) and United States Census Bureau (2016, Table 3))

**Proposition 9** Present and future wellbeing can be enhanced if children grow up in households that are able to access adequate economic resources.

There are important policy debates about what are adequate economic resources (Ravallion 2016, Chap. 4). It is useful to begin in the United States, where official measures of child poverty are based on 1964 research by the Social Security Administration that set minimum adequate income thresholds for families of different size and composition (United States Census Bureau 2016). These thresholds were calculated using the cost of the cheapest nutritionally adequate food plan designed by the Department of Agriculture, multiplied by a factor based on survey data to cover other necessary expenditures such as accommodation, clothing and transport (U.S. Bureau of the Census 1982, p. 185). The thresholds are adjusted annually to compensate for inflation, but not for increases in the country's average living standards. Because the thresholds do not change with economic growth, these data are termed *absolute poverty* indicators.

Figure 3.4 presents data for the last 50 years on the percentage of people living in households with income below the absolute poverty thresholds for two demographic groups: people aged under 18 years (children) and people aged 18 to 64 years (the working-age population). The shaded bars show the level of real per capita gross domestic product (GDP) in each year. GDP has shortcomings as discussed in Chap. 1, but continues to indicate a country's average material living standards. Over the five decades, real per capita GDP increased from just over $12,000 in 1966 to just under $52,000 in 2015, an increase of 140 per cent.

Two observations stand out from Fig. 3.4. First, child poverty in the United States is more extensive than adult poverty; the proportion of young people living in households with inadequate income is well above the proportion of working-age adults in this situation. Second, despite a 140 per cent increase in real per capita GDP, there has been no sustained improvement in the country's level of child poverty, using absolute standards set in the 1960s. There have been oscillations, but child poverty has remained above 15 per cent since 1974, and has been 20 per cent or higher since 2009, damaging the care and development of large numbers of children. Economic growth has failed to improve this important aspect of a country's wellbeing.

The UK approach to measuring child poverty is different. Children need access to sufficient economic resources for their cultural development; hence, official poverty thresholds are defined relative to the country's living standards. The Family Resources Survey samples more than 19,000 private households in the United Kingdom (Department for Work and Pensions 2017a, p. 18). Adjustments to each household's income are made to reflect its size and composition, which results in *household equivalised income*. Ranking these data from poorest to richest, the result for the middle household is the median equivalised income. The poverty threshold is set at 60 per cent of this median equivalised income.[4] When the median equivalised income changes, so does the threshold; hence, it is a measure of socially determined relative poverty.

Figure 3.5 presents three poverty measures for the United Kingdom between 1994–1995 and 2015–2016, against a background showing the country's real per capita GDP. The GDP data show steady growth before the impact of the global financial crisis in 2007–2008 and 2008–2009.

The bottom measure in the graph is the poverty rate of working-age adults, calculated before housing costs (BHC) are considered. This sits at 14–16 per cent throughout the 22 years. The lighter shaded line in the graph is the poverty rate of children, again before housing costs. Like in the United States, child poverty in the United Kingdom is more extensive than adult poverty. Unlike America, there is a downward trend in the child poverty data (at least until the last two years), to the extent that the gap with working-age adult poverty almost closed in 2012–2013.

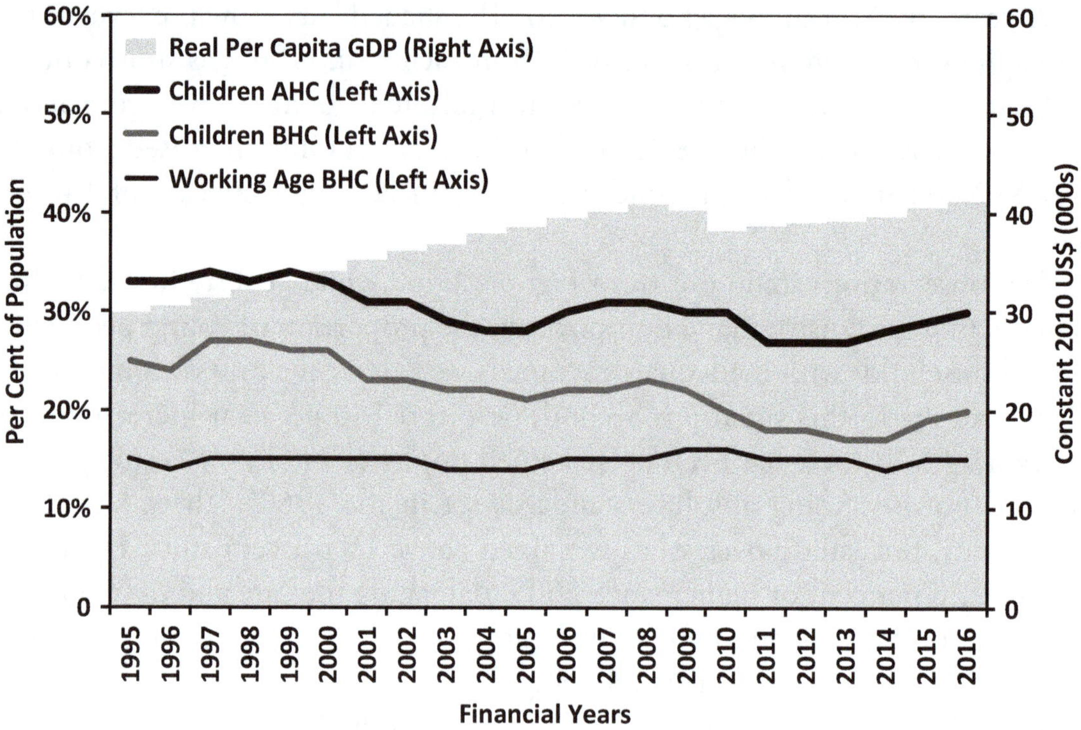


**Fig. 3.5** Real per capita gross domestic product and relative poverty status of children, United Kingdom, 1994–1995 to 2015–2016. (Notes: Data are for Great Britain prior to 2002–2003. AHC is After Housing Costs. BHC is Before Housing Costs. Source: World Bank (2017, Indicator NY.GDP.PCAP.KD) and Department for Work and Pensions (2017a, Table 4.1tr and 5.1tr))

Finally, the top line depicts child poverty after housing costs (AHC); that is, after accounting for: rent (gross of housing benefit); water rates, community and council water charges; mortgage interest payments (net of tax relief); structural insurance premiums (for owner occupiers); and ground rent and service charges (Department for Work and Pensions 2017b, p. 45). This series is better for comparing living standards of individuals whose housing costs are high relative to their quality of accommodation and where their Housing Benefit has risen to offset higher rents (idem, p. 27). On this definition, child relative poverty in 2015–2016 was 30 per cent, back to its value a decade earlier.

This represents 4 million children recorded as living in households with inadequate economic resources. This has two consequences. First, it limits the capabilities of parents and children to co-create the kinds of lives they value and have reason to value according to the country's social norms of the day. Second, the lack of access to adequate economic resources hampers the children's educational and cultural development, which is creating long-term costs. Such high child poverty is a blight on the country's wellbeing.

## Conclusion

The central idea of this chapter is expressed in Proposition 7: Investment in cultural capital can enhance the wellbeing of households and families by expanding opportunities to express, develop, transform and pass on to the next generation their cultural inheritance. Although a clumsy term for the richness and dynamism of the experiences it signifies, the metaphor of cultural capital emphasises that cultural inheritance is an important asset for persons co-creating the kinds of lives they value, and have reason to value, in their households and families.

There is robust evidence of serious wellbeing challenges experienced by UK households and families. Parental sacrifices of time and financial costs are carried disproportionately by mothers, and large numbers of women do not have the same capability for wellbeing as most men, reflected in far greater vulnerability to intimate violence. After accounting for housing costs, nearly one in three children in the United Kingdom are growing up in households with income below 60 per cent of median equivalised income. These children are likely to be missing opportunities for cultural and educational development, with long-term adverse consequences for their personal wellbeing, for the wellbeing of their parents and for the wellbeing of wider society.

The urgency of integrated action to address child care arrangements, intimate violence, affordable housing and child poverty is lost when the primary focus is on economic growth as "the essential foundation of all our aspirations" (Cameron 2010, par. 4). In contrast, the lived experiences of families and households reflected in the data presented in this chapter must challenge the dominant cultural values in our society. How can it be culturally acceptable for such high levels of parental inequality, intimate violence, poor housing and child poverty to be allowed to persist?

This chapter has focused on households and families. The next step in the wellbeing economics framework is to analyse how people can collaborate outside their homes to pursue greater wellbeing for themselves and for their communities. This analysis begins in Chap. 4.

## Notes

1. See also Belzil (2007, p. 1076).
2. More recently, Miles and Sullivan (2012, p. 321) draw on UK data to "confirm the powerful role of the family in transmitting tastes and participation [in culture] during childhood, and of community cultures in maintaining and reinforcing them".

The term is now part of the economics lexicon; see, for example, Berkes and Folke (1992), Johnson et al. (1995), de Bruin (1998, 1999), Klamer (2002), Cheng (2006), Cochrane (2006), Dalziel et al. (2009) and Throsby (1999, 2011, 2014).

3. Consistent with the way we use "cultural capital" in this chapter, Article 1 of the UNESCO Universal Declaration on Cultural Diversity (2001) describes cultural diversity as "the common heritage of humanity [that] should be recognized and affirmed for the benefit of present and future generations".
4. Other proportions of median equivalised income can be used; the OECD, for example, uses 50 per cent of median household income for its international comparisons (see https://data.oecd.org/inequality/poverty-rate.htm). A child is a person aged under 16 years or a person between 16 and 19 years who is: not married nor in a civil partnership nor living with a partner; living with parents or a responsible adult; and in full-time non-advanced education or in unwaged government training (Department for Work and Pensions 2017b, p. 39).

## References

Back, Les. 2015. Why Everyday Life Matters: Class, Community and Making Life Livable. *Sociology* 49 (5): 820–836.

Becker, Gary. 1991. *A Treatise on the Family*, Enlarged Edition. Cambridge, MA: Harvard University Press.

———. 1992. The Economic Way of Looking at Life. Nobel Lecture 9 December. Reprinted in Torsten Persson, Ed. Nobel Lectures, Economics 1991–1995. Singapore: World Scientific Publishing, pp. 38–58.

Belzil, Christian. 2007. The Return to Schooling in Structural Dynamic Models: A Survey. *European Economic Review* 51 (5): 1059–1105.

Berkes, Fikret, and Carl Folke. 1992. A Systems Perspective on the Interrelations between Natural, Human-made and Cultural Capital. *Ecological Economics* 5 (1): 1–8.

Bjarnason, Thoroddur, Pernille Bendtsen, Arsaell M. Arnarsson, Ina Borup, Ronald J. Iannotti, Petra Löfstedt, Ilona Haapasalo, and Birgit Niclasen. 2012. Life Satisfaction among Children in Different Family Structures: A Comparative Study of 36 Western Societies. *Children & Society* 26 (1): 51–62.

Blanden, Jo, Kirstine Hansen, and Stephen Machin. 2008. *The GDP Cost of the Lost Earning Potential of Adults who Grew Up in Poverty*. York: Joseph Rowntree Foundation.

Bok, Derek. 2010. *The Politics of Happiness: What Government Can Learn from the New Research on Well-being*. Princeton, NJ: Princeton University Press.

Bourdieu, Pierre. 1973. Cultural Reproduction and Social Reproduction. In *Knowledge, Education and Cultural Change: Papers in the Sociology of Education*, ed. Richard K. Brown, 71–112. London: Tavistock.

———. 1983. Ökonomisches Kapital, Kulturelles Kapital, Soziales Kapital. In *Soziale Ungleichheiten* (Soziale Welt, Sonderheft 2), ed. Reinhard Kreckel, 183–98. Goettingen: Otto Schartz. Translated by Richard Nice and republished as The Forms of Capital in *Handbook of Theory and Research for the Sociology of Education*, ed. John C. Richardson, 241–258. Westport, CT: Greenwood Publishing Group, 1986.

Bourdieu, Pierre, and Jean-Claude Passeron. 1964. *Les héritiers: Les étudiants et la culture*. Paris: Les Editions de Minuit. Translated by Richard Nice and republished as *The Inheritors: French Students and their Relation to Culture*. Chicago: University of Chicago Press.

Bramley, Glen, and David Watkins. 2008. *The Public Service Costs of Child Poverty*. York: Joseph Rowntree Foundation.

Browning, Martin, Pierre-André Chiappori, and Yoram Weiss. 2014. *Economics of the Family*. Cambridge: Cambridge University Press.

Budig, Michelle J., Joya Misra, and Irene Boeckmann. 2012. The Motherhood Penalty in Cross-National Perspective: The Importance of Work–Family Policies and Cultural Attitudes. *Social Politics* 19 (2): 163–193.

Cameron, Rt. Hon. David. 2010. PM Speech on Wellbeing. A Transcript of a Speech Given by the Prime Minister on 25 November 2010. https://www.gov.uk/government/speeches/pm-speech-on-wellbeing.

CASE. 2010. *Understanding the Drivers, Impact and Value of Engagement in Culture and Sport: An Over-arching Summary of the Research*. London: The Culture and Sport Evidence Programme.

Caspi, Avshalom, Renate M. Houts, Daniel W. Belsky, Honalee Harrington, Sandhya Ramrakha, Richie Poulton, and Terrie E. Moffitt. 2016. Childhood Forecasting of a Small Segment of the Population with Large Economic Burden. *Nature Human Behaviour* 1, Article 0005, published at https://doi.org/10.1038/s41562-016-0005.

Cheng, Sao-Wen. 2006. Cultural Goods Creation, Cultural Capital Formation, Provision of Cultural Services and Cultural Atmosphere Accumulation. *Journal of Cultural Economics* 30 (4): 263–286.

Cochrane, Phoebe. 2006. Exploring Cultural Capital and its Importance in Sustainable Development. *Ecological Economics* 57 (2): 318–330.

Connelly, Rachel, and Jean Kimmel. 2015. If You're Happy and You Know It: How Do Mothers and Fathers in the US Really Feel about Caring for Their Children? *Feminist Economics* 21 (1): 1–34.

Convention on the Rights of the Child. 1990. Retrieved 25 March 2017 from: www.ohchr.org/EN/ProfessionalInterest/Pages/CRC.aspx.

Cooper, Adam. 2012. The Drivers, Impact and Value of CASE: A Short History from the Inside. *Cultural Trends* 21 (4): 281–289.

Dalziel, Paul and Caroline Saunders with Rosie Fyfe and Bronwyn Newton. 2009. Sustainable Development and Cultural Capital. *Official Statistics Research Series* 5, available at http://hdl.handle.net/10182/2427.

Davies, Hayley. 2015. *Understanding Children's Personal Lives and Relationships*. London: Palgrave Macmillan.

de Bruin, Anne. 1998. Cultural Capital. In *Encyclopedia of Political Economy*, ed. Phillip O'Hara, 169–171. London: Routledge.

———. 1999. Towards Extending the Concept of Human Capital: A Note on Cultural Capital. *Journal of Interdisciplinary Economics* 10 (1): 59–70.

Deaton, Angus, and Arthur A. Stone. 2014. Evaluative and Hedonic Wellbeing among Those With and Without Children. *Proceedings of the National Academy of Sciences* 111 (4): 1328–1333.

Department for Work and Pensions. 2017a. *Households Below Average Income: 1994/95 to 2016/16*. Report and Supporting Data Tables. https://www.gov.uk/government/statistics/households-below-average-income-199495-to-201516. Accessed 12 Apr 2017.

———. 2017b. *Households Below Average Income (HBAI) Quality and Methodology Information Report 2015/16*. London: Department for Work and Pensions.

Dew, Jeffrey, and W. Bradford Wilcox. 2011. If Momma Ain't Happy: Explaining Declines in Marital Satisfaction Among New Mothers. *Journal of Marriage and Family* 73 (1): 1–12.

Dunn, Judy, and Kirby Deater-Deckard. 2001. *Children's Views of their Changing Families*. Layerthorpe: York Publishing Services for the Joseph Rowntree Foundation.

Ebrey, Jill. 2016. The Mundane and Insignificant, the Ordinary and the Extraordinary: Understanding Everyday Participation and Theories of Everyday Life. *Cultural Trends* 25 (3): 158–168.

Ermisch, John F. 2003. *An Economic Analysis of the Family*. Princeton and Oxford: Princeton University Press.

Fawcett, James T. 1988. The Value of Children and the Transition to Parenthood. *Marriage & Family Review* 12 (3-4): 11–34.

Fujiwara, Daniel, Laura Kudrna, and Paul Dolan. 2014. *Quantifying and Valuing the Wellbeing Impacts of Culture and Sport*. London: Department for Culture Media & Sport.

Gangl, Markus, and Andrea Ziefle. 2009. Motherhood, Labor Force Behavior, and Women's Careers: An Empirical Assessment of the Wage Penalty for Motherhood in Britain, Germany, and the United States. *Demography* 46 (2): 341–369.

Gash, Vanessa. 2009. Sacrificing Their Careers for Their Families: An Analysis of the Penalty to Motherhood in Europe. *Social Indicators Research* 93 (3): 569–586.

Gaviria, Alejandro. 2002. Intergenerational Mobility, Sibling Inequality and Borrowing Constraints. *Economics of Education Review* 21 (4): 331–340.

Genesoni, Lucia, and Maria Anna Tallandini. 2009. Men's Psychological Transition to Fatherhood: An Analysis of the Literature, 1989–2008. *Birth* 36 (4): 305–317.

Gershuny, Jonathan. 2011. *Time-Use Surveys and the Measurement of National Well-being*. Report prepared for the Office for National Statistics. Oxford: Centre for Time Use Research, University of Oxford.

Gershuny, Jonathan, and Oriel Sullivan. 2017. *United Kingdom Time Use Survey, 2014-2015*. Data collection. UK Data Service. SN: 8128, https://doi.org/10.5255/UKDA-SN-8128-1.

Greenfield, Emily A., and Nadine F. Marks. 2006. Linked Lives: Adult Children's Problems and Their Parents' Psychological and Relational Well-Being. *Journal of Marriage and Family* 68 (2): 442–454.

Griggs, Julia, and Robert Walker. 2008. *The Costs of Child Poverty for Individuals and Society: A Literature Review*. York: Joseph Rowntree Foundation.

Hammack, Phillip L., and Erin Toolis. 2015. Identity, Politics, and the Cultural Psychology of Adolescence. In *The Oxford Handbook of Human Development and Culture: An Interdisciplinary Perspective*, ed. Lene Arnett Jensen, 396–409. Oxford: Oxford University Press.

Hansen, Thomas. 2012. Parenthood and Happiness: a Review of Folk Theories Versus Empirical Evidence. *Social Indicators Research* 108 (1): 29–64.

Harkness, Susan E. 2016. The Effect of Motherhood and Lone Motherhood on the Employment and Earnings of British Women: A Lifecycle Approach. *European Sociological Review* 32 (6): 850–863.

Haugen, Gry Mette D. 2010. Children's Perspectives on Everyday Experiences of Shared Residence: Time, Emotions and Agency Dilemmas. *Children & Society* 24 (2): 112–122.

Highmore, Ben. 2002. *Everyday Life and Cultural Theory. An Introduction*. London/New York: Routledge.

Hirsch, Donald. 2008. *Estimating the Costs of Child Poverty*. York: Joseph Rowntree Foundation.

Hirsch, Donald. 2013. *An Estimate of the Cost of Child Poverty in 2013*. London: Child Poverty Action Group.

Hook, Jennifer L. 2010. Gender Inequality in the Welfare State: Sex Segregation in Housework. *American Journal of Sociology* 115 (5): 1480–1523.

Johnson, James H., Elisa Jayne Bienenstock, and Jennifer A. Stoloff. 1995. An Empirical Test of the Cultural Capital Hypothesis. *Review of Black Political Economy* 23 (4): 7–27.

Keane, Michael P., and Kenneth I. Wolpin. 1997. The Career Decisions of Young Men. *Journal of Political Economy* 105 (3): 473–522.

Klamer, Arjo. 2002. Accounting for Social and Cultural Values. *De Economist* 150 (4): 453–473.

Lake, Anthony. 2014. Children's Rights, Equity and Our Common Future. In *25 Years of the Convention on the Rights of the Child: Is the World a Better Place for Children?*, 1–5. New York: United Nations Children's Fund.

Lersch, Philipp M., Marita Jacob, and Karsten Hank. 2017. Parenthood, Gender, and Personal Wealth. *European Sociological Review* 33 (3): 410–422.

Mackenzie, Catriona. 2007. Relational Autonomy, Sexual Justice and Cultural Pluralism. In *Sexual Justice/Cultural Justice: Critical Perspectives on Political Theory and Practice*, ed. Barbara Arneil, Monique Deveaux, Rita Dhamoon, and Avigail Eisenberg, 103–121. London/New York: Routledge.

Marsh, Kevin, and Evelina Bertranou. 2012. Can Subjective Well-being Measures be Used to Value Policy Outcomes? The Example of Engagement in Culture. *Cultural Trends* 21 (4): 299–310.

McCall, Becky. 2016. Child Poverty Continues to Rise in the UK. *The Lancet* 388 (10046): 747.

Miles, Andrew. 2016. Telling Tales of Participation: Exploring the Interplay of Time and Territory in Cultural Boundary Work using Participation Narratives. *Cultural Trends* 25 (3): 182–193.

Miles, Andrew, and Alice Sullivan. 2012. Understanding Participation in Culture and Sport: Mixing Methods, Reordering Knowledges. *Cultural Trends* 21 (4): 311–324.

Morrow, Virginia. 1998. *Understanding Families: Children's Perspectives*. London: National Children's Bureau in Association with the Joseph Rowntree Foundation.

Musick, Kelly, Ann Meier, and Sarah Flood. 2016. How Parents Fare: Mothers' and Fathers' Subjective Well-Being in Time with Children. *American Sociological Review* 81 (5): 1069–1095.

Nussbaum, Martha C. 2000. *Women and Human Development: The Capabilities Approach*. Cambridge: Cambridge University Press.

———. 2003. Capabilities as Fundamental Entitlements: Sen and Social Justice. *Feminist Economics* 9 (2–3): 33–59.

Nussbaum, Martha, and Jonathan Glover, eds. 1995. *Women, Culture and Development: A Study of Human Capabilities*. Oxford: Clarendon Press.

OECD. 2017. *How's Life? 2017: Measuring Well-being*. Paris: OECD Publishing, https://doi.org/10.1787/how_life-2017-en.

ONS. 2003. *The United Kingdom 2000 Time Use Survey: Technical Report*. Norwich: Her Majesty's Stationery Office.

———. 2015. *2011 Census: United Kingdom Submission for United Nations Questionnaire on Population and Housing Censuses, Part 2*. London: Office for National Statistics. https://www.ons.gov.uk/peoplepopulationandcommunity/populationandmigration/populationestimates/datasets/2011censusunitedkingdomsubmissionforunitednationsquestionnaireonpopulationandhousingcensuses. Spreadsheet accessed 16 Jan 2017.

———. 2016a. *Families and Households in the UK: 2016*. Statistical Bulletin released 4 November. London: Office for National Statistics.

———. 2016b. Changes in the Value and Division of Unpaid Care Work in the UK: 2000 to 2015. https://www.ons.gov.uk/economy/nationalaccounts/satelliteaccounts/articles/changesinthevalueanddivisionofunpaidcareworkintheuk/2000to2015. Article accessed 4 Apr 2017.

———. 2017. *Focus on Violent Crime and Sexual Offences, England and Wales, Year Ending March 2016*. Compendium released 9 February. London: Office for National Statistics.

Pettit, Becky, and Jennifer L. Hook. 2009. *Gendered Tradeoffs: Family, Social Policy, and Economic Inequality in Twenty-one Countries*. New York: Russell Sage Foundation.

Pollmann-Schult, Matthias. 2014. Parenthood and Life Satisfaction: Why Don't Children Make People Happy? *Journal of Marriage and Family* 76 (2): 319–335.

Poulton, Richie, Terrie E. Moffitt, and Phil A. Silva. 2015. The Dunedin Multidisciplinary Health and Development Study: Overview of the First 40 Years, with an Eye to the Future. *Social Psychiatry and Psychiatric Epidemiology* 50 (5): 679–693.

Ravallion, Martin. 2016. *The Economics of Poverty: History, Measurement and Policy*. New York: Oxford University Press.

Reay, Diane. 1998. *Class Work: Mothers' Involvement in their Children's Primary Schooling*. London: UCL Press.

Sandberg, Kirsten. 2014. The Genesis and Spirit of the Convention on the Rights of the Child. In *25 Years of the Convention on the Rights of the Child: Is the World a Better Place for Children?*, 59–65. New York: United Nations Children's Fund.

Sen, Amartya. 1995. Gender Inequality and Theories of Justice. In *Women, Culture and Development: A Study of Human Capabilities*, ed. Martha Nussbaum and Jonathan Glover, 259–273. Oxford: Clarendon Press.

Sligo, Judith L., Helena M. McAnally, John E. Tansley, Joanne M. Baxter, Aroha E. Bolton, Katherine M. Skillander, and Robert J. Hancox. 2017. The Dynamic, Complex and Diverse Living and Care Arrangements of Young New Zealanders: Implications for Policy. *Kōtuitui: New Zealand Journal of Social Sciences Online* 12 (1): 41–55.

Taylor, Mark. 2016. Nonparticipation or Different Styles of Participation? Alternative Interpretations from Taking Part. *Cultural Trends* 25 (3): 169–181.

Throsby, David. 1995. Culture, Economics and Sustainability. *Journal of Cultural Economics* 19 (3): 199–206.

———. 1999. Cultural Capital. *Journal of Cultural Economics* 23 (1): 3–12.

———. 2011. Cultural Capital. In *A Handbook of Cultural Economics*, ed. Ruth Towse, 2nd ed., 142–146. Cheltenham: Edward Elgar.

———. 2014. The Role of Culture in Sustainable Urban Development: Some Economic Issues. *International Journal of Global Environmental Issues* 13 (2–4): 89–99.

Trommsdorff, Gisela. 2015. Cultural Roots of Values, Morals, and Religious Orientations in Adolescent Development. In *The Oxford Handbook of Human Development and Culture: An Interdisciplinary Perspective*, ed. Lene Arnett Jensen, 377–395. Oxford: Oxford University Press.

Umberson, Debra, Tetyana Pudrovska, and Corinne Reczek. 2010. Parenthood, Childlessness, and Well-Being: A Life Course Perspective. *Journal of Marriage and Family* 72 (3): 612–629.

UNESCO Universal Declaration on Cultural Diversity. 2001. http://www.unesco.org/fileadmin/MULTIMEDIA/HQ/CLT/pdf/5_Cultural_Diversity_EN.pdf. Accessed 25 Mar 2017.

United States Census Bureau. 2016. Historical Poverty Tables: People and Families – 1959 to 2015. https://www.census.gov/data/tables/time-series/demo/income-poverty/historical-poverty-people.html. Website accessed 18 Apr 2017.

U.S. Bureau of the Census. 1982. *Characteristics of the Population Below the Poverty Level: 1980*. Current Population Reports, Series P-60, No. 133. Washington, DC: U.S. Government Printing Office.

Walmsley, Ben. 2012. Towards a Balanced Scorecard: A Critical Analysis of the Culture and Sport Evidence (CASE) Programme. *Cultural Trends* 21 (4): 325–334.

World Bank. 2017. World Development Indicators. http://data.worldbank.org/. Database accessed 18 Apr 2017.

# 4

# Civil Society and Social Capital

**Abstract** This chapter explores how humans collaborate with others outside their families and households to expand capabilities for wellbeing, particularly by creating and participating in civil society institutions. The chapter also analyses social capital and how it can be increased through mechanisms that include: learning in schools; participation in networks; enforcement of norms; development of societal aspirations; and efforts for social inclusion. There are tensions between cultural capital (discussed in the previous chapter) and social capital (this chapter) since access to the services of social capital—especially to bridging social capital—is much easier for people who share the cultural capital of the community's dominant social group. Policy can enhance capabilities for wellbeing by ensuring persons are not disadvantaged as a result of ethnicity or other personal characteristic in their equitable access to services from all forms of capital.

**Keywords** Social capital • Wellbeing • Civil society • Structural racism • Interculturalism

We humans are social beings. Consistent with that observation, Chap. 3 has described how most of us cohabit with other people for long periods of our lives. This book now turns to how we humans collaborate outside our families and households to expand capabilities for wellbeing. This chapter focuses on


P. Dalziel et al., *Wellbeing Economics*, Wellbeing in Politics and Policy,
https://doi.org/10.1007/978-3-319-93194-4_4

collaboration in what is termed the third sector (Etzioni 1973; Corry 2010) or civil society (Seligman 1992; Dekker and van den Broek 1998; Fukuyama 2001; Office for Civil Society 2010).

Despite nuanced differences in definitions offered for this aspect of social life, there is general agreement that the institutional core of civil society is "constituted by voluntary associations outside the sphere of the state and the economy" (Flyvbjerg 1998, p. 210; see also Kumar 1993, and Seligman 2002). Persons support these associations by donating time and finance to pursue common interests and shared values. In the UK Community Life Survey of 2015–2016, for example, 47 per cent of respondents reported providing unpaid service to a volunteer organisation at least once a month (70 per cent reported doing so at least once a year), and 73 per cent reported making a financial donation to charity during an average four-week period (Cabinet Office 2016). The first section of this chapter discusses these civil society institutions and their contribution to wellbeing.

A closely related idea, which is adopted in many wellbeing frameworks, is *social capital* (see the survey in Scrivens and Smith 2013, part 3). This conveys the idea that social collaboration is easier when people are strongly connected to each other through established relationships in diverse social networks and by sharing accepted social norms (such as trust and civic co-operation; see Knack and Keefer 1997). This concept is explored in the second section, with a discussion of how social capital can be strengthened through learning in schools, participation in networks, enforcement of norms, development of societal aspirations and efforts for social inclusion.

The chapter's third section focuses on social capital and ethnicity, observing that there are tensions between the concept of cultural capital discussed in the previous chapter and the concept of social capital discussed in this chapter. These tensions exist because access to services from social capital—especially from what is termed bridging social capital—is much easier for people who share the cultural capital of a community's dominant cultural group. This creates and maintains privilege for the dominant group, to the disadvantage of outsiders' wellbeing, so that reflective action is required to redress the balance. The chapter finishes with a brief conclusion.

## The Institutions of Civil Society

In an open society, people create diverse social institutions to pursue common goals and shared values.[1] The National Council for Voluntary Organisations, for example, publishes data on UK institutions that inhabit the civil society space between state, businesses and individuals (NCVO 2017). Table 4.1 presents a count of the 390,000 formally incorporated organisations fitting that description. This sizeable number is not the full extent of voluntary collaboration by British citizens; the NCVO suggests 600,000 to 900,000 unincorporated associations could also be included in a broader definition of civil society (idem). The scale of activity that takes place in these incorporated and unincorporated institutions gives rise to our tenth proposition.

**Proposition 10** Persons can access enhanced capabilities for wellbeing by participating in institutions of civil society to collaborate with others in the pursuit of common interests and shared values.

Civil society collaborations can be motivated by a desire to exclude outsiders (this is discussed below), but there are also strong elements of altruism and philanthropy. The largest category in Table 4.1 is comprised of *general charities*, which covers institutions that satisfy six criteria:

**Table 4.1** Number of civil society incorporated organisations by organisation type, United Kingdom, 2013–2014

| Organisation Type | Number of Organisations |
|---|---|
| General charities (2014–2015 data) | 165,801 |
| Sports clubs | 135,900 |
| Companies limited by guarantee | 46,238 |
| Religious bodies | 38,383 |
| Community interest companies | 9177 |
| Co-operatives | 5568 |
| Trade associations and professional bodies | 3900 |
| Independent schools | 2598 |
| Housing associations | 1862 |
| Benevolent societies | 1681 |
| Credit unions | 521 |
| Political parties | 447 |
| Employee owned businesses | 250 |
| Football/rugby supporter trusts | 185 |
| Trade unions | 163 |
| Universities | 163 |
| Leisure trusts | 125 |
| Friendly societies and mutual insurers | 100 |
| Common investment funds | 55 |
| Building societies | 44 |
| LESS: Duplicates in the above list | (23,510) |
| Total | **389,651** |

Source: NCVO (2017, Civil Society Data)

- Registration as a general charity (including a public benefit test)
- Formality (institutionalised to some extent)
- Independence (separate from the state)
- Non-profit distributing (profits not returned to owners or directors)
- Self-governance
- Voluntarism (some meaningful degree of voluntary participation)

Table 4.2 gives further details of this category, grouping the general charities in a list of primary activities adapted from Salamon and Anheier (1996). The largest group has *social services* as the primary purpose. Members in this group volunteer time and money to provide assistance to people in their communities who are experiencing difficulties. Thus, the common interests and values in these institutions centre on philanthropy and altruism, which can be recognised as important elements in civil society.

A good example is the network of Citizens Advice Bureaux operating in about 3000 locations throughout the United Kingdom. In 2015–2016, the Bureaux provided help to 3.1 million people directly, as well as many more who accessed Citizens Advice web pages. That assistance was offered by professional staff and

**Table 4.2** Number of voluntary organisations registered as charities by area of activity, United Kingdom, 2014–2015

| | Number of Organisations |
|---|---|
| Social services | 30,265 |
| Culture and recreation | 23,586 |
| Religion | 14,357 |
| Grant-making foundations | 12,753 |
| Parent-teacher associations | 12,252 |
| Development | 10,286 |
| Education | 7914 |
| Village halls | 7662 |
| Playgroups and nurseries | 6960 |
| Health | 6710 |
| Scout groups and youth clubs | 6462 |
| International | 6055 |
| Environment | 5922 |
| Law and advocacy | 4270 |
| Housing | 3662 |
| Research | 3504 |
| Employment and training | 1985 |
| Umbrella bodies | 1156 |
| Not classified | 40 |
| Total | **165,801** |

Source: NCVO (2017, Scope Data)

more than 24,200 volunteers. The volunteered time was a substantial commitment, shown by calculating how much it would have cost for the same services to be provided by the professional staff (Citizens Advice 2014, fn. 2, p. 4). In 2015–2016, this was estimated to be £114 million in England and Wales, and £10 million in Scotland.[2]

Moving beyond this example, the Office of National Statistics uses survey data to estimate the value of volunteer time across all UK civil society institutions (ONS 2016; 2017). It focuses on people engaged in frequent formal volunteering; that is, residents who donate time at least once a month to a recognised institution. Figure 4.1 shows estimates for the decade 2005–2014. The impact of inflation has been removed from the series. Despite population growth over the same period, there is a downward trend. This is because the average time volunteered per person declined significantly over the decade, by 19.3 per cent (ONS 2016, pp. 40–41).

The estimates in Fig. 4.1 indicate the income volunteers might have earned if they had offered the same services in paid employment. Recall that Chap. 2 used this conceptualisation to estimate the opportunity cost of time spent by people in any valued activity (see the discussion around Fig. 2.1). The same understanding can be applied here, with some caveats. Volunteers participate in

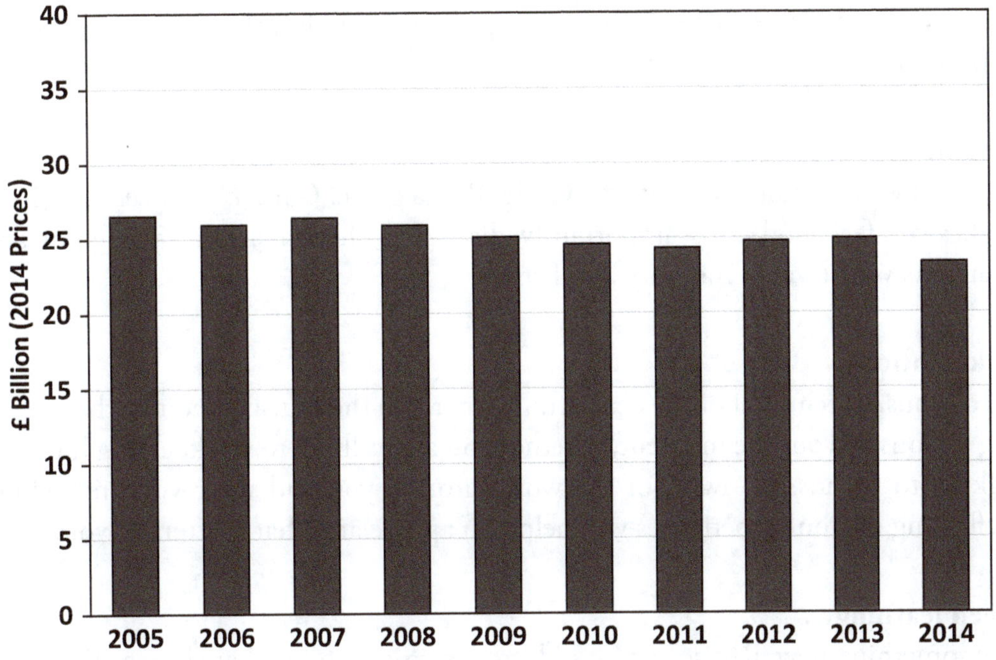


**Fig. 4.1** Gross value added of frequent formal volunteering measured in 2014 prices, United Kingdom, 2005–2014. (Note: The impact of inflation has been removed using the GDP Deflator at Market Prices. Source: ONS (2016, Fig. 8.2, p. 41) and HM Treasury (2017))

training and gain experience; hence, some of the time represents investment in developing human capital. Similarly, volunteering introduces persons to new social networks, opening up access to the community's social capital (see the following section). Even allowing for these caveats, however, the high opportunity cost of volunteered time recorded in Fig. 4.1 suggests that, at least for some persons, living a valued kind of life includes helping other people (see Fujiwara et al. 2013; Jenkinson et al. 2013).

## Social Capital

In 2008, the UK Government's Foresight Project on mental capital and wellbeing commissioned the New Economics Foundation to develop a set of evidence-based actions that people can take to improve personal wellbeing. The resulting review of the science literature identified five actions that can be good for mental wellbeing if built into daily life. They are worth citing in full (Aked et al. 2008, p. iii; Aked and Thompson 2011, p. 8):

> **Connect…**
> With the people around you. With family, friends, colleagues and neighbours. At home, work, school or in your local community. Think of these as the cornerstones of your life and invest time in developing them. Building these connections will support and enrich you every day.
>
> **Be active…**
> Go for a walk or run. Step outside. Cycle. Play a game. Garden. Dance. Exercising makes you feel good. Most importantly, discover a physical activity you enjoy and that suits your level of mobility and fitness.
>
> **Take notice…**
> Be curious. Catch sight of the beautiful. Remark on the unusual. Notice the changing seasons. Savour the moment, whether you are walking to work, eating lunch or talking to friends. Be aware of the world around you and what you are feeling. Reflecting on your experiences will help you appreciate what matters to you.
>
> **Keep learning…**
> Try something new. Rediscover an old interest. Sign up for that course. Take on a different responsibility at work. Fix a bike. Learn to play an instrument or how to cook your favourite food. Set a challenge you will enjoy achieving. Learning new things will make you more confident as well as being fun.

**Give...**
Do something nice for a friend, or a stranger. Thank someone. Smile. Volunteer your time. Join a community group. Look out, as well as in. Seeing yourself, and your happiness, linked to the wider community can be incredibly rewarding and creates connections with the people around you.

These five ways to wellbeing involve going outside a person's immediate family and household. Moving beyond the relative safety of kith and kin, however, is also associated with risks to wellbeing, including potential harm arising from public shame and humiliation (Sen 1983, p. 159; Zavaleta Reyles 2007). This was recognised in a famous passage of *The Wealth of Nations* (Smith 1776, Vol. 2, pp. 399–400):

> But in the present times, through a greater part of Europe, a creditable day-labourer would be ashamed to appear in public without a linen shirt, the want of which would be supposed to denote that disgraceful degree of poverty which, it is presumed, nobody can well fall into without extreme bad conduct.

More recently, Wilkinson and Pickett (2009) have drawn on research by Scheff (1988) and Dickerson and Kemeny (2004) to argue that residents who live in countries with more inequality are vulnerable to greater anxiety about potential shame for low or falling social status. Anxiety leads to poorer national outcomes across multiple indicators of wellbeing. On this theme, Walker and Chase (2013) and Kent (2016) have documented how poverty debates in the United Kingdom have become dominated by private and public sector efforts to shame citizens judged as undeserving of welfare assistance.

Further social barriers exist when it is not always safe to trust others in day-to-day social relations (Fukuyama 1995), particularly if social and political institutions are not trustworthy (O'Neill 2002). In some countries, this can be because the State actively suppresses civil society institutions (Bernhard 1993; Chamberlain 1993). In some societies, it can be socially accepted for a person to promote interests of family and friends over the civil rights of a stranger, even when acting as a public official (Fukuyama 2001, p. 9). Indeed, a country's legal system can include laws and regulations designed to prevent members of specified social groups from participating in high status occupations or engaging in important public activities (Dasgupta 2005; Clark and Worger 2016).

Observations such as these lead to the idea that social collaboration is easier in some communities than in others. Expressing this idea using the capital stock metaphor, communities in which people find it easier to co-operate are said to have higher levels of *social capital* than communities where collaboration is more difficult (Knack and Keefer 1997; Woolcock 1998). This metaphor is not easily explained (Scrivens and Smith 2013, p. 11), to the extent that Manski (2000, p. 123) suggests "economists should use 'social capital' only as a lesson in the ambiguity of words". Nevertheless, the following definitions capture different aspects of the term:

> … "social capital" refers to features of social organization such as networks, norms, and social trust that facilitate coordination and cooperation for mutual benefit. (Putnam 1995a, p. 67)

> The social capital of a society includes the institutions, the relationships, the attitudes and values that govern interactions among people and contribute to economic and social development. (World Bank 1998, p. 1)

> Social capital is the shared knowledge, understandings, norms, rules, and expectations about patterns of interactions that groups of individuals bring to a recurrent activity. (Ostrom 2000, p. 176)

> … the definition of social capital is: networks together with shared norms, values and understandings that facilitate co-operation within or among groups. (OECD 2001, p. 41)

> Social capital generally refers to trust, concern for one's associates, a willingness to live by the norms of one's community and to punish those who do not. (Bowles and Gintis 2002, p. F419)

A widely adopted classification recognises three forms of social capital (Szreter and Woolcock 2004; Keeley 2007, p. 103; Poortinga 2012). *Bonding* social capital draws together groups of relatively homogenous people bound by considerations such as family, ethnicity, gender or social class. *Bridging* social capital supports collaboration among diverse social groups in a region or country. *Linking* social capital makes it easier for people to connect with the country's major institutions exercising power, including local, regional and national government.

Bonding capital may be strong within each community of a country at the same time that bridging capital between different communities is weak. Sectarian conflict in Northern Ireland has been cited as an example (Leonard 2004; Campbell et al. 2010). Similarly, access to linking social capital may be far easier for members of some communities than for others, to the extent that some groups of citizens can be systematically disadvantaged in interactions with the country's education, health, police and justice systems (Eddo-Lodge 2017, Chap. 2; see also the following section).

The capital metaphor recognises that social capital can deteriorate with neglect, just as physical capital depreciates without maintenance, but can also be increased with suitable investment.[3] The first of these characteristics motivated Robert Putnam (1995a, 2000) to lament what he saw as the decline of social capital in the United States over the previous three decades, reflected in his symbol of an individual "bowling alone" rather than participating with others in organised competitions.

Putnam's diagnosis has been criticised for overstating the extent of the problem and for failing to distinguish causes and effects of changes in the stock of social capital (Portes 1998, pp. 18–21). Hall (1999), for example, found no evidence of an equivalent erosion of social capital in the United Kingdom (although this may be changing this century; see Richards and Heath 2015, and Fig. 4.1 above). Nevertheless, there has been progress in understanding how investment in social capital can take place, summarised in the following proposition and explained in the remainder of this section.

**Proposition 11** Investment in social capital can occur through mechanisms that include: learning in schools; participation in networks; enforcement of norms; development of societal aspirations and efforts for social inclusion.

**Learning in Schools** Fukuyama (1999, p. 257) observes that "one of the most important sources of social capital in contemporary societies is the educational system". At school, young people learn how to collaborate with others outside their immediate family circle, including through participation in well-structured programmes of physical education (Bailey et al. 2013). Citizenship programmes may be included in a national curriculum (Department for Education 2013).

Putnam (1995b, p. 667) observes the powerful effects of schooling on later social and political participation, concluding: "highly educated people are much more likely to be joiners and trusters, partly because they are better off economically, but mostly because of the skills, resources, and inclinations that were imparted to them at home and in school". Hall (1999, pp. 435–437) similarly observes that radical transformation in the British education system between the 1950s and 1990s reduced segregation by class and gender, and increased attainment, which positively affected the country's social capital.

**Participation in Networks** A key idea in Coleman's (1986) original essay is that social capital grows when persons participate in social networks, but this does not occur to the extent needed to maximise aggregate wellbeing because a large share of the benefits accrues to people other than the decision-maker. This is because the personal benefits of greater social capital are not restricted to a person's own individual contribution.

Thus, social capital has a "public good" element (see Chap. 6 for further discussion on economic public goods), which tends to limit the scope for collaboration. To be successful, voluntary organisations must find ways to foster "a cooperative spirit, norms of reciprocity, and collective thinking beyond the boundaries of the group itself" (Stolle and Rochon 1998, p. 49). The public good element of participation in social networks can justify supportive public policies (Hall 1999, pp. 440–443).[4]

**Enforcement of Norms** The social capital definition of Bowles and Gintis (2002) cited above includes willingness to punish violations of community norms (see also Paldam and Svendsen 2000, section 4, and Dasgupta 2005, pp. S6–S7). To illustrate, suppose a person travelling on a bus is subjected to sustained verbal abuse; can the person rely on other passengers to intervene so that community norms of courtesy and respect are enforced? If the answer is no, then social capital is weak.

Similar to participation in networks, enforcement of norms has a public good element (benefits are enjoyed by a wider group than the enforcer), which is one of several reasons for funding judicial systems from the public purse. The development of human rights legislation has been important for building social capital, by providing a mechanism to enforce fundamental rights such as freedom from unfair discrimination and protection of private property.

**Development of Societal Aspirations** There is a substantial literature on tensions between individual freedoms and societal aspirations. Margaret Thatcher famously claimed while UK Prime Minister that "there is no such thing as society"; instead "there is living tapestry of men and women and people" (Thatcher 1987, pp. 30–31). That attitude reflects what Francis Fukuyama (1999, pp. 5–6) has labelled a Great Disruption in social values from the mid-1960s to the early 1990s, which he suggests resulted in a culture of "intensive individualism" that "weakened the bonds holding families, neighborhoods, and nations together".

In contrast, social capital can be strengthened when countries develop societal aspirations or common goals. This involves, but is not limited to, the political process. Societal aspirations must be supported by community rules that Fukuyama observes will always entail some limits to individual freedoms to facilitate new forms of collaboration and connectedness (idem, p. 15).

**Efforts for Social Inclusion** In his UK study, Peter Hall reported that access to social capital is unevenly distributed among the British population, to the extent that "the more accurate image is of a nation divided between a well-connected and highly-active group of citizens with generally prosperous lives and another set of citizens whose associational life and involvement in politics are very limited" (Hall 1999, p. 455). A later study similarly concluded that social capital in Britain operates to entrench privilege within and across generations, so that "encouraging greater formal civic engagement without tackling the root causes of socio-economic disadvantage may well aggravate rather than ameliorate social division" (Li et al. 2008, p. 407).

These observations suggest that efforts to promote social inclusion, initiated in both the private and public sectors, are required to strengthen access by all citizens to the services provided by the country's social capital. This is discussed in the following section.

## Social Capital and Ethnicity

The social capital definitions listed in the previous section all refer to shared values or norms. Cultural values and accepted norms were discussed in Chap. 3, which observed that they are learned by young persons within families and households. This was labelled as cultural capital, which differs from social capital in two important respects.

First, cultural capital in its primary sense is *embodied* in persons, whereas social capital "exists in the *relations* among persons" (Coleman 1986, pp. S100–S101).[5] Second, while both types of capital are continuously transformed in a healthy society, cultural capital is conceptualised as connecting a person with previous and future generations (through the transmission of cultural heritage), whereas social capital connects a person with others in the current generation of living people.

There are inevitable tensions between cultural and social capital, since history shows repeatedly that access to services from a community's social capital (as well as access to other private and public resources) is much easier for people who share the cultural capital of the community's dominant social group. Indeed, this was a central message of Pierre Bourdieu's (1973, 1983) research, which developed the concept of cultural capital to explain why children from wealthy households achieve better results at school than children from lower socioeconomic groups.

Recall the example in the previous section of a bus passenger subjected to sustained verbal abuse. The answer to whether the passenger can rely on others to intervene may depend on the abused person's ethnicity (see, for example, Qureshi 2017). If so, this is a community where access to services from social capital—especially from bridging social capital—is limited for people outside the dominant cultural group.

Further, shared norms held by the dominant group may include general acceptance, perhaps unvoiced, that it is legitimate for its members to treat people from other ethnic groups in a hostile manner that would be sanctioned if applied to anyone from the dominant group. This can include using humiliating language, acting with dishonest intent, providing discriminatory standards of service, denying entry to certain networks or clubs, or tolerating an ever-present threat of physical assault that generally goes unpunished (Coates 2015).

These possibilities represent "the dark side of social capital" (Portes 1998, pp. 15–18; Gargiulo and Benassi 1999; Putnam 2000, Chap. 22; Dasgupta 2005, p. S17; van Deth and Zmerli 2010; Scrivens and Smith 2013, p. 23). An often-cited study by Waldinger (1995) gave an example of how insiders of white ethnicity in the New York construction sector effectively mobilised social capital to sustain economic advantage at the expense of African-American, Caribbean and Korean outsiders.[6]

Reni Eddo-Lodge (2017, Chap. 3) has called this phenomenon "white privilege", which a black person can only watch "as an outsider to the insularity of whiteness" (idem, p. 86). She goes on to say (idem, p. 87):

> When I talk about white privilege, I don't mean that white people have it easy, that they've never struggled, or that they've never lived in poverty. But white privilege is the fact that if you're white, your race will almost certainly positively impact your life's trajectory in some way. And you probably won't even notice it.

The tendency for members of the dominant culture to be advantaged over outsiders is not restricted to individual behaviour. It can occur in the country's state and civil society organisations, where it is labelled institutional or cultural discrimination (Dovidio et al. 2010, pp. 10–11), or structural racism (Eddo-Lodge 2017, p. 64). The Stephen Lawrence inquiry, for example, acknowledged institutional racism in the Metropolitan Police Service, which it defined as (Macpherson 1999, section 6.34):

> The collective failure of an organisation to provide an appropriate and professional service to people because of their colour, culture, or ethnic origin. It can be seen or detected in processes, attitudes and behaviour which amount to discrimination through unwitting prejudice, ignorance, thoughtlessness and racist stereotyping which disadvantage minority ethnic people.

Eddo-Lodge observes that the dominant group tend not to notice their advantage, while Macpherson speaks of prejudice that is unwitting. This is often how social capital operates. It is a resource that insiders find they can draw upon easily, or without conscious thought, while outsiders find they must collectively organise sustained social action to obtain some degree of equitable access to its services. Using terms introduced in Chap. 2, the result of this social structure is that persons with similar *personal abilities* find they have unequal *social capabilities* depending on their ethnicity or some other personal characteristic.

Such an outcome is a fundamental challenge to policy. In the language of this book, equitable access to services from all forms of capital is necessary for citizens to have reasoned capabilities for leading valued lives. When large numbers of citizens, because of ethnicity or some other characteristic, face systematic limitations on their access to services from the country's shared social capital, the capabilities of those citizens for leading valued lives are reduced and wellbeing is stunted. This leads to the following proposition.

**Proposition 12** Policy can enhance capabilities for wellbeing by ensuring persons are not disadvantaged in their equitable access to services from the country's capital stocks because of ethnicity or other personal characteristics.

Note that Proposition 12 goes well beyond the Pareto efficiency criterion for policy advice discussed in the opening chapter. This criterion supports economic policies if at least one person's wellbeing is improved and no one is made worse off. In contrast, Proposition 12 sanctions proposals in which members of the dominant cultural group sacrifice historical privilege in order to improve equitable access of other people to the country's social capital. It is possible that increasing the capabilities of people from minority groups would raise aggregate economic productivity to everyone's potential benefit (see Arrow et al. 2000), but this is not presumed in Proposition 12.

One way to address Proposition 12 is through efforts by individuals, private businesses, public officials and civil society institutions to foster interaction and dialogue among different cultural traditions. A term that has emerged for these efforts is *interculturalism* (Cantle 2012; Meer and Modood 2012; Taylor 2012; Zapata-Barrero 2015; Meer et al. 2016). The Council of Europe, for example, funds an Intercultural Cities Programme (Wood and Landry 2008; ICC 2016) that builds capacity, offers strategies and initiates projects to strengthen inclusive approaches that support diversity in cities.

## Conclusion

Collaborations with people outside a person's immediate family and household can greatly expand personal and social capabilities for wellbeing. In a free society, there is scope for a large number of diverse organisations to bring persons together to collaborate in the pursuit of common interests and shared values, supported by financial donations and volunteered time. These institutions make up the core of civil society.

Social capital is a metaphor reflecting the idea that interconnections among people contribute to wellbeing in a number of important ways. Social capital can be strengthened by conscious efforts in the private and public spheres, including through: learning in schools; participation in networks; enforcement of norms; development of societal aspirations; and efforts for social inclusion.

This chapter discussed social capital and ethnicity. This drew on Eddo-Lodge's (2017) recent book, supporting its insistence that members of the dominant social group take active measures to sacrifice historical privilege in order to improve equitable access of other people to the country's social capital. This finished by highlighting efforts by individuals, private businesses, public officials and civil society institutions to foster interculturalism.

Having considered choices made at the levels of individual persons, of households and families, and of communities, the stage is now set for the middle chapter of this book. It examines how participation in the market economy can contribute to expanded wellbeing, especially as a result of firms maintaining specialised capabilities for supplying goods and services needed by persons to live the kinds of lives they value.

## Notes

1. The key philosophical text on open societies is Karl Popper's *The Open Society and Its Enemies*, first published in two volumes in 1945, republished as one volume by Princeton University Press in Popper (2013).
2. These and other data in this paragraph are drawn from Citizens Advice (2016), Citizens Advice Northern Island (2015) and Citizens Advice Scotland (2016).
3. Bowles and Gintis (2002, pp. F420–F421) object to this metaphor on the grounds that "capital refers to something that can be owned". They therefore propose an alternative conceptualisation of "community governance".
4. The value of participation in social networks leads Layard (2006, p. C32) to warn economists not to advocate greater worker mobility (to generate higher incomes) without considering the associated effects on the quality of relationships in the community and in families.
5. Glaeser et al. (2002, p. F438) object to the view of social capital as a community-level attribute "because economists find it difficult to think of communities as decision-makers" (ibid). They therefore define individual social capital to be embodied in a person, and aggregate social capital is calculated as a function of these individual social characteristics. We do think that approach is fruitful; the key issue in our view is access to services provided by social capital.
6. Insider-outside behaviour is well understood by economists, especially in a labour market context; see, for example, Solow (1985) and Lindbeck and Snower (1988, 2001).

## References

Aked, Jody, and Sam Thompson. 2011. *Five Ways to Wellbeing: New Applications, New Ways of Thinking*. London: New Economics Foundation.

Aked, Jody, Nic Marks, Corrina Cordon, and Sam Thompson. 2008. *Five Ways to Wellbeing*. London: New Economics Foundation.

Arrow, Kenneth, Samuel Bowles, and Steven Durlauf, eds. 2000. *Meritocracy and Economic Inequality*. Princeton, NJ: Princeton University Press.

Bailey, Richard, Charles Hillman, Shawn Arent, and Albert Petitpas. 2013. Physical Activity: An Underestimated Investment in Human Capital. *Journal of Physical Activity & Health* 10 (3): 289–308.

Bernhard, Michael. 1993. Civil Society and Democratic Transition in East Central Europe. *Political Science Quarterly* 108 (2): 307–326.

Bourdieu, Pierre. 1973. Cultural Reproduction and Social Reproduction. In *Knowledge, Education and Cultural Change: Papers in the Sociology of Education*, ed. Richard K. Brown, 71–112. London: Tavistock.

———. 1983. Ökonomisches Kapital, Kulturelles Kapital, Soziales Kapital. In *Soziale Ungleichheiten* (Soziale Welt, Sonderheft 2), ed. Reinhard Kreckel, 183–198. Goettingen: Otto Schartz. Translated by Richard Nice and republished as The Forms of Capital in *Handbook of Theory and Research for the Sociology of Education*, ed. John C. Richardson, 241–258. Westport, CT: Greenwood Publishing Group, 1986.

Bowles, Samuel, and Herbert Gintis. 2002. Social Capital and Community Governance. *Economic Journal* 112 (483, Features): F419–F436.

Cabinet Office. 2016. *Community Life Survey 2015–16 Statistical Bulletin*. London: Cabinet Office Official Statistics.

Campbell, Andrea, Joanne Hughes, Miles Hewstone, and Cairns Ed. 2010. Social Capital as a Mechanism for Building a Sustainable Society in Northern Ireland. *Community Development Journal* 45 (1): 22–38.

Cantle, Ted. 2012. *Interculturalism: The New Era of Cohesion and Diversity*. Houndmills: Palgrave Macmillan.

Chamberlain, Heath B. 1993. On the Search for Civil Society in China. *Modern China* 19 (2): 199–215.

Citizens Advice. 2014. *CAB Volunteering – How Everyone Benefits*. London: Citizens Advice.

———. 2016. *Helping People Find a Way Forward: A Snapshot of Our Impact in 2015/16*. London: Citizens Advice.

Citizens Advice Northern Ireland. 2015. *One Service, Looking Forward: Annual Report 2014–2015*. Belfast: Citizens Advice Northern Ireland.

Citizens Advice Scotland. 2016. *Face Value: Impact Report 2015/16*. Edinburgh: Citizens Advice Scotland.

Clark, Nancy L., and William H. Worger. 2016. *South Africa: The Rise and Fall of Apartheid*. 3rd ed. London/New York: Routledge.

Coates, Ta-Neshi. 2015. *Between the World and Me*. Melbourne: Text Publishing.

Coleman, James S. 1986. Social Capital in the Creation of Human Capital. *American Journal of Sociology* 94 (Supplement): S95–S120.

Corry. Olaf. 2010. Defining and Theorizing the Third Sector. In *Third Sector Research*, ed. Rupert Taylor, 11–20. New York: Springer.

Dasgupta, Partha. 2005. Economics of Social Capital. *Economic Record* 81 (S1): S2–S21.

Dekker, Paul, and Andries van den Broek. 1998. Civil Society in Comparative Perspective: Involvement in Voluntary Associations in North America and Western Europe. *Voluntas: International Journal of Voluntary and Nonprofit Organisations* 9 (1): 11–38.

Department for Education. 2013. *Citizenship Programmes of Study: Key Stages 3 and 4*. GOV.UK website. https://www.gov.uk/government/collections/national-curriculum. Accessed 3 Oct 2017.

Dickerson, Sally, and Margaret E. Kemeny. 2004. Acute Stressors and Cortisol Responses: A Theoretical Integration and Synthesis of Laboratory Research. *Psychological Bulletin* 130 (3): 355–391.

Dovidio, John F., Miles Hewstone, Peter Glick, and Victoria M. Esses. 2010. Prejudice, Stereotyping and Discrimination: Theoretical and Empirical Overview. In *The SAGE Handbook of Prejudice, Stereotyping and Discrimination*, ed. John F. Dovidio, Miles Hewstone, Peter Glick, and Victoria M. Esses, 3–28. London: SAGE Publications.

Eddo-Lodge, Reni. 2017. *Why I'm No Longer Talking to White People About Race*. London: Bloomsbury Circus.

Etzioni, Amitai. 1973. The Third Sector and Domestic Missions. *Public Administration Review* 33 (4): 314–323.

Flyvbjerg, Bent. 1998. Habermas and Foucault: Thinkers for Civil Society? *British Journal of Sociology* 49 (2): 210–233.

Fujiwara, Daniel, Paul Oroyemi, and Ewen McKinnon. 2013. Wellbeing and Civil Society: Estimating the Value of Volunteering using Subjective Wellbeing Data. Working Paper No. 112. Sheffield: Department for Work and Pensions.

Fukuyama, Francis. 1995. *Trust: The Social Virtues and the Creation of Prosperity*. New York: Free Press.

———. 1999. *The Great Disruption: Human Nature and the Reconstitution of Social Order*. New York: Free Press.

———. 2001. Social Capital, Civil Society and Development. *Third World Quarterly* 22 (1): 7–20.

Gargiulo, Martin, and Mario Benassi. 1999. The Dark Side of Social Capital. In *Corporate Social Capital and Liability*, ed. Roger T.A.J. Leenders and Shaul M. Gabba, 298–322. Boston, MA: Springer.

Glaeser, Edward L., David Laibson, and Bruce Sacerdote. 2002. An Economic Approach to Social Capital. *Economic Journal* 112 (483, Features): F437–F458.

Hall, Peter A. 1999. Social Capital in Britain. *British Journal of Political Science* 29 (3): 417–461.

HM Treasury. 2017. *GDP Deflators at Market Prices, and Money GDP: March 2017 (Spring Budget 2017)*. GOV.UK website. https://www.gov.uk/government/statistics/gdp-deflators-at-market-prices-and-money-gdp-march-2017-spring-budget-2017. Accessed 23 Nov 2017.

ICC. 2016. *Intercultural Cities Annual Report 2016: Sharing Our Cities Sharing the Future*. Council of Europe Intercultural Cities Programme. https://rm.coe.int/16806c9674. Accessed 6 October 2017.

Jenkinson, Caroline E., Andy P. Dickens, Kerry Jones, Thompson-Coon Jo, Rod S. Taylor, Morwenna Rogers, Clare L. Bambra, Iain Lang, and Suzanne H. Richards. 2013. Is volunteering a public health intervention? A systematic review and meta-analysis of the health and survival of volunteers. *BMC Public Health* 13: 773. https://doi.org/10.1186/1471-2458-13-773.

Keeley, Brian. 2007. *Human Capital: How What You Know Shapes Your Life*. OECD Insights. Paris: OECD Publishing.

Kent, Gabi. 2016. Shattering the Silence: The Power of *Purposeful Storytelling* in Challenging Social Security Policy Discourses of 'Blame and Shame' in Northern Ireland. *Critical Social Policy* 36 (1): 124–141.

Knack, Stephen, and Philip Keefer. 1997. Does Social Capital Have an Economic Payoff? A Cross-Country Investigation. *Quarterly Journal of Economics* 112 (4): 1251–1288.

Kumar, Krishan. 1993. Civil Society: An Inquiry into the Usefulness of an Historical Term. *British Journal of Sociology* 44 (3): 375–395.

Layard, Richard. 2006. Happiness and Public Policy: A Challenge to the Profession. *Economic Journal* 116 (510): C24–C33.

Leonard, Madeleine. 2004. Bonding and Bridging Social Capital: Reflections from Belfast. *Sociology* 38 (5): 927–944.

Li, Yaojun, Mike Savage, and Alan Warde. 2008. Social Mobility and Social Capital in Contemporary Britain. *British Journal of Sociology* 59 (3): 391–411.

Lindbeck, Assar, and Dennis J. Snower. 1988. Cooperation, Harassment, and Involuntary Unemployment: An Insider-Outsider Approach. *American Economic Review* 78 (1): 167–188.

———. 2001. Insiders versus Outsiders. *Journal of Economic Perspectives* 15 (1): 165–188.

Macpherson, Sir William. 1999. *The Stephen Lawrence Inquiry*, Cm 4262-I. https://www.gov.uk/government/publications/the-stephen-lawrence-inquiry. Accessed 9 July 2017.

Manski, Charles F. 2000. Economic Analysis of Social Interactions. *Journal of Economic Perspectives* 14 (3): 115–136.

Meer, Nasar, and Tariq Modood. 2012. How Does Interculturalism Contrast with Multiculturalism? *Journal of Intercultural Studies* 33 (2): 175–196.

Meer, Nasar, Tariq Modood, and Richard Zapata-Barrero, eds. 2016. *Multiculturalism and Interculturalism: Debating the Dividing Lines*. Edinburgh: Edinburgh University Press.

NCVO. 2017. *UK Civil Society Almanac 2017*. London: National Council for Voluntary Organisations. https://data.ncvo.org.uk/. Database and text accessed 24 May 2017.

O'Neill, Onora. 2002. *A Question of Trust: The BBC Reith Lectures 2002*. Cambridge: Cambridge University Press.

OECD. 2001. *The Well-being of Nations: The Role of Human and Social Capital*. Paris: OECD Publishing https://doi.org/10.1787/9789264189515-en.

Office for Civil Society. 2010. *Building a Stronger Civil Society: A Strategy for Voluntary and Community Groups, Charities and Social Enterprises*. London: HM Government.

ONS. 2016. *Household Satellite Accounts: 2005 to 2014*. Compendium released 7 April. London: Office for National Statistics.

———. 2017. Changes in the Value and Division of Unpaid Volunteering in the UK: 2000 to 2015. Article released 16 March. London: Office for National Statistics.

Ostrom, Elinor. 2000. Social Capital: A Fad or a Fundamental Concept? In *Social Capital: A Multifaceted Approach*, ed. Partha Dasgupta and Ismail Serageldin, 172–214. World Bank: Washington, DC.

Paldam, Martin, and Gert Tinggaard Svendsen. 2000. An Essay on Social Capital: Looking for the Fire behind the Smoke. *European Journal of Political Economy* 16 (2): 339–366.

Poortinga, Wouter. 2012. Community Resilience and Health: The Role of Bonding, Bridging, and Linking Aspects of Social Capital. *Health & Place* 18 (2): 286–295.

Popper, Karl. 2013. *The Open Society and Its Enemies*. Princeton, NJ: Princeton University Press.

Portes, Alejandro. 1998. Social Capital: Its Origins and Applications in Modern Sociology. *American Review of Sociology* 24: 1–24.

Putnam, Robert D. 1995a. Bowling Alone: America's Declining Social Capital. *Journal of Democracy* 6 (1): 65–78.

———. 1995b. Tuning In, Tuning Out: The Strange Disappearance of Social Capital in America. *PS: Political Science and Politics* 28 (4): 664–683.

———. 2000. *Bowling Alone: The Collapse and Revival of American Community*. New York: Simon & Schuster.

Qureshi, Sadiah. 2017. *Black and British: A Forgotten History* by David Olusoga. *London Review of Books* 39 (14): 39–40.

Richards, Lindsay and Anthony Heath. 2015. The Uneven Distribution and Decline of Social Capital in Britain. CSI Briefing Note 15, Centre for Social Investigation, Nuffield College, Oxford. http://csi.nuff.ox.ac.uk/?page_id=89. Accessed 3 Oct 2017.

Salamon, Lester M. and Helmut K. Anheier. 1996. The International Classification of Nonprofit Organizations: ICNPO-Revision 1, 1996. Working Papers of the Johns Hopkins Comparative Nonprofit Sector Project, no. 19. Baltimore: The Johns Hopkins Institute for Policy Studies.

Scheff, Thomas J. 1988. Shame and Conformity: The Deference-Emotion System. *American Sociological Review* 53 (3): 395–406.

Scrivens, Katherine, and Conal Smith. 2013. Four Interpretations of Social Capital: An Agenda for Measurement. OECD Statistics Working Papers 2013/06. Paris: OECD Publishing at doi: https://doi.org/10.1787/5jzbcx010wmt-en.

Seligman, Adam B. 1992. *The Idea of Civil Society*. New York: The Free Press.

———. 2002. Civil Society as Idea and Ideal. In *Alternative Conceptions of Civil Society*, ed. Simone Chambers and Will Kymlicka, 13–33. Princeton, NJ: Princeton University Press.

Sen, Amartya. 1983. Development: Which Way Now? Presidential Address of the Development Studies Association. *Economic Journal* 93 (December): 745–762.

Smith, Adam (1776) *An Enquiry into the Nature and Causes of the Wealth of Nations*, 2 vols., University Paperbacks edition, ed. Edwin Cannan. London: Methuen.

Solow, Robert M. 1985. Insiders and Outsiders in Wage Determination. *Scandinavian Journal of Economics* 87 (2): 411–428.

Stolle, Dietlind, and Thomas R. Rochon. 1998. Are All Associations Alike? Member Diversity, Associational Type, and the Creation of Social Capital. *American Behavioral Scientist* 42 (1): 47–65.

Szreter, Simon, and Michael Woolcock. 2004. Health by Association? Social Capital, Social Theory, and the Political Economy of Public Health. *International Journal of Epidemiology* 33 (4): 650–667.

Taylor, Charles. 2012. Interculturalism or Multiculturalism. *Philosophy and Social Criticism* 38 (4–5): 413–423.

Thatcher, Margaret. 1987. Interview for *Woman's Own*. Transcript of Interview with Journalist Douglas Keay, 23 September. https://www.margaretthatcher.org/document/106689. Accessed 3 Oct 2017.

van Deth, Jan W., and Sonja Zmerli. 2010. Introduction: Civicness, Equality, and Democracy–A "Dark Side" of Social Capital? *American Behavioral Scientist* 53 (5): 631–639.

Waldinger, Roger. 1995. The "Other Side" of Embeddedness: A Case-Study of the Interplay of Economy and Ethnicity. *Ethnic and Racial Studies* 18 (3): 555–580.

Walker, Robert, and Elaine Chase. 2013. Separating the Sheep from the Goats: Tackling Poverty in Britain for over Four Centuries. In *The Shame of It: Global Perspectives on Anti-poverty Policies*, ed. Erika K. Gubrium, Sony Pellissery, and Ivar Lødemel, 133–156. Bristol: Policy Press.

Wilkinson, Richard G., and Kate Pickett. 2009. *The Spirit Level: Why More Equal Societies Almost Always Do Better*. London: Allen Lane.

Wood, Phil, and Charles Landry. 2008. *The Intercultural City: Planning for Diversity Advantage*. London: Earthscan.

Woolcock, Michael. 1998. Social Capital and Economic Development: Toward a Theoretical Synthesis and Policy Framework. *Theory and Society* 27 (2): 151–208.

World Bank. 1998. The Initiative on Defining, Monitoring and Measuring Social Capital: Overview and Program Description. Social Capital Working Paper Series. Washington, DC: World Bank, Social Development Department.

Zapata-Barrero, Ricard. 2015. *Interculturalism in Cities: Concept, Policy, and Implementation*. Cheltenham: Edward Elgar.

Zavaleta Reyles, Diego. 2007. The Ability to go about Without Shame: A Proposal for Internationally Comparable Indicators of Shame and Humiliation. *Oxford Development Studies* 35 (4): 405–430.

# 5

# Market Participation and Economic Capital

**Abstract** The market economy supports human wellbeing. This chapter offers evidence for this observation, while recognising that markets need rules, customs and institutions to work well. A key market institution is the firm, which combines different types of capital to maintain specialist capabilities for supplying goods and services valued by their customers. This expands the potential for wellbeing, but a large number of jobs pay less than the real living wage, with a strong gender bias, which diminishes wellbeing. The chapter analyses economic capital, comprised of physical capital and financial capital. Growth in economic capital has increased material living standards for billions of people, but recent economic development is also associated with cumulative environmental damage, episodes of financial instability and greater concentration of wealth.

**Keywords** Economic capital • Market strength • Capability theory of the firm • Unemployment • Living wage

To lead valued lives, people must access goods and services for meeting basic needs, and then for pursuing other goals (Maslow 1943, 1954). There are moral limits to the use of markets for this purpose (Sandel 2012), and the following two chapters will analyse other important cases of market failure. Nevertheless, goods and services necessary for wellbeing are often supplied by firms that



P. Dalziel et al., *Wellbeing Economics*, Wellbeing in Politics and Policy,
https://doi.org/10.1007/978-3-319-93194-4_5

operate in markets for inputs and outputs. Participation in the market economy therefore enhances capabilities for wellbeing beyond what persons could achieve through social networks alone.

The chapter begins by analysing four features of competitive markets that make this possible: specialised production, rewards for creating new value, decentralised decision-making and Pareto efficient outcomes. The potential is not always realised, however, and so the chapter also pays attention to how markets need well-designed rules, customs and institutions to work well.

The chapter then analyses a key institution in every market economy: the firm. Firms develop specialised capabilities for supplying valued goods and services, and provide access to the market economy by offering people opportunities for paid employment. Both roles support wellbeing.

Economic capital is a term used to cover physical capital (such as buildings and machinery) and financial capital (such as shares and bonds). Growth in these assets can promote wellbeing, but with important policy issues analysed in the third section of the chapter. The Global Financial Crisis in 2007–2008, for example, had a sharp impact on physical capital investment and exposed vulnerabilities in the global architecture for financial capital (Crotty 2009). Piketty (2013) has documented how capital accumulation can concentrate financial wealth and increase economic inequality.

The chapter finishes with a brief summary. It accepts the potential of the market economy and of economic capital for expanding the capabilities of persons to lead valued lives, but argues there is more to understand about how to harness the benefits of these institutions for wellbeing.

## Markets and Wellbeing

John McMillan (2002) showed how markets have emerged in human history wherever there were enough people for their operation and no political or military forces acting to suppress them. This is itself evidence that markets can be useful for wellbeing, but McMillan recognises a crucial caveat (idem, pp. 13–14):

> Markets, then, are the most potent antipoverty engine there is – but only where they work well. The caveat is crucial. … Left to themselves, markets can fail. To deliver their full benefits, they need support from a set of rules, customs, and institutions. They cannot operate efficiently in a vacuum.

Based on that insight, Proposition 13 recognises the potential of markets for contributing to enhanced wellbeing, while acknowledging that achievement of this potential requires a well-designed institutional structure.

**Proposition 13** Persons can enhance wellbeing by participating as sellers and as buyers in the market economy; but markets need rules, customs and institutions to work well.

This does not mean all possible market transactions are morally or socially acceptable. Human trafficking and exploitative child labour, for example, are universally rejected, as codified in international agreements such as the 2003 Protocol to Prevent, Suppress and Punish Trafficking in Persons, especially Women and Children and the 1990 Convention on the Rights of the Child. There is also a strong public consensus that access to life-changing services such as housing, education and health should not be restricted by a person's low market income.

Within limits such as these, four features help explain the potential of markets for contributing to enhanced wellbeing. First, a key insight in Smith's (1776) *Wealth of Nations* was its recognition that a market economy allows producers to specialise in their range of outputs and in their production. This is feasible because producers can rely on markets to buy inputs and sell outputs. Smith's opening chapter introduced this feature using the example of pins manufacture (Smith 1776, Volume 1, p. 8):

> One man draws out the wire, another straightens it, a third cuts it, a fourth points it, a fifth grinds it at the top for receiving the head; to make the head requires two or three distinct operations; to put it on is a peculiar business, to whiten the pins is another; it is even a trade by itself to put them into the paper; and the important business of making a pin is, in this manner, divided into about eighteen distinct operations…

Smith estimated that in his time, ten workers could make upwards of 48,000 pins a day, whereas not more than 200 were possible without this division of labour. Thus, specialisation can greatly increase the productivity of workers (measured as the value of their output per hour of work), which is an important driver of higher material living standards.[1]

Second, the market economy rewards successful developments of new ways to deliver value to consumers. This was explained by Joseph Schumpeter (1943) in his influential book *Capitalism, Socialism and Democracy*. Emphasising benefits from the "creative destruction" of capitalism, Schumpeter explained how market dynamism is driven by the innovation of entrepreneurs (idem, p. 83):

> The fundamental impulse that sets and keeps the capitalist engine in motion comes from the new consumers' goods, the new methods of production or transportation, the new markets, the new forms of industrial organization that capitalist enterprise creates.

Third, the market supports decentralised decision-making that is able to respond to economic shocks such as discoveries of new technologies or changes in consumer preferences. In competitive markets, these shocks result in relative price adjustments, which cause producers and consumers to shift resources to where they have become more highly valued, in a way that no central planner could hope to achieve. This feature was emphasised by Friedrich Hayek (1945, p. 520):

> The marvel is that in a case like that of a scarcity of one raw material, without an order being issued, without more than perhaps a handful of people knowing the cause, tens of thousands of people whose identity could not be ascertained by months of investigation, are made to use the material or its products more sparingly; i.e., they move in the right direction.

Fourth, the First Fundamental Theorem of Welfare Economics, introduced by economists including Nobel Laureates Ken Arrow (1951) and Gérard Debreu (1959), demonstrates that a system of perfectly competitive markets, involving private goods with no externalities (so that private costs equal social costs), produces an outcome where no one's preference satisfaction can be increased without reducing the satisfaction of someone else. This property is termed Pareto efficiency (Pareto 1906; Hicks 1939). It prevails because the price in a competitive market equals the cost to society of producing one more unit of the traded item (its marginal cost) and equals the amount consumers are willing to pay for that extra unit (its marginal benefit).

Thus, a consumer choosing to pay the market price of an item is forced to recognise the marginal benefit of that item to other consumers and the marginal cost of supplying a replacement. Similarly, producers are forced to recognise in their decision-making the marginal costs of other producers and the marginal benefits to all consumers.

These features make competitive markets a potentially powerful mechanism for supplying goods and services needed to enhance wellbeing. Specialisation allows greater value to be delivered to diverse customers. Firms pay the marginal cost of each input and create outputs for which consumers are willing to pay more than the total cost of their production. There are incentives for successful innovation. The economic outcome is efficient in the sense that no one's preferences can be further satisfied without diminishing the satisfaction of someone else.

This potential is not always realised for all consumers. Market outcomes depend on the distribution of resources among households. This is because purchasing power is the principal factor determining access to market goods and services, and so resources flow towards high-wealth households, while low-wealth persons are vulnerable to exploitation by those holding greater market power. Consequently, it is reasonable for citizens to be concerned about poverty and income inequality in the market economy (Rawls 1971; Sen 2009) and for public policy to be designed so that all persons can access housing, health and education services independently of their household income (see Chap. 7).

Further, markets often fail to meet the strict requirements for the theories of perfect competition to apply. Market transactions may involve externalities or the traded item may be an economic public good (see Chaps. 6 and 7). There may be only one seller (monopoly) or one buyer (monopsony). If there are few buyers or sellers, the market may produce outcomes considered unjust without countervailing power on the other side (Galbraith 1952). Sellers may use customer loyalty to take advantage of an inefficient market structure known as monopolistic competition (Robinson 1933; Chamberlin 1933). Consumers may be unable to judge the quality of a potential purchase, unsure whether to trust supplier claims about product safety or professional expertise (Darby and Karni 1973; Caswell and Mojduszka 1996).

Hence, there is room for good public policy to restrict anti-competitive behaviour in established markets. The UK regulatory regime for promoting competition, for example, has four main elements (Seely 2016, p. 12): investigating markets that might be working poorly for consumers; controlling mergers that might be anti-competitive; enforcing prohibitions against anti-competitive business agreements, price fixing and other abuses of market strength; and generally advocating for the benefits of competition. The emergence of new technologies supporting on-line markets has created new challenges for competition policy (see the analysis of Google, Facebook, Amazon and eBay by Haucap and Heimeshoff 2013).

## Firms and Capabilities

Firms are a key institution in any market economy. At the beginning of 2016, there were 5.5 million private sector businesses in the United Kingdom (Rhodes 2016, p. 5). Of these, 4.2 million were operated by sole proprietors with no employees. This section focuses on the other 1.3 million private sector businesses with at least one employee, which we call firms. The vast majority of firms employed fewer than ten people, but 40 per cent of total employment in all firms was accounted for by 7000 large businesses with at least 250 employees (ibid).

An important question posed initially by Ronald Coase (1937, p. 390) is "why a firm emerges at all in a specialised exchange economy". Given the strengths of market transactions discussed in the previous section, why are any economic activities managed within firms, rather than all persons being self-employed and all transactions being organised through markets?

Coase's insight was that market trades have their own *transaction costs*, including the cost of time needed to discover relevant market prices, negotiate separate contracts, and make allowances for contingencies and risks. Under some circumstances, these transaction costs are avoided "when the direction of resources is dependent on an entrepreneur" within a firm (idem, p. 393).

Coase's explanation has been developed further, including by Nobel Laureates Oliver Williamson (2010) and Oliver Hart (2017). This research has highlighted other factors giving rise to firms. A firm is better able to invest in assets specifically designed for its chosen outputs, for example, and a firm might reduce the unit costs of production as the scale of its activity increases.

Building on that tradition, David Teece (1982) has created a capability theory of the firm.[2] This conceptualises a firm as an ongoing institution that sustains two types of capabilities: *operational capabilities*, necessary for supplying to market the firm's chosen outputs; and *dynamic capabilities*, driving entrepreneurial innovation within the firm (see also Teece et al. 1997). Dynamic capabilities are the more important, reflecting the crucial function of senior management to identify and exploit opportunities (Teece 2017a, p. 698):

> For applied purposes, dynamic capabilities can usefully be broken down into three primary clusters of activities: (1) identification, development, co-development and assessment of technological opportunities in relationship to customer needs (*sensing*); (2) mobilization of resources to address needs and opportunities, and to capture value from doing so (*seizing*); and (3) continued renewal (*transforming*).

The emphasis on technology opportunities in relationship to customer needs is consistent with this book's understanding of knowledge capital as an essential input into production systems (see Chap. 7). Knowledge capital includes intellectual property, customer relationship management systems and other intangible assets based on specialised knowledge. This form of capital is particularly valuable because "knowledge, capabilities and other intangibles are not only scarce; they are often difficult to imitate" (Teece 2017a, p. 699).

All capital types considered in this book are important for a market firm. Consider a high street retail business. It leases a fitted-out store (economic capital) and employs skilled staff (human capital). It develops internal norms for daily operations (cultural capital) and maintains good relations with other businesses and people (social capital). It operates a sophisticated customer relationship management system and protects a distinctive brand (knowledge capital). Its logistics, energy and waste disposal systems use environmental resources (natural capital). Its supply chain relies on contracts and trusted relationships with partners around the globe (diplomatic capital).

Combining these capitals allows a firm to build its capability for quality goods and services that customers come to understand and trust. Proposition 14 therefore draws on the capability theory of the firm to provide a definition that fits the wellbeing economics framework.

**Proposition 14** Firms operating in the market economy can combine different types of capital to maintain specialist capabilities for supplying goods and services valued by their customers.

Throughout history, some firms have damaged wellbeing, including through large-scale dispossession of indigenous peoples during the global expansion of the market system in the nineteenth century (Polanyi 1944). As discussed earlier in this book, current activities of firms continue to cause environmental damage (Jackson 2017), although there are also consumer-led movements aiming to reward firms that demonstrate social and environmental responsibility (PwC 2013; GRI 2016).[3] Proposition 14 also indicates why the market economy favours households with high wealth. Customer values are expressed in the market economy by willingness-to-pay, so that low-wealth households have weak purchasing power to access goods and services produced by firms, even if those goods and services would greatly increase their wellbeing.

Nevertheless, the capability theory also explains how firms can improve human wellbeing. Proposition 2 states that wellbeing can be enhanced by expanding the *capabilities* of persons to lead the kinds of lives they value. Proposition 14 states that firms operating in the market economy maintain specialist *capabilities*. Thus, firms can expand opportunities for wellbeing by increasing capabilities, at least for those who can find employment in firms or otherwise have the financial means to purchase the goods and services that firms provide.

Drawing on this discussion, Fig. 5.1 presents a model of Proposition 14, depicting a firm's capabilities as the result of integrating different types of capital. This is designed to complement the skills model in Fig. 2.2 of Chap. 2 (both diagrams feature in the final chapter). Knowledge capital is highlighted because of its centrality in the dynamic capabilities of a firm. Human capital is highlighted because it is embodied in the firm's staff and so is central to the employment opportunities offered in the enterprise.

Employment is the primary means by which persons earn market income to purchase goods and services that contribute to the kind of life they value. It also offers social connections and may contribute to a person's social identity. It is not surprising, therefore, that one of the strongest findings in the wellbeing literature is that unemployed people generally report lower values for happiness and life satisfaction than do employed people, influenced by a range of personal and social factors.[4]

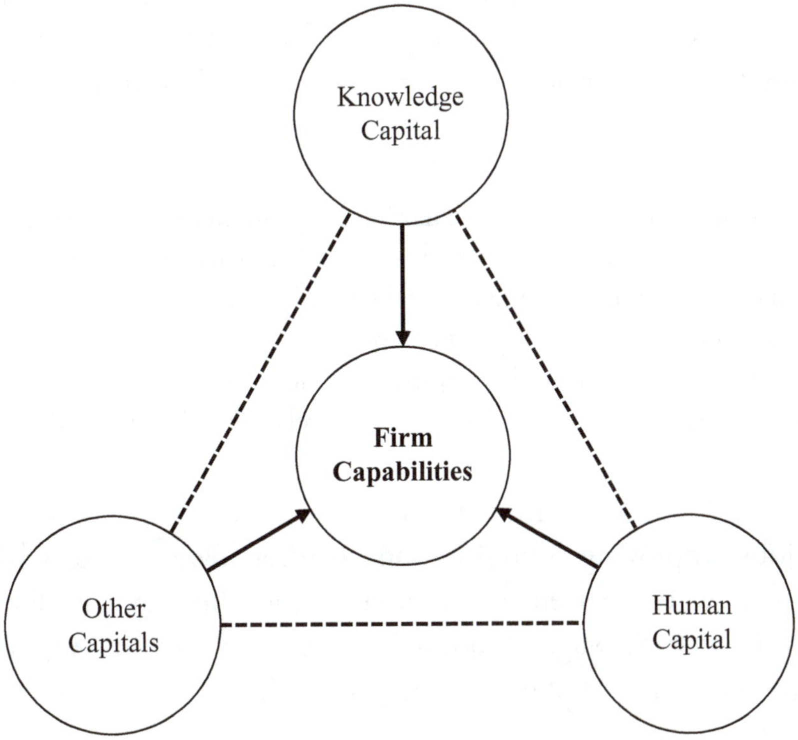


**Fig. 5.1** Firm capabilities as the integration of human, knowledge and other capitals

Winkelmann (2014) observes that reduced life satisfaction upon becoming unemployed is associated with a sense of departing from accepted social norms towards paid work. Hence, the impact tends to be smaller when a greater number of local people also have no job (Clark 2003). The loss of subjective wellbeing is more than can be explained by lost earnings. Psychological damage comes from factors such as lost economic identity, a sense of personal failure, feelings of insecurity, and reduced self-confidence in the ability to determine personal outcomes (Winkelmann 2014, p. 8).

Further, the need to focus on urgent problems caused by unemployment "captures the mind", which can lead to poor decision-making that neglects other sources of wellbeing (Shah et al. 2012; Mullainathan and Shafir 2013). Unemployment leaves scarring effects such as lower future wages (Gregory and Jukes 2001; Arulampalam 2001), higher risks of further spells of unemployment (Gregg 2001) and lower subjective wellbeing even when re-employed (Clark et al. 2001). Wellbeing reported by those who are not unemployed is also lower when there is higher unemployment among peers (Clark 2003; De Neve and Ward 2017, p. 154).

Employment is therefore important for wellbeing, but quality of employment should not be overlooked since "insecure and poor quality employment is also associated with increased risks of poor physical and mental health" (Marmot 2010, p. 26). De Neve and Ward (2017) report that blue-collar jobs and low-income jobs are associated with lower levels of subjective wellbeing, while other evidence shows strong connections between job quality and wellbeing (idem, p. 145)[5]:

> Work-life balance emerges as a particularly strong predictor of people's happiness. Further factors include job variety and the need to learn new things, as well the level of individual autonomy enjoyed by the employee. Moreover, job security and social capital (as measured through the support one receives from fellow workers) are also positively correlated with happiness, while jobs that involve risks to health and safety are generally associated with lower levels of subjective wellbeing.

A critical consideration is income earned in a job. It may be reasonable for entry-level jobs employing school-leavers to offer lower wages while a young person builds relevant experience, but older people who may have family responsibilities require decent wages (taking into account income support through social security policies; see Chap. 7) to lead lives they have reason to value by the standards of their peers.

**Table 5.1** Statutory national minimum wage, statutory national living wage, and voluntary or real living wage, United Kingdom, April 2017

| Age Band | Rate Per Hour |
|---|---|
| Statutory National Minimum Wage | |
| Under 18 | £4.05 |
| 18–20 | £5.60 |
| 20–24 | £7.05 |
| Statutory National Living Wage | |
| 25 and over | £7.50 |
| Voluntary or real living wage | |
| 18 and over | £9.75 in London<br>£8.45 in rest of United Kingdom |

Note: These figures exclude Apprentice Rates

Sources: https://www.gov.uk/national-minimum-wage-rates and https://www.livingwage.org.uk/what-real-living-wage

In the United Kingdom, this difference is recognised in a distinction between minimum wages and living wages. Table 5.1 shows the statutory national minimum wage and the statutory national living wage, plus a third category that is referenced as either the *voluntary* living wage (IHS Markit 2017) or the *real* living wage (Living Wage Foundation 2017).

The principle behind the voluntary or real living wage is "that work should bring dignity and should pay enough to provide families the essentials of life" (Hirsch and Moore 2011, p. 4). Its calculation is therefore based on actual living costs, which are higher in London than elsewhere in the United Kingdom, taking into account income support received through social security. In April 2017, the voluntary real living wage was estimated to be £9.75 per hour in London and £8.45 in the rest of the country.

Table 5.1 shows that the statutory rates in the United Kingdom increase with the employee's age, reaching £7.50 per hour at 25 years. Even this highest rate is well below the voluntary or real living wage, however, so that the minimum wage that employers must pay by statute is less than the rate considered sufficient to provide families with the essentials of life.

IHS Markit is commissioned annually by KPMG to analyse jobs paying less than the voluntary living wage. The analysis for 2017 estimated that 5.5 million people aged 18 or older were employed on these terms. Where the employee was aged between 18 and 21, two-thirds of the jobs paid below the voluntary living wage (see Fig. 5.2). One-quarter of jobs did not meet the threshold where employees were aged 22 to 29. Even for employees in their 30s, 40s and 50s, the percentage of jobs not paying the voluntary living wage was 15–16 per cent (IHS Markit 2017, p. 11).

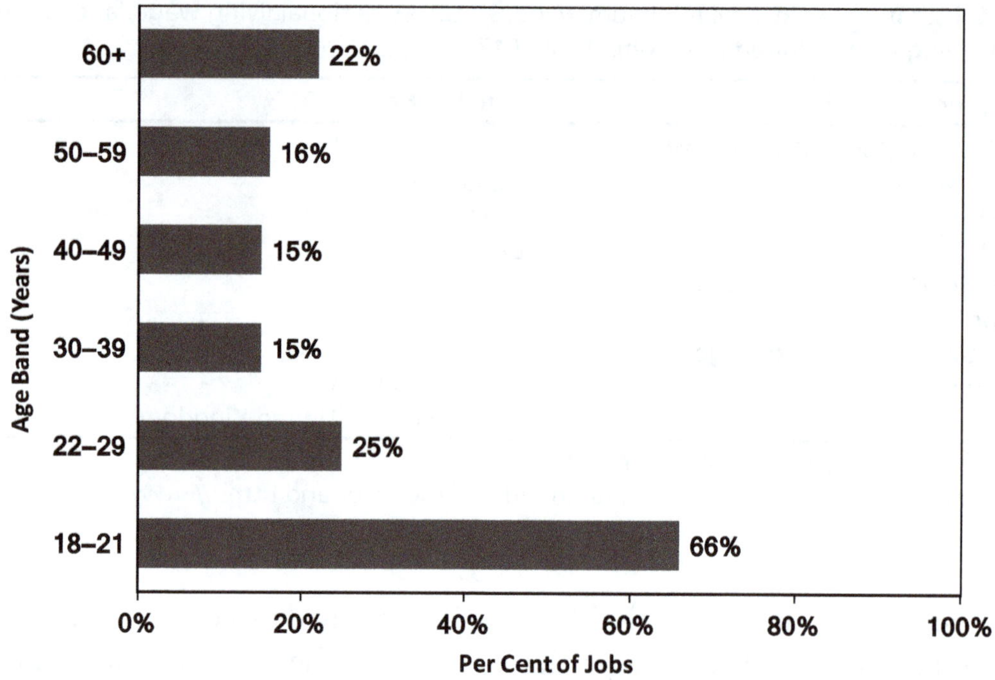


**Fig. 5.2** Estimated percentage of jobs paying less than the voluntary living wage, by employee age, England, Scotland and Wales, 2017. (Source: IHS Markit (2017, Table 3.6.1, p. 11))

These data indicate a major policy challenge within a wellbeing economics framework. Even with social security support, more than one in seven employed people aged between 30 and 59 are in jobs that do not pay a wage deemed high enough to provide families with the essentials of life. The proportion is higher for younger and older age groups. In other words, employment is not sufficient to guarantee that a person can afford to purchase the market goods and services needed to create a level of wellbeing judged reasonable by the standards of the day.

Further, there is a strong gender disparity in this experience: 26 per cent of employed females are paid less than the voluntary living wage, compared to 16 per cent of employed males (idem, p. 9). This difference is contrary to Proposition 8 that men and women can have equal capabilities for wellbeing. More than one in four women in paid work are not earning the real living wage; this must restrict capabilities for creating wellbeing for themselves and their families.

## Economic Capital

Economic capital encompasses physical capital and financial capital. Physical capital refers to long-lasting human-made material assets such as buildings, factories, roads, vehicles, machinery, equipment and the like. Financial capital refers to nominal assets such as equities, shares, securities, bonds, debentures, bank deposits and cash.

Physical and financial capitals are closely connected. A firm includes physical capital on the assets side of its balance sheet, funded by financial capital on the liabilities side. A household with savings distributes its wealth between physical capital (such as home ownership) and a portfolio of financial capital. The financial assets are backed by physical and other types of capital, whose profit streams underpin the portfolio's economic value.

Economic policy pays close attention to investment in new physical capital (OECD 2015). This is justified by its importance in the national economy. In the United Kingdom, for example, this expenditure was valued in 2016 at £260 billion, which was 13.5 per cent of that year's gross domestic product.[6] As Keynes (1936) first explained, the amount of investment expenditure influences a nation's level of economic activity, so that a large drop in investment can push the economy into recession. In the medium term, the neoclassical growth model shows that a country tends to have a higher value of output produced per hour of work if a greater share of its output is devoted to physical capital investment (see Chap. 1).

A further reason for close attention to physical capital investment is that firms and households rely on the public sector to maintain and expand core infrastructure such as transport networks and essential utilities such as water and sewer networks (Aschauer 1989; Munnell 1992; Gramlich 1994; Pereira and Andraz 2013). These networks and utilities are essential for promoting wellbeing, to the extent that the UK Government has created the Infrastructure and Projects Authority whose purpose is "to continuously improve the way infrastructure and major projects are delivered in order to support government priorities and improve people's lives" (IPA 2017, p. 1).

Experiences over the last two decades indicate some deep-seated problems in the role of economic capital in promoting wellbeing. First, and arguably the most pressing issue, current patterns of physical capital investment and technological development are having cumulative and potentially irreversible impacts on the environment (OECD 2011, p. 10).

Recognising this challenge, the OECD recommends strategies to foster *green growth*, including: carbon emission pricing to reflect its full environmental and economic costs, temporary support for new technologies with lower environmental impacts, reduced barriers to the development and diffusion of green technologies globally, and investment in public network infrastructure that supports next-generation technologies (idem, p. 12). The UK Government's *Clean Growth Strategy* (HM Government 2017) is an example of an integrated public strategy that aims to support investment in innovation for clean growth.

A second issue from recent experience can be seen in Fig. 5.3, which depicts the United Kingdom's physical capital investment from 2001 to 2016. The sharp fall in physical capital investment during the Global Financial Crisis of 2007–2008 is clearly visible. Investment fell from £250 billion in 2007 to £196 billion in 2009, a reduction of 21.6 per cent. It returned to its 2007 value only in 2015. Fluctuations of this size are a serious challenge to policy goals of maintaining stable and full employment.

That episode also illustrates the close connection between physical and financial capital, since it is universally agreed that the origins of the crisis lay in financial markets. The Financial Crisis Inquiry Commission was appointed by the US Government to examine what led to the greatest financial crisis since the Great Depression. It reported as follows (Financial Crisis Inquiry Commission 2011, p. xvi):

> While the vulnerabilities that created the potential for crisis were years in the making, it was the collapse of the housing bubble – fuelled by low interest rates, easy and available credit, scant regulation, and toxic mortgages – that was the spark that ignited a string of events, which led to a full-blown crisis in the fall of 2008. …

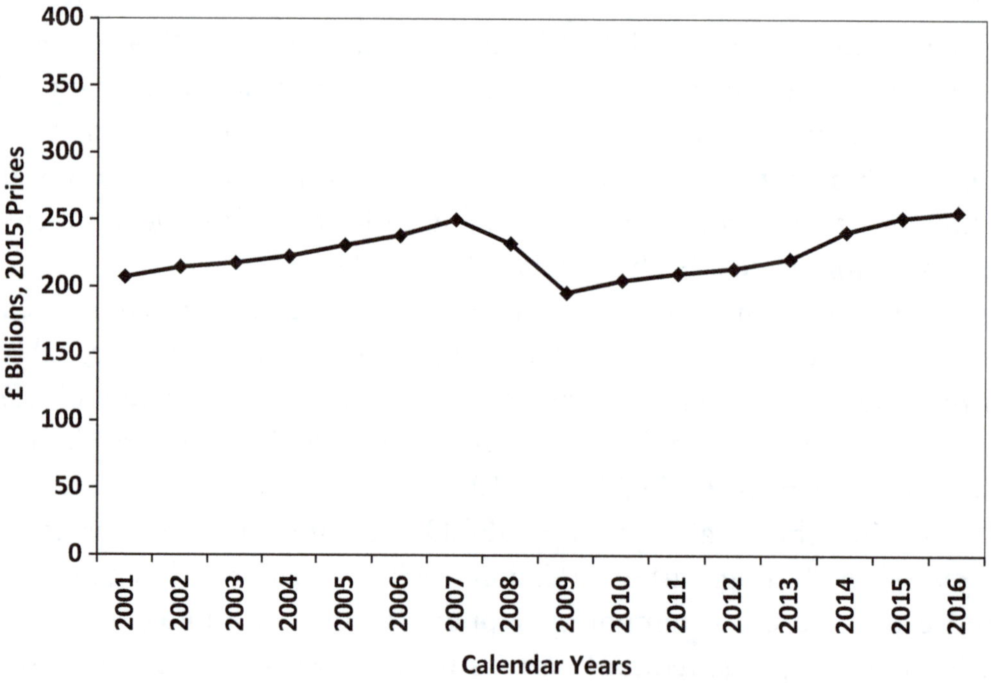


**Fig. 5.3** Annual gross fixed capital formation, excluding cultivated assets and intellectual property products, United Kingdom, 2001 to 2016. (Note: The series is the chained volume measure (CVM), which removes the impact of price changes; the values are presented at 2015 prices. Source: Calculated from ONS (2017a))

> When the bubble burst, hundreds of billions of dollars in losses in mortgages and mortgage-related securities shook markets as well as financial institutions that had significant exposures to those mortgages and had borrowed heavily against them.

Thomas Piketty (2013) has published long-term data from different countries to demonstrate that income inequality has generally been increasing in recent decades. He hypothesises that this trend is amplified by financial returns to the ownership of capital exceeding the rate of economic growth.[7] This means income from capital ownership typically grows faster than income from wages, with straightforward consequences for concentration of wealth and power (idem, p. 26):

> Under such conditions, it is almost inevitable that inherited wealth will dominate wealth amassed from a lifetime's labor by a wide margin, and the concentration of capital will attain extremely high levels – levels potentially incompatible with the meritocratic values and principles of social justice fundamental to modern democratic societies.

Thus, economic capital is important for wellbeing, but there are issues that must be addressed for it to contribute to its full potential. This is summarised in Proposition 15.

**Proposition 15** Investment in physical capital and the growth of financial capital can contribute to enhanced wellbeing, but recent patterns of economic development are also associated with cumulative environmental damage, episodes of financial instability and greater concentration of wealth.

## Conclusion

The market economy supports substantial expansion of human wellbeing, yet markets do not always work well. Firms maintain specialist capabilities for supplying market goods and services that enhance wellbeing; yet firms also offer a large number of jobs paying less than the real living wage. Growth in economic capital has increased material living standards for billions of people; yet recent economic development is also associated with cumulative environmental damage, episodes of financial instability and greater concentration of wealth.

Chapter 3 concluded with the question: How can it be culturally acceptable for such high levels of parental inequality, intimate violence, poor housing and child poverty to be allowed to persist? This chapter has highlighted a key causal mechanism of these outcomes. More than one in seven employed persons aged between 30 and 59 are in employment that does not pay a living wage sufficient to support family life, with a strong gender bias. This must limit capabilities for wellbeing. It is a glaring example of how economic policies that do not pay attention to *how* the economy is growing (in this case, through the creation of large numbers of low-wage jobs) can harm personal and social wellbeing.

The book now turns to how local and central governments can contribute to enhanced wellbeing.

## Notes

1. Specialisation may also contribute to workers' experience of powerlessness, meaninglessness, normlessness, isolation and self-estrangement, expressed in the concept of "alienation" (Seeman 1959; Neal and Rettig 1963).
2. See Teece (2017a, b) for recent overviews. Kay (1993) also emphasises the importance of a firm's distinctive capabilities, especially its architecture, reputation, innovation and strategic assets.
3. There are also social enterprises operating in the market economy with explicit commitments to social purposes (Besley and Ghatak 2017; Social Enterprise UK 2017).
4. See Feather (1990), Clark and Oswald (1994), Winkelmann and Winkelmann (1998), Clark (2003), Dockery (2005), Winkelmann (2009, 2014), Grün et al. (2010), Knabe et al. (2010), Brown et al. (2012), Gielen and van Ours (2014), Helliwell and Huang (2014), Hetschko et al. (2014), Wulfgramm (2014) and De Neve and Ward (2017).
5. Oswald et al. (2015) provide experimental evidence of a possible connection in the reverse direction, suggesting worker happiness might contribute to labour productivity.
6. This is gross fixed capital formation, excluding investment in intellectual property products and in cultivated assets, taken from ONS (2017a). Intellectual property products are part of knowledge capital, and cultivated assets (livestock for breeding) are part of natural capital; see ONS (2017b).
7. Piketty's empirical findings are generally accepted by economists, but not his theoretical explanation; see, for example, Summers (2014), Acemoglu and Robinson (2015), Auerbach and Hassett (2015), Blume and Durlauf (2015), Krusell and Smith (2015) and Mankiw (2015). Piketty (2015) addresses some of these criticisms.

## References


Acemoglu, Daron, and James A. Robinson. 2015. The Rise and Decline of General Laws of Capitalism. *Journal of Economic Perspectives* 29 (1): 3–28.

Arulampalam, Wiji. 2001. Is Unemployment Really Scarring? Effects of Unemployment Experiences on Wages. *Economic Journal* 111 (475): 585–606.

Arrow, Kenneth J. 1951. An Extension of the Basic Theorems of Classical Welfare Economics. In *Proceedings of the Second Berkeley Symposium on Mathematical Statistics and Probability*, ed. Jerzy Neyman, 507–532. Berkeley: University of California Press.

Aschauer, David Alan. 1989. Is Public Expenditure Productive? *Journal of Monetary Economics* 23 (2): 177–200.

Auerbach, Alan J., and Kevin Hassett. 2015. Capital Taxation in the Twenty-First Century. *American Economic Review* 105 (5): 38–42.

Besley, Timothy, and Maitreesh Ghatak. 2017. Profit with Purpose? A Theory of Social Enterprise. *American Economic Journal: Economic Policy* 9 (3): 19–58.

Blume, Lawrence E., and Steven N. Durlauf. 2015. Capital in the Twenty-First Century: A Review Essay. *Journal of Political Economy* 123 (4): 749–777.

Brown, Denise, Julie Woolf, and Conal Smith. 2012. An Empirical Investigation into the Determinants of Life Satisfaction in New Zealand. *New Zealand Economic Papers* 46 (3): 239–251.

Caswell, Julie A., and Eliza M. Mojduszka. 1996. Using Informational Labeling to Influence the Market for Quality in Food Products. *American Journal of Agricultural Economics* 78 (5): 1248–1253.

Chamberlin, Edward H. 1933. *The Theory of Monopolistic Competition: A Re-orientation of the Theory of Value*. Cambridge, MA: Harvard University Press.

Clark, Andrew E. 2003. Unemployment as a Social Norm: Psychological Evidence from Panel Data. *Journal of Labor Economics* 21 (2): 323–351.

Clark, Andrew E., Yannis Georgellis, and Peter Sanfey. 2001. Scarring: The Psychological Impact of Past Unemployment. *Economica* 68 (270): 221–241.

Clark, Andrew E., and Andrew J. Oswald. 1994. Unhappiness and Unemployment. *Economic Journal* 104 (42): 648–659.

Coase, Ronald H. 1937. The Nature of the Firm. *Economica* 4 (16): 386–405.

Crotty, James. 2009. Structural Causes of the Global Financial Crisis: A Critical Assessment of the 'New Financial Architecture'. *Cambridge Journal of Economics* 33 (4): 563–580.

Darby, Michael R., and Edi Karni. 1973. Free Competition and the Optimal Amount of Fraud. *Journal of Law and Economics* 16 (1): 67–88.

De Neve, Jan-Emmanuel, and George Ward. 2017. Happiness at Work. In *World Happiness Report 2017*, ed. John Helliwell, Richard Layard, and Jeffrey Sachs, 144–177. New York: Sustainable Development Solutions Network.

Debreu, Gérard. 1959. *Theory of Value: An Axiomatic Analysis of Economic Equilibrium*. New York: John Wiley.

Dockery, Alfred M. 2005. The Happiness of Young Australians: Empirical Evidence on the Role of Labour Market Experience. *Economic Record* 81 (255): 322–335.

Feather, Norman T. 1990. *The Psychological Impact of Unemployment*. New York: Springer-Verlag.

Financial Crisis Inquiry Commission. 2011. *The Financial Crisis Inquiry Report: The Final Report of the National Commission on the Causes of the Financial and Economic Crisis in the United States, Including Dissenting Views*. New York: Cosmo Reports.

Galbraith, John Kenneth. 1952. *American Capitalism – The Concept of Countervailing Power*. Boston MA: Houghton Mifflin.

Gielen, Anne C., and Jan C. van Ours. 2014. Unhappiness and Job Finding. *Economica* 81 (323): 544–565.

Gramlich, Edward M. 1994. Infrastructure Investment: A Review Essay. *Journal of Economic Literature* 32 (4): 1176–1196.

Gregg, Paul. 2001. The Impact of Youth Unemployment on Adult Unemployment in the NCDS. *Economic Journal* 111 (475): 626–653.

Gregory, Mary, and Robert Jukes. 2001. Unemployment and Subsequent Earnings: Estimating Scarring among British Men 1984–94. *Economic Journal* 111 (475): 607–625.

GRI. 2016. *Empowering Sustainable Decisions: GRI's Annual Report 2015–2016*. Global Reporting Initiative (GRI). https://www.globalreporting.org/information/about-gri/Pages/GRIs-own-reports.aspx. Accessed 4 Oct 2017.

Grün, Carola, Wolfgang Hauser, and Thomas Rhein. 2010. Is Any Job Better than No Job? Life Satisfaction and Re-employment. *Journal of Labour Research* 31 (3): 285–306.

Hart, Oliver. 2017. Incomplete Contracts and Control. *American Economic Review* 107 (7): 1731–1752.

Haucap, Justus, and Ulrich Heimeshoff. 2013. Google, Facebook, Amazon, eBay: Is the Internet Driving Competition or Market Monopolization? *International Economics and Economic Policy* 11 (1–2): 49–61.

Hayek, Friedrich. 1945. The Use of Knowledge in Society. *American Economic Review* 35 (4): 519–530.

Helliwell, John F., and Haifang Huang. 2014. New Measures of the Costs of Unemployment: Evidence from the Subjective Well-being of 3.3 Million Americans. *Economic Inquiry* 52 (4): 1485–1502.

Hetschko, Clemens, Andreas Knabe, and Ronnie Schöb. 2014. Changing Identity: Retiring from Unemployment. *Economic Journal* 124 (575): 149–166.

Hicks, John R. 1939. The Foundations of Welfare Economics. *Economic Journal* 49 (196): 696–712.

Hirsch, Donald, and Rhys Moore. 2011. *The Living Wage in the United Kingdom: Building on Success*. London: Living Wage Foundation.

HM Government. 2017. *The Clean Growth Strategy: Leading the Way to a Low Carbon Future*. London: Department for Business, Energy & Industrial Strategy.

IHS Markit. 2017. *Living Wage Research for KPMG*. Henley on Thames: IHS Markit Ltd.

IPA. 2017. *Annual Report on Major Projects 2016–17*. London: Infrastructure and Projects Authority.

Jackson, Tim. 2017. *Prosperity without Growth: Foundations for the Economy of Tomorrow*. 2nd ed. Abingdon/New York: Routledge.

Kay, John. 1993. *Foundations of Corporate Success: How Business Strategies Add Value*. Oxford: Oxford University Press.

Keynes, John Maynard. 1936. *The General Theory of Employment, Interest and Money*. London: Macmillan.

Knabe, Andreas, Steffen Rätzel, Ronnie Schöb, and Joachim Weimann. 2010. Dissatisfied with Life but Having a Good Day: Time-use and Well-being of the Unemployed. *Economic Journal* 120 (547): 867–889.

Krusell, Per, and Anthony A. Smith, Jr. 2015. Is Piketty's "Second Law of Capitalism" Fundamental? *Journal of Political Economy* 123 (4): 725–748.

Living Wage Foundation. 2017. What is the Real Living Wage. https://www.livingwage.org.uk/what-real-living-wage. Webpage accessed 30 Oct 2017.

Mankiw, N. Gregory. 2015. Yes, r > g. So What? *American Economic Review* 105 (5): 43–47.

Marmot, Michael. 2010. *Fair Society, Healthy Lives: A Strategic Review of Health Inequalities in England Post-2010*. London: The Marmot Review.

Maslow, Abraham H. 1943. A Theory of Human Motivation. *Psychological Review* 50 (4): 370–396.

———. 1954. *Motivation and Personality*. New York: Harper.

McMillan, John. 2002. *Reinventing the Bazaar: A Natural History of Markets*. New York/London: W. W. Norton.

Mullainathan, Sendhil, and Eldar Shafir. 2013. *Scarcity: Why Having Too Little Means So Much*. New York: Times Books, 2013.

Munnell, Alicia H. 1992. Policy Watch: Infrastructure Investment and Economic Growth. *Journal of Economic Perspectives* 6 (4): 189–198.

Neal, Arthur G., and Salomon Rettig. 1963. Dimensions of Alienation among Manual and Non-Manual Workers. *American Sociological Review* 28 (4): 599–608.

OECD. 2011. *Towards Green Growth*. Paris: OECD Publishing https://doi.org/10.1787/9789264111318-en.

———. 2015. *Policy Framework for Investment, 2015 Edition*. Paris: OECD Publishing https://doi.org/10.1787/9789264208667-en.

ONS. 2017a. Annual Gross Fixed Capital Formation by Industry and Asset. Database released 29 September, Office for National Statistics.

———. 2017b. A Short Guide to Gross Fixed Capital Formation and Business Investment. Article released 25 May, Office for National Statistics.

Oswald, Andrew J., Eugenio Proto, and Daniel Sgroi. 2015. Happiness and Productivity. *Journal of Labor Economics* 33 (4): 789–822.

Pereira, Alfredo M., and Jorge M. Andraz. 2013. On the Economic Effects of Public Infrastructure Investment: A Survey of the International Evidence. *Journal of Economic Development* 38 (4): 1–37.

Pareto, Vilfredo. 1906. *Manuale di Economia Politica*. Milan: Societa Editrice Libraria.

Piketty, Thomas. 2013. *Le capital au XXIe siècle*. Paris: Éditions du Seuil. Translated by Arthur Goldhammer and published in English as *Capital in the Twenty-First Century*. Cambridge, MA: Belknap Press, 2014.

———. 2015. About *Capital in the Twenty-First Century*. *American Economic Review* 105 (5): 48–53.

Polanyi, Karl. 1944. *The Great Transformation: The Political and Economic Origins of Our Time*. New York: Farrar & Rinehart.

PwC. 2013. *Measuring and Managing Total Impact: A New Language for Business Decisions*. PwC Network, downloaded 3 October 2017 at www.pwc.com/totalimpact.

Rawls, John. 1971. *A Theory of Justice*. Cambridge, MA: Harvard University Press.

Rhodes, Chris. 2016. Business Statistics. Briefing Paper Number 06152. London: House of Commons Library.

Robinson, Joan. 1933. *The Economics of Imperfect Competition*. London: Macmillan.

Sandel, Michael. 2012. *What Money Can't Buy: The Moral Limits of Markets*. New York: Farrar, Straus and Giroux.

Schumpeter, Joseph. 1943. *Capitalism, Socialism and Democracy*. London: George Allen & Unwin.

Seely, Antony. 2016. The UK Competition Regime. Briefing Paper Number 04814. London: House of Commons Library.

Seeman, Melvin. 1959. On the Meaning of Alienation. *American Sociological Review* 24 (6): 783–791.

Sen, Amartya. 2009. *The Idea of Justice*. Cambridge, MA: Harvard University Press.

Shah, Anuj K., Sendhil Mullainathan, and Eldar Shafir. 2012. Some Consequences of Having Too Little. *Science* 338 (6107): 682–685.

Smith, Adam. 1776. *An Enquiry into the Nature and Causes of the Wealth of Nations*, 2 vols., University Paperbacks edition, ed. by Edwin Cannan. London: Methuen.

Social Enterprise UK. 2017. *The Future of Business: State of Social Enterprise Survey 2017*. London: Social Enterprise UK.

Summers, Lawrence H. 2014. The Inequality Puzzle. *Democracy* 33 (Summer). https://democracyjournal.org/magazine/33/the-inequality-puzzle/. Accessed 6 Feb 2017.

Teece, David J. 1982. Towards an Economic Theory of the Multiproduct Firm. *Journal of Economic Behavior & Organization* 3 (1): 39–63.

———. 2017a. Towards a Capability Theory of (Innovating) Firms: Implications for Management and Policy. *Cambridge Journal of Economics* 41 (3): 693–720.

———. 2017b. A Capability Theory of the Firm: An Economics and (Strategic) Management Perspective. *New Zealand Economic Papers*, forthcoming, https://doi.org/10.1080/00779954.2017.1371208.

Teece, David J., Gary Pisano, and Amy Shuen. 1997. Dynamic Capabilities and Strategic Management. *Strategic Management Journal* 18 (7): 509–533.

Williamson, Oliver E. 2010. Transaction Cost Economics: The Natural Progression. *American Economic Review* 100 (3): 673–690.

Winkelmann, Liliana, and Rainer Winkelmann. 1998. Why are the Unemployed so Unhappy? Evidence from Panel Data. *Economica* 65 (257): 1–15.

Winkelmann, Rainer. 2009. Unemployment, Social Capital, and Subjective Well-Being. *Journal of Happiness Studies* 10 (4): 421–430.

———. 2014. Unemployment and Happiness. *IZA World of Labor* 94. https://doi.org/10.15185/izawol.94.

Wulfgramm, Melike. 2014. Life Satisfaction Effects of Unemployment in Europe: The Moderating Influence of Labour Market Policy. *Journal of European Social Policy* 24 (3): 258–272.

# 6

# Local Government and Natural Capital

**Abstract** This chapter marks a significant change in the book's narrative, as the analysis moves from private citizens to the public sphere. Its starting point is that good government can develop distinctive capabilities to ensure that certain types of goods and services, especially those involving externalities and economic public goods, are provided for persons to use to enhance wellbeing. For some policies, particularly where local residents can improve outcomes by participating in policy design or implementation, local government can do this better than central government. In this context, the chapter explains Ostrom's theory of co-production of local government services and applies it to regional economic development. The chapter also discusses natural capital. Since ecosystem services provided by the natural environment can be diminished by human activity, investment in natural capital is required to maintain wellbeing.

**Keywords** Natural capital • Externalities • Economic public goods • Co-production • Regional economic development

Previous chapters have examined how private citizens can enhance wellbeing through personal time-use choices, through co-creating culturally valued lives within households and families, through collaboration in institutions of civil society, and through participation as producers and consumers in the market



P. Dalziel et al., *Wellbeing Economics*, Wellbeing in Politics and Policy,
https://doi.org/10.1007/978-3-319-93194-4_6

economy. This chapter marks a significant change, as the analysis turns to activities in the public sphere, introducing terms such as public sector, public services, public works, public economics, public goods, public policy and the public interest.

Discussion of the public sphere touches on strongly contested debates about the role of government in promoting wellbeing. These debates reflect diverse perspectives between views that favour a more expansive public sector and views that advocate smaller government. The wellbeing economics framework does not address this question directly, but emphasises that the public sector offers *distinctive* opportunities for private citizens to expand their capabilities for enhanced wellbeing, beyond what they could achieve through voluntary associations and market transactions.

A founding contribution to this insight was made by Mancur Olson (1965). Recall from Chap. 4 that persons can enhance wellbeing by participating in institutions of civil society to collaborate with others in the pursuit of common interests and shared values. Olson's analysis supported that proposition, but also explained that voluntary organisations tend to be limited in what they can achieve. This is because the personal reward to any member offering additional effort to advance the group's mission is reduced as the scale of its activities increases. Olsen therefore concluded, "the larger the group, the less it will further its common interests" (idem, p. 36).

Turning to the market economy, Chap. 5 began by acknowledging two important types of goods and services not well supplied by market firms: transactions involving externalities affecting people not directly involved, and items with the characteristics of an economic public good. Both examples are analysed in this chapter, demonstrating that market firms tend to supply too little or too much of an item with externalities (depending on whether the externalities create additional benefits or cause harm) and tend to supply too little of an economic public good (or perhaps none at all).

Thus, voluntary groups and market firms are unable to provide certain goods and services that enhance wellbeing. This creates room for local and central government to support greater wellbeing by ensuring these gaps are filled. As the following sections explain, this distinctive capability is due to the unique authority of governments to collect taxes and to promulgate legally enforced regulations.

There is no guarantee, of course, that this capability will always be exercised well. Throughout history, there have been oppressive governments acting tyrannically to cause great harm to wellbeing (Locke 1690, Chap. 18). Even in well-functioning democracies, just as markets can fail to provide optimal quantities of certain goods and services, so too can governments fail to deliver all they could to enhance wellbeing (Buchanan and Tullock 1962; Wolf 1979, 1989; Le Grand 1991). These limitations are an important part of the discussion that follows, but Proposition 16 expresses the core idea that good government can make distinctive contributions to the promotion of wellbeing.

**Proposition 16** Good government can develop distinctive capabilities for managing the provision of certain types of goods and services, especially those with externalities or the characteristics of an economic public good.

This chapter focuses on local government (including the governance of large cities), leaving the analysis of central government to Chap. 7. It begins with two sections examining externalities and economic public goods. This lays foundations for the chapter's main section, which analyses the distinctive contribution of local government to promoting wellbeing. This draws on the research of Nobel laureate, Elinor Ostrom, who emphasised the importance of co-production of services by local government and resident communities. It also draws on research exploring how local government can collaborate to strengthen place-based capabilities for wellbeing through regional economic development (Sotarauta 2005; Barca 2009; OECD 2009a, b; Barca et al. 2012; Foray 2015; McCann and Ortega-Argilés 2015).

An important example of a public good is a locality's natural environment. The wellbeing of residents in any given place is affected by items such as air and water quality, green spaces in liveable cities, facilities for outdoor recreation and the management of regional parks. The chapter's fourth section therefore introduces the next use of the capital metaphor in the wellbeing economics framework—natural capital. The chapter finishes with a brief conclusion.

## Externalities

Consider a household that regularly hosts parties involving loud music into the early hours of the morning. The parties are presumably part of the kind of life valued by the household's residents, and the partygoers are there by choice, free to leave if they find the hour too late or the music disagreeable. Thus, the direct participants in this activity—the hosts and their guests—can be presumed to value the experience, but the same may not be true for the neighbours. The noise may interfere with their own enjoyment of an evening at home, or it may interrupt the sleep of children and adults.

In the language of economics, activities like this create an *externality* by impacting on others not directly involved (Pigou 1932; Coase 1960; Baumol 1972). The loud music example is a negative externality, since the impacts are harmful, but externalities can be positive. Consider a property developer who purchases a row of derelict warehouses and converts them into quality residential housing. The developer and the buyers of the new homes can be presumed to have greater wellbeing, but the development may improve the quality of life for others in the neighbourhood—a positive externality.

The presence of a market externality is not sufficient reason for government intervention. Coase (1960) pointed out that if property rights concerning the externality are clearly defined, then those affected can negotiate a market transaction to reach some mutually accepted solution, as long as the transaction costs of negotiating and enforcing the agreement are not too high. This is known as the Coase Theorem and is a further illustration of how private persons can use the market economy to advance wellbeing.

The caveat in the Coase Theorem is crucial. The market option is not feasible if the costs of negotiating and enforcing agreements are too high, which is likely to be the case when the number of persons involved is large. Thus, an externality involving many people is typically an example of *market failure*, meaning that the market economy cannot be relied upon to produce a Pareto efficient outcome.

Under these circumstances, local government might use statutory powers to improve outcomes. In the United Kingdom, for example, local councils are responsible for investigating complaints about excessive noise from 11 pm to 7 am, and can impose fines or prosecute if the noise is not kept below fixed limits (DEFRA 2017). In the property development example, a council might fund a local development agency to negotiate incentives for developers to create neighbourhood regeneration projects that generate positive externalities.

## Economic Public Goods

A good or service is an economic public good if it has two characteristics (Samuelson 1954). First, using the good or service must not prevent other persons from benefiting from the same item simultaneously. This is termed *non-rivalry in consumption*. Second, if an economic public good is provided to any person, then it must not be possible to prevent others from enjoying its benefits; the good or service is said to be *non-excludable*.[1]

A good example is street lighting installed by a local council to increase safety at night. One person using the street lighting does not prevent others from doing likewise at the same time (non-rivalry in consumption). When the lights are operating, it is not possible to prevent anyone in the streets from using them (non-excludable).

The first characteristic means that a small financial sacrifice by each person in a community can produce large wellbeing benefits for all residents. Consider a city with a population of 400,000 adults. If each adult agrees to contribute £20 a year for street lighting, the result is £8 million available to fund an annual service whose benefits can be enjoyed by all, because the street lighting is non-rival in consumption. Thus, each resident can access services costing £8 million to operate, while paying only £20.

However, because the services are non-excludable, economic public goods are unlikely to be funded by voluntary collaboration, at least not beyond a small scale. Suppose a resident is asked to volunteer £20 for the street lighting. The person might decline, judging that an extra £20 for operating an £8 million system would not be as beneficial as an extra £20 of personal spending. Other residents might reason in the same way and so the lighting project would be underfunded. A market firm trying to sell the service to individual residents would face the same issue.

This is the free-rider problem: "Not all people can be expected to contribute voluntarily to a good cause, and any voluntary system is likely to produce too little of the public good" (Dawes and Thaler 1988, p. 196).[2] It provides a rationale for government, which can resolve the problem by its authority to collect compulsory taxes and rates. As the street lighting example illustrates, economic public goods have the potential to deliver large benefits to residents in return for a relatively small tax levied on each property owner or income-earner.

This reasoning does not require a local government to collect its own revenue. In England, for example, Parishes and Charter Trustees charge a precept collected on their behalf by larger billing authorities (DCLG 2017, pp. 4–5). Also, local authorities receive funds through central government. Some funds are from general taxation (including grants tied to specific purposes such as education or policing) and some are from the rates on non-domestic properties (also known as business rates) that are collected and distributed according to rules set by central government.

Figure 6.1 shows the transfers from central to local government in England from 1997–1998 to 2016–2017. The data are measured using 2016–2017 prices

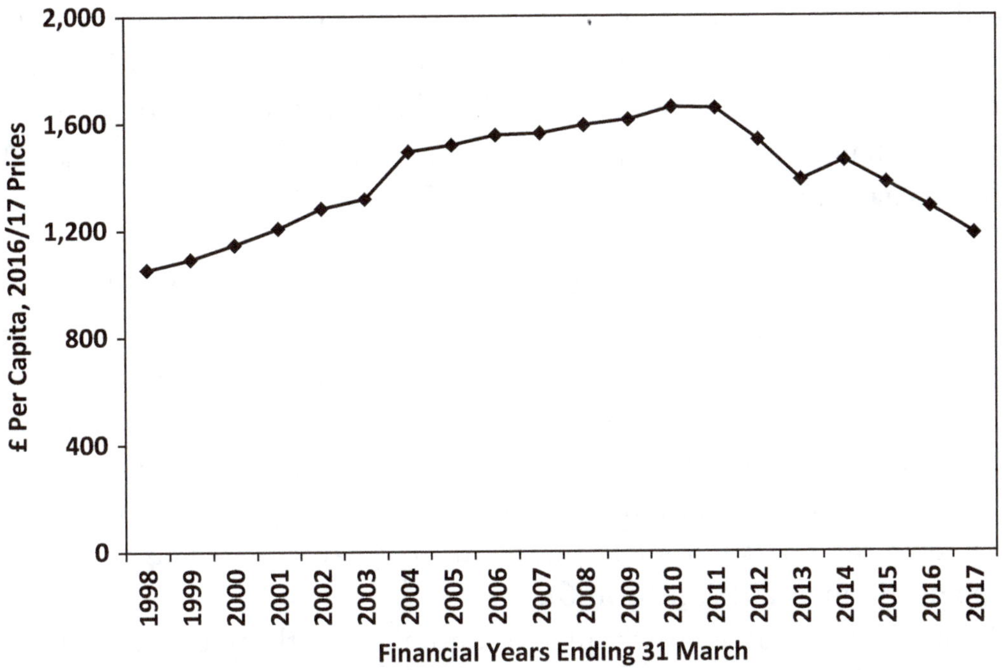


**Fig. 6.1** Transfers from central government to local government, per capita, England, 1997–1998 to 2016–2017. (Note: Transfers include government grants and non-domestic rates; the values are presented at 2017 GDP Deflator prices and have been divided by mid-year population for England in the previous calendar year. Source: Calculated from DCLG (2014, Table 3.2e) and DCLG (2017, Table 3.2a) using ONS estimates for the GDP Deflator and mid-year population)

to remove the impact of inflation, and are shown in per capita terms to account for increased demand on services due to population growth. Comparisons between years must still be made cautiously because policy changes can affect the need for local government finance (such as the increase in academy schools, which are funded by central rather than local government). Nevertheless, three distinctive periods are clear in the graph.

First, per capita transfers grew strongly between 1997–1998 and 2003–2004, from just under £1100 to nearly £1500, as central government sought to address longstanding problems of social exclusion in some parts of the United Kingdom. Second, transfers then rose at a slower rate, peaking at £1658 per person in 2009–2010. Third, as part of the central government's austerity measures after the Global Financial Crisis, a sharp fall resulted in per capita transfers reducing to £1186 in 2016–2017. This was 28.5 per cent lower than in 2009–2010.

The scale of these cuts has put pressure on the ability of local governments to fund public goods and services for residents (Kennett et al. 2015, p. 640; Hastings et al. 2015). Further, this burden has not been distributed evenly;

instead, there was a marked association with deprivation: "Between 2010/11 and 2013/14, authorities in the least deprived quintile lost 16% of their spending power compared with 21% for those in the most deprived three quintiles" (Bailey et al. 2015, pp. 574–575; see also Keep and Berman 2013, p. 10; Meegan et al. 2014, pp. 141–142).

The changes were designed to support the government's prioritisation of economic growth, discussed in Chap. 1. This can be illustrated with the policy change for non-domestic rates collected from businesses. These were previously distributed to local governments using a formula based on each authority's relative needs and ability to raise income locally (Keep and Berman 2011, pp. 5–8). The Local Government Finance Act 2012 introduced a new scheme, under which each local authority receives a greater or lesser share depending on whether the real value of its local business rates is increasing or falling (Keep and Berman 2013, section 6).

The new scheme aims to stimulate economic growth by creating incentives for an authority to support local economic development, since the authority now retains a share of any increase in local business rates (idem, p. 31). At the same time, however, the scheme creates greater financial risks for local authorities (National Audit Office 2013, par. 3.17). Further, some local authorities face higher risks than others, because they have fewer opportunities for fostering local economic growth.

Paul Krugman, for example, introduced the theory of *agglomeration economics* to show how modern technologies can result in situations where "manufactures production will tend to concentrate where there is a large market, but the market will be large where manufactures production is concentrated" (Krugman 1991, p. 486).[3] This means that patterns of strong economic growth in large cities, accompanied by relative deprivation in other regions, tend to persist (McCann 2008).

Several authors have argued that the financial cutbacks imposed on local governments are part of "the great risk shift" in recent years from social security to individual responsibility.[4] Hastings et al. (2015, p. 618), for example, place the cuts within a wider objective for local government "to behave more entrepreneurially; to take on more responsibility for economic growth and the distribution of benefits; and to take on new risks in relation both to the demands placed on services such as social care and for balancing budgets". They conclude that England's local government "will have to change to a very substantial extent" (ibid), which provides a context for the following analysis on distinctive contributions local government can make to wellbeing.

## Local Government, Co-production and Capabilities

As noted earlier, there is no guarantee that local and national governments will always promote wellbeing effectively, even in well-functioning democracies. As Downs (1957, p. 149) was one of the first to analyse, "apathy among citizens towards elections, ignorance of the issues, the tendency of parties in a two-party system to resemble each other, and the anti-consumer bias of government action can all be explained logically as efficient reactions to imperfect information in a large democracy".

Buchanan and Tullock (1962) have proposed *constitutional democracy* as a system for mitigating some of these tendencies by allowing majority decision-making for ordinary issues of the day, while requiring all decisions to satisfy rules that have been codified in a higher-level document that is hard to change. For local government, this system is achieved through State legislation defining its duties and powers. In England, for example, Section 2 of the Local Government Act 2000 used language for this purpose that resonates with major themes of this book:

> Every local authority are to have power to do anything which they consider is likely to achieve any one or more of the following objects—
>
> (a) the promotion or improvement of the economic well-being of their area,
> (b) the promotion or improvement of the social well-being of their area, and
> (c) the promotion or improvement of the environmental well-being of their area.

Authorities made limited use of that wellbeing power, however, tending to rely on other powers that were more specific and so less open to legal challenge (DCLG 2008a, b). The Localism Act 2011 therefore replaced the wellbeing power with a general power of competence: "A local authority has power to do anything that individuals generally may do." This phrase gives local authorities scope for a wide range of initiatives on behalf of communities (Sandford 2016), but obscures the key idea in Proposition 16 that governments have *distinctive* capabilities for contributing to enhanced wellbeing, *beyond* "anything that individuals generally may do".

There remains the question of the division of responsibility between local and central governments. The principle of subsidiarity holds that "decisions should be made at the lowest possible spatial scale – being closest to the people affected" (Wills 2016, p. 11). This principle helps guide the allocation of responsibilities at different levels of government, as enshrined, for example, in the Treaty on European Union, signed at Maastricht on 7 February 1992 (Article 5, Clause 3):

> Under the principle of subsidiarity, in areas which do not fall within its exclusive competence, the Union shall act only if and in so far as the objectives of the proposed action cannot be sufficiently achieved by the Member States, either at central level or at regional and local level, but can rather, by reason of the scale or effects of the proposed action, be better achieved at Union level.

The policy of having decision-making closest to the people affected is termed *localism*. It has a long history in the United Kingdom (Lyons 2007, pp. 45–49; Wilson and Game 2011; Wills 2016). An implication is that if a public initiative can be greatly improved by local residents actively participating in its design or implementation, then this is a reason for the initiative to be overseen by local rather than central government (Lyons 2007, par. 2.8).

This insight was explored in the research of Nobel laureate Elinor Ostrom (1990, 2005, 2010), who demonstrated how *co-production* of public services by local residents and local government officials, respecting different levels and nodes of decision-making in local communities, can result in positive outcomes for well-being. A good summary is the following statement (Ostrom 1996, p. 1073):

> By coproduction, I mean the process through which inputs used to produce a good or service are contributed by individuals who are not "in" the same organization. … All public goods and services are potentially produced by the regular producer and by those who are frequently referred to as the client. The term "client" is a passive term. Clients are acted upon. Coproduction implies that citizens can play an active role in producing public goods and services of consequence to them.

Note that Ostrom placed persons at the centre of their own lives in a way that resonates strongly with Sen's capabilities approach (Tully 2013). Indeed, her Nobel Prize lecture criticised policies imposed on communities as if "the momentum for change must come from outside the situation rather than from the self-reflection and creativity of those within a situation to restructure their own patterns of interaction" (Ostrom 2010, p. 648).

An important application is place-based regional economic development. Barca et al. (2012, p. 149) observe: "The place-based argument suggests that development strategies should thus focus on mechanisms which build on local capabilities and promote innovative ideas through the interaction of local and general knowledge and of endogenous and exogenous actors in the design and delivery of public policies". This accepts the importance of insiders and outsiders interacting in policy design and delivery, and emphasises *local capabilities* (see also Barca 2009; OECD 2009a, b).

Recall that the previous chapter explained how market firms combine different types of capital to maintain specialist capabilities for supplying goods and services (Proposition 14). Similarly, although at a higher level of generality, regions can develop capabilities for wellbeing as a result of integrated investment in the seven capitals analysed in this book.[5] This observation is expressed in Proposition 17.

**Proposition 17** Local government, sharing leadership with other actors in their communities, can develop and sustain regional capabilities for wellbeing through integrated investment in different types of capital.

Thus, public sector investments in large-scale physical capital projects typically involve regional infrastructure strategies (see, e.g., Solé-Ollé et al. 2012). Similarly, regional skills ecosystems aim to connect human capital investment with demands for labour skills by local industries (Finegold 1999; Hall and Lansbury 2006; Buchanan and Jakubauskas 2010; Dalziel 2015, 2017). Further, regional innovation systems are designed to support the expansion and utilisation of knowledge capital to strengthen regional competitive advantage (Cooke 1992; de la Mothe and Paquet 1998; Asheim and Gertler 2005; Corrocher and Cusmano 2014).

Recent scholarship recognises the value of integrating these types of strategies. Crescenzi and Rodríguez-Pose (2012), for example, found that isolated investments by the European Union in transport infrastructure projects had shown little evidence of improved regional growth. They therefore concluded that transport infrastructure should be linked to "more integrated and inclusive development policies based on human capital and innovation" (idem, p. 508). This echoes similar recommendations by the OECD (2009a, pp. 17–18).

Strategies for investment in other types of capital can also be beneficial. Considering social capital, Malecki (2012, p. 1028) cites Rutten and Boekema (2007) to suggest that "regional social capital is what transforms technology into regional economic development through regional innovation networks". Warner (1999, 2001) explains how local government can foster social capital, but concludes both papers with the observation that deeper structural issues—economic and political, as well as social issues—impact on local wellbeing, so that a focus on social capital development is only one aspect of a broader transformation required in local government institutions.

Similarly, investment in cultural capital is important for *place-shaping*, defined as "the creative use of powers and influence to promote the general well-being of a community and its citizens" (Lyons 2007, par. 2.43). This includes local government initiatives that support creative lives and the vibrancy of creative endeavours (Florida 2002, p. 232).[6] Local governments pay attention to the ongoing renewal of heritage in public spaces (Graham 2002; Carmona 2014), as well as creating spaces for communities to engage with each other through programmes such as intercultural cities (Wood and Landry 2008; Cantle 2012; Zapata-Barrero 2015; ICC 2016).

A strong theme in regional policy is the importance of connections beyond a region, including with other regions, with central government and with the global market economy (Harrison 2013; McCann 2016, pp. 10–13). An important driver of European Union cohesion policy, for example, is the smart specialisation concept (Foray 2006; Foray et al. 2009; OECD 2013; Foray 2015; McCann and Ortega-Argilés 2015). This concept proposes that regions can be helped to identify areas of research and development where they have strengths and opportunities based on their existing capabilities and connections to the global market economy. Chap. 8 of this book will discuss connections of this nature under the heading of diplomatic capital.

Finally, all local governments operate in particular places with specific environmental characteristics requiring management. The following section addresses this important feature under the heading of natural capital.

## Natural Capital

The term *natural capital* is widely used (Schumacher 1973, p. 2; Jansson et al. 1994; Helm 2015), but not always accepted. The metaphor of "capital" is associated with four key elements of an item:

1. The item is an asset, which may be owned privately (e.g., human capital, embodied cultural capital and private physical capital) or collectively (e.g., material cultural capital, social capital and public physical capital).
2. The item provides ongoing services that can be used by persons, organisations and communities to enhance wellbeing.
3. The item has a tendency to deteriorate in quantity or quality over time.
4. The stock of the item can grow through well-designed investment, which always has an opportunity cost.

The natural environment clearly meets items 2, 3 and 4 in this list. Nature provides essential services for human wellbeing. These are sometimes called *ecosystem services* (Costanza et al. 1997; Boyd and Banzhaf 2007; Fisher et al. 2009), although there is disagreement about how their economic value should be calculated, if at all (Boehnert 2016, pp. 404–40). Human activity is having detrimental impacts on environmental quality. These impacts can be mitigated through costly investment.

The first item in the list is open to challenge. The suggestion that nature is an asset owned by humans seems to overlook that we humans are a subset of nature (Schumacher 1973, p. 2). Professor Brian Cox, Fellow of the Royal Society and recipient of the 2010 Kelvin Medal and Prize awarded by the Institute of Physics, has expressed this reality on a cosmic scale (Cox and Cohen 2011, p. 135):

> When we look out into space, we are looking into our own origins, because we are truly children of the stars. Written into every atom and every molecule of our bodies is the entire history of the Universe.

Hence, to treat nature as a type of capital can be "a procedure by which the higher is reduced to the level of the lower and the priceless is given a price" (Schumacher 1973, p. 46). Boehnert (2016, p. 404) similarly argues that there are deep philosophical objections to the idea that nature might be considered a subsystem of the economy.

> The global ecological commons are the source of life and the basis for all activities—economic and noneconomic. Economics is a construct made possible by ecological processes. Ecological processes are simply too complex to be captured absolutely through financial valuation processes because they are the context of economics, not a subsystem of economics…

Some scholars therefore argue that nature has an *intrinsic value*, independent of the instrumental value to human wellbeing resulting from the provision of ecosystem services (Batavia and Nelson 2017; Piccolo 2017).

These points can be accepted while still retaining a place for the metaphor of natural capital. It would be folly to suggest that *all nature*, reaching out to the edges of the Universe, is encapsulated within this metaphor. Rather, the metaphor refers only to the interaction of nature with human activities, which is what makes nature subject to items 2, 3 and 4 in the above list. Since these items are profoundly important for the natural environment and for human wellbeing, natural capital should not be excluded from a wellbeing economics framework.

This is well discussed by Dieter Helm (2015). Helm makes the point that natural damage from human activity is accelerating. This will continue, since current trends suggest that the global economy could multiply perhaps 16 times by the end of the century. Consequently, an unavoidable issue for economic policy is how much effort should be spent preserving and enhancing the environment: "Not much will be left on a business-as-usual basis, and current policies are utterly feeble when confronted with this scale of destruction coming down the track" (idem, p. 5). This is expressed in the final proposition for this chapter.

**Proposition 18** Human activity can diminish ecosystem services provided by the natural environment, and so investment in natural capital is required to maintain and enhance wellbeing.

The question arises: *Who owns this problem?* This is the sense in which arrangements must be made for the ownership of natural capital (the first key element of the capital metaphor listed above). It is not ownership in the sense of assigning exclusive property rights, but ownership in the sense of exercising stewardship by managing investment in natural capital required to maintain and enhance its quality.

Who owns this problem depends on the scale of a particular investment decision. Issues such as climate change affect the whole global community; hence, it is the major focus of Chap. 8. At the local level, all communities have their own natural capital investment decisions to make. These are typically made through co-production with local government services to invest in amenities such as open spaces, community parks, the countryside, natural waterways, protected coastlines, green spaces in cities and good air quality.

## Conclusion

Local government has distinctive capabilities for improving wellbeing, primarily through its ability to address the free-rider problem in the provision of economic public goods and externalities in voluntary transactions. Local authorities provide a range of facilities and services that would otherwise be under-provided.

Best outcomes are achieved through co-production of public services by local residents and local government officials, respecting different levels and nodes of decision-making in local communities. An important application is that a local government, sharing leadership with other actors in their communities, can develop and sustain regional capabilities for wellbeing (including, but not restricted to, regional economic development) through integrated investment in different types of capital. This includes investment in natural capital, since ecosystem services provided by the environment are being diminished by human activity.

Local governments are most effective where public decision-making needs to be close to the people affected. In other cases of public goods and services, a larger scale at the national level is more sensible. Chap. 7 therefore turns to the Nation State and wellbeing.

## Notes

1. If an item is rival in consumption but is non-excludable, this gives rise to "The Tragedy of the Commons" (Hardin 1968). This possibility will be discussed in Chap. 8 as part of the analysis of climate change.
2. McMillan (1979) provides an overview of mechanisms proposed by economists for mitigating the free-rider problem.
3. This theory is the starting point for modern economic geography (Krugman 2008, p. 344). The feature that gives rise to this effect is termed *increasing returns to scale*, meaning that if all inputs into production double, then the volume of output increases by more than double.
4. The cutbacks in funding mean that local authorities are forced to reduce their services, shifting risks to residents. See Meegan et al. (2014); Bailey et al. (2015), Hastings et al. (2015), Kennett et al. (2015) and Scott (2015). Hacker (2008) introduced the term in a US context.
5. Sotarauta (2005) used the theory of the dynamic capabilities of firms to discuss the development of a region's leadership capabilities. Note that place-based policies are not universally supported. Two high-profile critiques were provided by Glaeser and Gottlieb (2008) and World Bank (2009).
6. An impact of austerity measures in the United Kingdom has been significant withdrawals of local government subsidies from arts and culture activities (Hastings et al. 2015, p. 611).

## References

Asheim, Bjørn T., and Meric S. Gertler. 2005. The Geography of Innovation: Regional Innovation Systems. In *The Oxford Handbook of Innovation*, ed. Jan Fagerberg and David C. Mowery, 291–317. Oxford: Oxford University Press.

Bailey, Nick, Glen Bramley, and Annette Hastings. 2015. Symposium Introduction: Local Responses to 'Austerity'. *Local Government Studies* 41 (4): 571–581.

Barca, Fabrizio. 2009. *An Agenda for a Reformed Cohesion Policy: A Place-Based Approach to Meeting European Union Challenges and Expectations*. Independent report prepared for the Commissioner for Regional Policy, European Commission. http://ec.europa.eu/regional_policy/archive/policy/future/barca_en.htm. Accessed 29 Dec 2017.

Barca, Fabrizio, Philip McCann, and Andrés Rodríguez-Pose. 2012. The Case for Regional Development Intervention: Place-based versus Place-neutral Approaches. *Journal of Regional Science* 52 (1): 134–152.

Batavia, Chelsea, and Michael Paul Nelson. 2017. For Goodness Sake! What is Intrinsic Value and Why Should We Care? *Biological Conservation* 209: 366–376.

Baumol, William J. 1972. On Taxation and the Control of Externalities. *American Economic Review* 62 (3): 307–322.

Boehnert, Joanna. 2016. The Green Economy: Reconceptualizing the Natural Commons as Natural Capital. *Environmental Communication* 10 (4): 395–417.

Boyd, James, and Spencer Banzhaf. 2007. What are Ecosystem Services? The Need for Standardized Environmental Accounting Units. *Ecological Economics* 63 (2–3): 616–6126.

Buchanan, James, and Gordon Tullock. 1962. *The Calculus of Consent: Logical Foundations of Constitutional Democracy*. Ann Arbor, MI: University of Michigan Press.

Buchanan, John, and Michelle Jakubauskas. 2010. The Political Economy of Work and Skill in Australia: Insights from Recent Applied Research. In *Beyond Skill: Institutions, Organisations and Human Capability*, ed. Jane Bryson, 32–57. London: Palgrave Macmillan.

Cantle, Ted. 2012. *Interculturalism: The New Era of Cohesion and Diversity*. Houndmills: Palgrave Macmillan.

Carmona, Matthew. 2014. The Place-shaping Continuum: A Theory of Urban Design Process. *Journal of Urban Design* 19 (1): 2–36.

Coase, Ronald H. 1960. The Problem of Social Cost. *Journal of Law and Economics* 3 (1): 1–44.

Cooke, Philip. 1992. Regional Innovation Systems: Competitive Regulation in the New Europe. *Geoforum* 23 (3): 365–382.

Corrocher, Nicoletta, and Lucia Cusmano. 2014. The 'KIBS Engine' of Regional Innovation Systems: Empirical Evidence from European Regions. *Regional Studies* 48 (7): 1212–1226.

Costanza, Robert, Ralph d'Arge, Rudolf de Groot, Stephen Farberk, Monica Grasso, Bruce Hannon, Karin Limburg, Shahid Naeem, Robert V. O'Neill, Jose Paruelo, Robert G. Raskin, Paul Sutton, and Marjan van den Belt. 1997. The Value of the World's Ecosystem Services and Natural Capital. *Nature* 387: 253–260.

Cox, Brian, and Andrew Cohen. 2011. *Wonders of the Universe*. Glasgow: Collins.

Crescenzi, Riccardo, and Andrés Rodríguez-Pose. 2012. Infrastructure and Regional Growth. *Papers in Regional Science* 91 (3): 487–513.

Dalziel, Paul. 2015. Regional Skill Ecosystems to Assist Young People Making Education Employment Linkages in Transition from School to Work. *Local Economy* 30 (1): 53–66.

———. 2017. Education and Qualifications as Skills. In *The Oxford Handbook of Skills and Training*, ed. John Buchanan, David Finegold, Ken Mayhew, and Chris Warhurst, 143–160. Oxford: Oxford University Press.

Dawes, Robyn M., and Richard H. Thaler. 1988. Anomalies: Cooperation. *Journal of Economic Perspectives* 2 (3): 187–197.

DCLG. 2008a. *Evaluation of the Take-up and Use of the Well-Being Power: Research Summary*. London: Department for Communities and Local Government.

———. 2008b. *Practical Use of the Well-Being Power*. London: Department for Communities and Local Government.

———. 2014. *Local Government Financial Statistics England, No. 24 2014*. London: Department for Communities and Local Government.

———. 2017. *Local Government Financial Statistics England, No. 27 2017*. London: Department for Communities and Local Government.

de la Mothe, John, and Gilles Paquet, eds. 1998. *Local and Regional Systems of Innovation*. New York: Kluwer Academic Publishers.

DEFRA. 2017. Noise Nuisances: How Councils Deal with Complaints Department for Environment, Food & Rural Affairs webpage accessed 30 December 2017 at https://www.gov.uk/guidance/noise-nuisances-how-councils-deal-with-complaints.

Downs, Anthony. 1957. An Economic Theory of Political Action in a Democracy. *Journal of Political Economy* 65 (2): 135–150.

Finegold, David. 1999. Creating Self-sustaining, High-skill Ecosystems. *Oxford Review of Economic Policy* 15 (1): 60–81.

Fisher, Brendan, R. Kerry Turner, and Paul Morling. 2009. Defining and Classifying Ecosystem Services for Decision Making. *Ecological Economics* 68 (3): 643–653.

Florida, Richard. 2002. *The Rise of the Creative Class: And How It's Transforming Work, Leisure, Community and Everyday Life*. New York: Perseus Book Group.

Foray Dominique. 2006. Globalization of R&D: Linking Better the European Economy to "Foreign" Sources of Knowledge and Making EU a More Attractive Place for R&D Investment. Knowledge Economists Policy Brief No. 1. http://ec.europa.eu/invest-in-research/monitoring/knowledge_en.htm. Accessed 10 Jan 2018.

———. 2015. *Smart Specialisation: Opportunities and Challenges for Innovation Policy*. London: Routledge.

Foray Dominique, Paul A. David and Bronwyn Hall. 2009. Smart Specialisation – The Concept. Knowledge Economists Policy Brief No. 9. http://ec.europa.eu/invest-in-research/monitoring/knowledge_en.htm. Accessed 10 Jan 2018.

Glaeser, Edward L., and Joshua D. Gottlieb. 2008. The Economics of Place-making Policies. *Brookings Papers on Economic Activity* (1): 155–239.

Graham, Brian. 2002. Heritage as Knowledge: Capital or Culture? *Urban Studies* 39 (5–6): 1003–1017.

Hacker, Jacob S. 2008. *The Great Risk Shift: The New Economic Insecurity and the Decline of the American Dream*. Revised and expanded edition. New York: Oxford University Press.

Hall, Richard, and Russell D. Lansbury. 2006. Skills in Australia: Towards Workforce Development and Sustainable Skill Ecosystems. *Journal of Industrial Relations* 48 (5): 575–592.

Hardin, Garrett. 1968. The Tragedy of the Commons. *Science* 162 (3859): 1243–1248.

Harrison, John. 2013. Configuring the New 'Regional World': On being Caught between Territory and Networks. *Regional Studies* 47 (1): 55–74.

Hastings, Annette, Nick Bailey, Maria Gannon, Kirsten Besemer, and Glen Bramley. 2015. Coping with the Cuts? The Management of the Worst Financial Settlement in Living Memory. *Local Government Studies* 41 (4): 601–621.

Helm, Dieter. 2015. *Natural Capital: Valuing the Planet*. New Haven/London: Yale University Press.

ICC. 2016. *Intercultural Cities Annual Report 2016: Sharing Our Cities Sharing the Future*. Council of Europe Intercultural Cities Programme. https://rm.coe.int/16806c9674. Accessed 6 Oct 2017.

Jansson, AnnMari, Monica Hammer, Carl Folke, and Robert Costanza, eds. 1994. *Investing in Natural Capital: The Ecological Economics Approach to Sustainability*. Washington, DC: Island Press.

Keep, Matthew and Gavin Berman. 2011. The Local Government Finance Settlement 2011–2013. Research Paper 11/16. London: House of Commons Library.

———. 2013. The Local Government Finance Settlement 2013/14 and 2014/15. Research Paper 13/10. London: House of Commons Library.

Kennett, Patricia, Gerwyn Jones, Richard Meegan, and Jaccqui Croft. 2015. Recession, Austerity and the 'Great Risk Shift': Local Government and Household Impacts and Responses in Bristol and Liverpool. *Local Government Studies* 41 (4): 622–644.

Krugman, Paul. 1991. Increasing Returns and Economic Geography. *Journal of Political Economy* 99 (3): 483–499.

———. 2008. The Increasing Returns Revolution in Trade and Geography. Nobel Prize speech, republished in Karl Grandin, Ed. *The Nobel Prizes 2008*. Stockholm: Nobel Foundation, 2009, pp. 335–348.

Le Grand, Julian. 1991. The Theory of Government Failure. *British Journal of Political Science* 21 (4): 423–442.

Locke, John. 1690. *Two Treatises of Government*, Book II. Available at www.gutenberg.org/ebooks/7370.

Lyons, Sir Michael. 2007. *Place-shaping: A Shared Ambition for the Future of Local Government*. London: The Stationery Office.

Malecki, Edward J. 2012. Regional Social Capital: Why it Matters. *Regional Studies* 46 (8): 1023–1039.

McCann, Philip. 2008. Globalization and Economic Geography: The World Is Curved, Not Flat. *Cambridge Journal of Regions, Economy and Society* 1 (3): 351–370.

———. 2016. *The UK Regional-National Economic Problem: Geography, Globalisation and Governance*. Abingdon: Routledge.

McCann, Philip, and Raquel Ortega-Argilés. 2015. Smart Specialization, Regional Growth and Applications to European Union Cohesion Policy. *Regional Studies* 49 (8): 1291–1302.

McMillan, John. 1979. The Free-Rider Problem: A Survey. *Economic Record* 55 (2): 95–107.

Meegan, Richard, Patricia Kennett, Gerwyn Jones, and Jacqui Croft. 2014. Global Economic Crisis, Austerity and Neoliberal Urban Governance in England. *Cambridge Journal of Regions, Economy and Society* 7 (1): 137–153.

National Audit Office. 2013. *Financial Sustainability of Local Authorities*. Report by the Comptroller and Auditor General, HC 888. London: The Stationery Office.

OECD. 2009a. *How Regions Grow: Trends and Analysis*. Paris: Organisation for Economic Cooperation and Development.

———. 2009b. *Regions Matter: Economic Recovery, Innovation and Sustainable Growth*. Paris: Organisation for Economic Cooperation and Development.

———. 2013. *Innovation-driven Growth in Regions: The Role of Smart Specialisation*. Paris: Organisation for Economic Cooperation and Development.

Olson, Mancur. 1965. *The Logic of Collective Action: Public Goods and the Theory of Groups*. Cambridge, MA: Harvard University Press.

Ostrom, Elinor. 1990. *Governing the Commons: The Evolution of Institutions for Collective Action*. Cambridge: Cambridge University Press.

———. 1996. Crossing the Great Divide: Coproduction, Synergy, and Development. *World Development* 24 (6): 1073–1087.

———. 2005. *Understanding Institutional Diversity*. Princeton, NJ: Princeton University Press.

———. 2010. Beyond Markets and States: Polycentric Governance of Complex Economic Systems. *American Economic Review* 100 (3): 641–672.

Piccolo, John J. 2017. Intrinsic Values in Nature: Objective Good or Simply Half of an Unhelpful Dichotomy? *Journal for Nature Conservation* 37: 8–11.

Pigou, Arthur Cecil. 1932. *The Economics of Welfare*. 4th ed. London: Macmillan.

Rutten, Roel, and Frans Boekama. 2007. Regional Social Capital: Embeddedness, Innovation Networks and Regional Economic Development. *Technological Forecasting and Social Change* 74 (9): 1834–1846.

Samuelson, Paul A. 1954. The Pure Theory of Public Expenditure. *Review of Economics and Statistics* 36 (4): 387–389.

Sandford, Mark. 2016. The General Power of Competence. Briefing Paper Number 05687. London: House of Commons Library.

Schumacher, Ernst F. 1973. *Small is Beautiful: Economics as if People Mattered*. New York: Harper and Row.

Scott, Karen. 2015. Happiness on Your Doorstep: Disputing the Boundaries of Wellbeing and Localism. *The Geographical Journal* 181 (2): 129–137.

Solé-Ollé, Albert, Andreas Stephan, and Timo Valilä. 2012. Introduction: Productivity and Financing of Regional Transport Infrastructure. *Papers in Regional Science* 91 (3): 481–485.

Sotarauta, Markku. 2005. Shared Leadership and Dynamic Capabilities in Regional Development. In *Regionalism Contested: Institution, Society and Governance*, ed. Iwona Sagan and Henrik Halkier, 53–72. Farnham: Ashgate.

Tully, James. 2013. Two Ways of Realizing Justice and Democracy: Linking Amartya Sen and Elinor Ostrom. *Critical Review of International Social and Political Philosophy* 16 (2): 220–232.

Warner, Mildred. 1999. Social Capital Construction and the Role of the Local State. *Rural Sociology* 64 (3): 373–393.

———. 2001. Building Social Capital: The Role of Local Government. *Journal of Socio-Economics* 30 (2): 187–192.

Wills, Jane. 2016. *Locating Localism: Statecraft, Citizenship and Democracy*. Bristol: Policy Press.

Wilson, David, and Chris Game. 2011. *Local Government in the United Kingdom*. 5th ed. Houndmills: Palgrave Macmillan.

Wolf, Charles, Jr. 1979. A Theory of Nonmarket Failure: Framework for Implementation Analysis. *Journal of Law and Economics* 22 (11): 107–139.

———. 1989. *Markets or Governments: Choosing Between Imperfect Alternatives*. Cambridge, MA: MIT Press.

Wood, Phil, and Charles Landry. 2008. *The Intercultural City: Planning for Diversity Advantage*. London: Earthscan.

World Bank. 2009. *Reshaping Economic Geography: Economic Development Report 2009*. Washington, DC: World Bank.

Zapata-Barrero, Ricard. 2015. *Interculturalism in Cities: Concept, Policy, and Implementation*. Cheltenham: Edward Elgar.

# 7

# The Nation State and Knowledge Capital

**Abstract** This chapter analyses how a Nation State can contribute to enhanced wellbeing. It begins with its responsibility to act on behalf of citizens as wise custodian of the market economy and welfare state within its borders. This requires central government to adopt an integrated and balanced approach to all its economic and welfare policies. The second half of the chapter focuses on the concept of knowledge capital as a driver of wellbeing. Knowledge creation can be an economic public good, which creates a distinctive opportunity for a well-functioning state to contribute to expanded capabilities for wellbeing through policies that foster the growth and use of knowledge. Knowledge is essential to the operations of the Nation State, whose civil service can offer a specialist capability for creating, collating, synthesising, utilising and disseminating knowledge capital for the common good.

**Keywords** Knowledge capital • Public policy • Welfare state • Endogenous growth • Civil service

Readers may be surprised that this book has not turned to the Nation State, and hence to central government policy, until Chap. 7. The delay is due to the core presumption in wellbeing economics that persons are able to exercise initiative in promoting personal wellbeing and the wellbeing of others through individual effort, co-creation in households and families, collaboration in community



P. Dalziel et al., *Wellbeing Economics*, Wellbeing in Politics and Policy,
https://doi.org/10.1007/978-3-319-93194-4_7

institutions, co-operation in the market economy and co-production of local government services. It has been important to analyse these diverse capabilities before analysing distinctive contributions of central government to enhanced wellbeing.

A useful introduction to this chapter's major themes is the theory of the Nation State presented by Max Weber (1919) just after World War I. Weber argued that the defining characteristic of a State is its monopoly on the legitimate use of physical force within a given territory, so that individuals or organisations may exercise force only to the extent permitted by the State. As persons seek to lead valued lives, conflicts arise. Nevertheless, all should be able to presume that it is illegitimate for these conflicts to result in violence.[1] Hence, the State accepts responsibility for maintaining law and order, and so provides trustworthy institutions for dispute resolution such as the armed forces, the police, the judiciary, the prisons and arbitration tribunals.

This theory of the Nation State is an application of Proposition 16: Good government can develop distinctive capabilities for managing the provision of certain types of goods and services, especially those with externalities or the characteristics of an economic public good. In this case, the economic public good being provided by the government is the maintenance of the rule of law (Heckman et al. 2010; Xu 2011).

Another application of Proposition 16 concerns the market economy. The previous chapter observed that markets need rules to work well. The London Stock Exchange, for example, maintains a Rulebook for the operation of that sophisticated market that runs to 98 pages (London Stock Exchange 2018). More generally, one of the key responsibilities of the Nation State is to define rules for the operation of markets under its jurisdiction.

A further application concerns the welfare state. Chapter 5 commented that it is reasonable for public policy to be designed so that *all* persons can access life-changing services such as housing, education and health independently of their household income. Public policy is also designed to provide a measure of social security to all citizens. The Nation State is responsible for designing and implementing these public policies. The chapter begins by considering these responsibilities, arguing that the Nation State acts as custodian of the market economy and the welfare state, *taken together*.

To fulfil its diverse roles, a well-functioning state must create, collate, synthesise, utilise and disseminate considerable amounts of knowledge. Further, existing knowledge and the discovery of new knowledge can have the characteristics of an economic public good. Central government therefore has a distinctive role in managing knowledge provision. Consequently, this chapter discusses the contribution of *knowledge capital* in the wellbeing economics framework. It explains its importance in economic models of growth and how governments address the issues raised by its economic public good characteristics. The chapter then ends with a discussion of the civil service's specialist capability for working with knowledge for the common good, before a brief conclusion.

## Custodian of the Market Economy and Welfare State

For most of the nineteenth and early twentieth centuries, the general disposition in public policy towards the wellbeing of citizens was based on "individualism and laissez-faire" (Keynes 1926, p. 272). This held that a Nation State might offer some limited remedies for addressing deserving cases of extreme poverty (the English Poor Laws, e.g.; see Boyer 1990), but otherwise outcomes were best left to individual enterprise and civil society operating within the market economy.

That disposition changed in the 1930s and 1940s. The Great Depression demonstrated that individual effort under laissez-faire policies is not always able to achieve reasonable standards of living, while World War II led to new understandings of how government action might enhance citizen wellbeing. International consensus in support of this change became sufficiently strong for the Universal Declaration of Human Rights, which was adopted by the United Nations General Assembly on 10 December 1948, to record social security as a universal right (Article 22):

> Everyone, as a member of society, has the right to social security and is entitled to realization, through national effort and international co-operation and in accordance with the organization and resources of each State, of the economic, social and cultural rights indispensable for his dignity and the free development of his personality.

In the United Kingdom, this transition from individualism and laissez-faire to what might be termed liberal collectivism (Cutler et al. 1986, Chap. 1) is evident in two landmark publications: Keynes (1936) and Beveridge (1942). The former was written in response to the Great Depression. Triggered by the New York stock market crash in August 1929, the Depression was transmitted to other countries as a result of substantial falls in world trade (Hamilton

1988; Eichengreen and Temin 2000). The volume of UK exports, for example, fell by more than a third between 1929 and 1931 (Maddison 1962, Table 25, p. 186).

The impact on the UK economy was not as severe as in the United States, but unemployment was already high in 1929 at 1.5 million, which was 7.3 per cent of the labour force. Unemployment peaked at 3.4 million in 1932, and remained above 1.8 million until 1937 (Middleton 2010, p. 417, citing Feinstein 1972). Of those unemployed in 1929, 10.7 per cent had been without a job for more than a year, but this figure had reached 27.1 per cent in 1937 (Crafts 1989, p. 247).

The laissez-faire policy response was to wait for wages to fall in order to restore full employment. Average annual earnings in the United Kingdom did indeed decline, by 8.7 per cent between 1929 and 1933 (Clark 2018). The retail price index, however, fell by a greater amount (14.4 per cent), so that the real wage rate (i.e., the real purchasing power of wages, defined as money wages divided by the price level) actually increased; see also Beenstock and Warburton (1986) and Hart (2001).

John Maynard Keynes wrote *The General Theory of Employment, Interest and Money* against that background (Skidelsky 1992). He developed two objections to the classical theory that high unemployment could always be addressed by lower wages. The first was that workers might reasonably resist a reduction in their individual wages, even if willing to accept a fall in real spending power imposed on all workers through an increase in consumer prices. That behavioural assumption was of its time and place and need not detain us any further. Keynes described his second objection as more fundamental and the subject of his new theory (Keynes 1936, p. 13):

> There may exist no expedient by which labour as a whole can reduce its *real* wage to a given figure by making revised *money* bargains with the entrepreneurs. We shall endeavour to show that primarily it is certain other forces which determine the general level of real wages. The attempt to elucidate this problem will be one of our main themes.

Keynes called his theory the principle of effective demand. Under certain circumstances, the level of employment becomes constrained by inadequate demand for the purchase of goods and services (Davidson 1998). During such a period, reduced money wages cannot achieve full employment, because lower wages do not stimulate demand.[2] Individuals are powerless, but the Nation State can restore balance by managing effective demand. Keynes (1936, p. 380) recognised such a responsibility meant enlarging the functions of central government, which he defended as necessary to protect the market economy and to support individual initiative within its system.

The second landmark publication was commissioned during World War II from a committee of civil servants headed by Sir William Beveridge as the independent chair (Abel-Smith 1992). Beveridge took for granted that the State had major responsibility for keeping unemployment to a minimum (Beveridge 1942, par. 22 and par. 440). He drew on surveys that had been made of British poverty to argue that full employment is insufficient for the abolition of want in the community. Instead, a plan for social security was required with two elements: (1) "provision against interruption and loss of earning power"; and (2) "adjustment of incomes, in periods of earning as well as in interruption of earning, to family needs" (idem, par. 12 and par. 13).

Beveridge adopted the principle that "social security must be achieved by co-operation between the State and the individual" and "should not stifle incentive, opportunity, responsibility" (idem, par. 9). In that partnership, the State's specific contribution is to use its authority to collect compulsory levies so that a system of *social insurance* could be implemented. This expansion in the role of government was justified in Beveridge's view by "the general tendency of public opinion" (idem, par. 26):

> After a trial of a different principle, it has be found to accord best with the sentiments of the British people that in insurance organised by the community by use of compulsory powers each individual should stand on the same terms; none should claim to pay less because he is healthier or has more regular employment. In accord with that view, the proposals of the Report mark another step forward to the development of State insurance as a new type of human institution…

The Beveridge Report became a cornerstone of the British welfare state (Hill 1993; Lowe 2004; Glennerster 2007; Fraser 2017, Chap. 9; Renwick 2017). The Education Act 1944 provided for free secondary education and set the school-leaving age at 15. The Family Allowances Act 1945, the National Insurance Act 1946 and the National Assistance Act 1948 created a comprehensive system of social security. The National Health Service Act 1946, with similar legislation for Scotland and Northern Ireland in 1947 and 1948, provided a system of medical care without user charges. The New Towns Act 1946 and the Town and Country Planning Act 1947 supported major post-war programmes of new housing.

It is beyond the scope of this book to trace further developments in the UK welfare state since the 1940s, or to discuss welfare policies in other countries.[3]

The key point is that it became generally accepted that wise management of the market economy and welfare state by central government has the potential to improve wellbeing beyond what individuals and civil society can achieve. This observation is expressed in the following proposition.

**Proposition 19** The Nation State can contribute to expanded capabilities for wellbeing by acting on behalf of citizens as wise custodian of the market economy and welfare state within its borders.

There are intense debates in every country about what "wise custodian" might mean in this proposition, or even whether central government can perform such a role adequately. These debates can be an indicator of a democracy's good health, since they address important questions about the kinds of lives that communities have reason to value, reflecting different histories and aspirations in each country. Proposition 19 does not address those debates, but conveys a key idea in the wellbeing economics framework, which is that this function of government is a *single* role. The Nation State is custodian of the market economy and the welfare state, *taken together*.

This insistence on an integrated approach is necessary because the market economy and the welfare state are not isolated from each other. To illustrate, recall the strong tendency identified in Chap. 5 for resources in the market economy to flow towards high-wealth households. If housing, education and health services were provided on a laissez-faire basis within the market economy, then this tendency would result in low-wealth households having restricted access to these services. This would reduce capabilities for wellbeing. It would also restrict the ability of low-wealth households to invest in human capital, which would limit labour productivity and so damage economic performance. Policies of the welfare state seek to prevent this by aiming to making certain standards of housing, education and healthcare (determined by social expectations and budget constraints) available to the whole population.

Similarly, economic performance impacts on the wellbeing functions of the welfare state. Cutler et al. (1986, p. 18) point out, for example, that the Beveridge Report assumed that jobs would pay decent wages, so that a person in employment could be presumed capable of achieving a satisfactory standard of living. As discussed in Chap. 5, this presumption is untenable given that more than one in seven jobs in the UK pay below the voluntary living wage. The failure of the market economy to create decent jobs puts pressure on the housing, education, health and social security systems of the welfare state.

Proposition 19 therefore requires a unified stance in public policies affecting the market economy and welfare state. In particular, it rejects the view, already criticised in Chap. 1, that "growth is the essential foundation of all our aspirations" (Cameron 2010, par. 4). Instead, an integrated and balanced approach is required across all policy areas.

## Knowledge Capital

It has long been recognised that a Nation State must adopt a sophisticated approach to how it obtains and uses knowledge. Consider the Haldane Report, for example, which was commissioned as a guide for reform of the civil service after World War I. It identified four main principles for reform, the first of which emphasised knowledge (Ministry of Reconstruction 1918, par. 56):

> Further provision is needed in the sphere of civil government for the continuous acquisition of knowledge and the prosecution of research, in order to furnish a proper basis for policy.

In the private sector, knowledge is recognised as a fundamental factor driving growth in material living standards. Recall that Solow's (1956) neoclassical growth model explains how growth in a country's average standard of living depends on technological progress. The contributions to technological progress were not explored, which was a weakness. Paul Romer (1986, 1990) therefore initiated a research programme to fill the gap. He accepted Solow's insights that the best measure of technological progress is labour productivity (i.e., the average value of output produced per hour of work) and that this depends on the stock of physical capital. He then added the idea that labour productivity also depends on the stock of *knowledge*, which increases through the dedicated activities of specialist workers engaged in research and development.

Romer's insight created *endogenous growth* theory, so-called because it explains technological progress within the model (Romer 1994; Aghion and Howitt 1998). The theory analyses a trade-off, since workers engaged in research and development are not available for other production. Thus, the creation of new knowledge has an opportunity cost in the form of foregone benefits that could have been realised from shifting the knowledge workers to the production of other goods and services. Balancing the costs and benefits of this trade-off allows the model to analyse an economy's equilibrium rate of technological progress, which determines its rate of economic growth.

Romer assumed that new knowledge created at any time is proportional to the amount of existing knowledge, depending on how many workers are engaged in research and development (see also Aghion and Howitt 1992). This produced the result that economic growth is higher with more knowledge workers, but Jones (1995a, 1995b) pointed out that this result is incompatible with experience. Large increases in the number of researchers over decades have not resulted in anything like comparable increases in economic growth rates. Consequently, as Ang and Madsen (2011, p. 1360) observe:

> Following Jones's (1995b) critique of the predictions of the first-generation endogenous growth models of Romer (1990) and Aghion and Howitt (1992), a positive relationship between the levels of R&D and productivity growth is generally no longer accepted as an empirical regularity in the growth literature.

Jones (1995a) suggested instead that the theory should recognise that research involves some wasted effort. He assumed that researchers find it increasingly hard to create new knowledge (implying more and more wasted effort) as the stock of knowledge expands. This assumption reproduced many features of the neoclassical growth model. Neither efforts to reduce wasted research or policies to increase the number of research workers could increase a country's rate of economic growth (Jones and Vollrath 2013, p. 106).

A second generation of endogenous growth theory was then introduced by scholars such as Young (1998), Howitt (1999), Ha and Howitt (2007) and Ang and Madsen (2011). They agreed there is some wasted effort in creating knowledge, but did not accept that this waste increases as knowledge expands. Instead, the new model assumed that the effectiveness of research effort diminishes with scale, since the effort must be spread over a greater variety of products. This restored Romer's hypothesis that knowledge increases in proportion to its current level, but the relationship now depended on the *proportion* of the labour force (not the absolute number) devoted to the task of research and development.

In all these models, knowledge acts as a *capital* stock that enhances labour productivity in providing market goods and services.[4] Unlike physical or natural capital, however, knowledge capital does not depend on material resources. It can also have the characteristics of an economic public good (World Bank 1998, pp. 131–133; Stiglitz 1999), which gives rise to important implications for wellbeing.

## Knowledge as an Economic Public Good

Consider two passenger flights crossing the Atlantic at the same hour. The flights require two planes, each of which represents a separate investment in physical capital. They also require separate flight crews, each with skilled human capital acquired through training and experience. In contrast, the two flights use the same knowledge capital. Both planes were designed using the same laws of aerodynamics, and the actions of pilots and cabin crew in both planes are guided by the same knowledge about flight safety.

Economists have long studied how advancing knowledge is embedded in physical capital (Solow 1962) and how access to global knowledge depends on human capital (Nelson and Phelps 1966). A feature of knowledge capital is that the same knowledge can be incorporated into any number of items of physical capital, and can be used simultaneously by any number of persons with the necessary human capital. In the language of economics, knowledge is non-rival in consumption (Stiglitz 1999).

This property means that the discovery and use of knowledge can be hugely beneficial to wellbeing. Discoveries can be used simultaneously by millions, even billions, of people to enhance wellbeing. "In short, knowledge gives people greater control over their destinies" (World Bank 1998, p. 2). Nor are there physical limits on the accumulation of a non-rival, non-material good like knowledge (Romer 1990, p. S74).

Further, production systems that use knowledge capital as an input exhibit the property of *increasing returns to scale* (Romer 1990, pp. S75–S76). This means that if all inputs into the production system double, including non-rival knowledge, then the level of output more than doubles. This is the property that gives rise to the result in endogenous growth theory that a higher rate of knowledge creation can lead to a higher rate of economic growth.

These observations offer a potential path for addressing the crucial question of how it might be feasible for humanity to raise the wellbeing of people in poverty across the globe, while respecting the planet's absolute limits to material consumption. Conceptually, this might be achieved, at least in part, by technological progress that substitutes (immaterial) knowledge capital for (material) physical and natural capital in economic production systems. If this path is to be followed, however, there is a critical problem to be addressed.

Once new knowledge is put to use, it is often impossible to prevent others from putting the same idea into practice for themselves. There are exceptions. A firm may be able to keep new knowledge secret until market dominance has been achieved. A new technology might require such large physical capital investment, or such specialist human capital, that only a few firms can take advantage of the discovery. Nevertheless, without public policies to address this issue, new knowledge often has the second characteristic of an economic public good—it is *non-excludable.*[5]

This characteristic severely weakens the incentive for efforts to discover new knowledge. A firm might spend large sums to undertake original research. It might then devote more human and financial resources to develop a discovery into a commercial product. These investments would not be recouped, however, if other firms are able simply to copy the idea without incurring the same research and development costs.

Consequently, investment in creating new knowledge may be valuable for wellbeing, but impossible for market firms to finance. This creates a distinctive opportunity for good government to contribute to wellbeing by addressing this conundrum, as recorded in Proposition 20.

**Proposition 20** Knowledge capital has the properties of an economic public good, so that Nation States can contribute to enhanced wellbeing by fostering the growth and use of knowledge.

A straightforward example is to create laws that protect intellectual property through copyright, patents and other legal instruments (World Bank 1998, pp. 16–17). These laws typically require details of a discovery to be placed on public record in return for the right to exclude others from using the new knowledge for a fixed period of time. The length of the exclusion period aims to balance the incentive benefits of rewarding successful efforts to create new knowledge with the wellbeing benefits of discoveries being made widely available.

To be effective, domestic laws must be reinforced by international agreements for the protection of intellectual property, taking into account different capabilities of developed and developing countries (Schneider 2005). The ability to make such agreements is an example of what this book terms *diplomatic capital,* which will be discussed in the following chapter.

Another example of Proposition 20 is the smart specialisation concept for regional development, mentioned in the previous chapter (Foray 2006, 2015, Foray et al. 2009; OECD 2013; McCann and Ortega-Argilés 2015). Creation of new knowledge is a global enterprise (Stiglitz 1999). Hence, it is sensible for regions to focus their research and development efforts on niches in the global innovation system where they have particular strengths and opportunities. Central government can assist by funding the design of generic institutional processes and analytical tools for regions to use for determining their own capabilities for smart specialisation.

## The Civil Service, Knowledge and Capabilities

The public sector is a significant part of a national economy. In September 2017, there were 5.5 million people employed in the UK public sector, which represented 17.1 per cent of all employed people in the country (ONS 2017). Figure Fig. 7.1 shows how the distribution of this employment by industry, with the three largest concentrations being in the National Health Service, in education and in public administration.

The civil service is a small but important subset of the public sector. It has been significantly reduced in the United Kingdom; see Fig. Fig. 7.2. At the beginning of the global financial crisis in September 2007, the seasonally adjusted full-time equivalent number in the civil service was 495,000. This number was reduced to its lowest level since World War II by the end of 2011 (HM Government 2012b, p. 9). In September 2017, it had been further reduced to 392,000, which was 20.8 per cent lower than a decade earlier.

The civil service offers a specialist service within the public sector (NAO 2017). Its primary responsibility is to help the government of the day, which it has been doing on a professional basis in the United Kingdom since the middle of the nineteenth century (Northcote and Trevelyan 1854, p. 3):

> It may safely be asserted that, as matters now stand, the Government of the country could not be carried on without the aid of an efficient body of permanent officers, occupying a position duly subordinate to that of the Ministers who are directly responsible to the Crown and to Parliament, yet possessing sufficient independence, character, ability, and experience to be able to advise, assist, and, to some extent, influence, those who are from time to time set over them.

Organised into departments, agencies and non-departmental government bodies, the civil service has three specific roles: operational delivery, advising on policy and supporting Ministers, and implementing programmes and projects (HM Government 2012a, pp. 8–9). The first is the largest duty; more than 70 per cent of all civil servants are employed in the delivery departments and their agencies of Work and Pensions, HM Revenue and Customs, Justice, Defence and the Home Office (ONS 2017, Table 9).

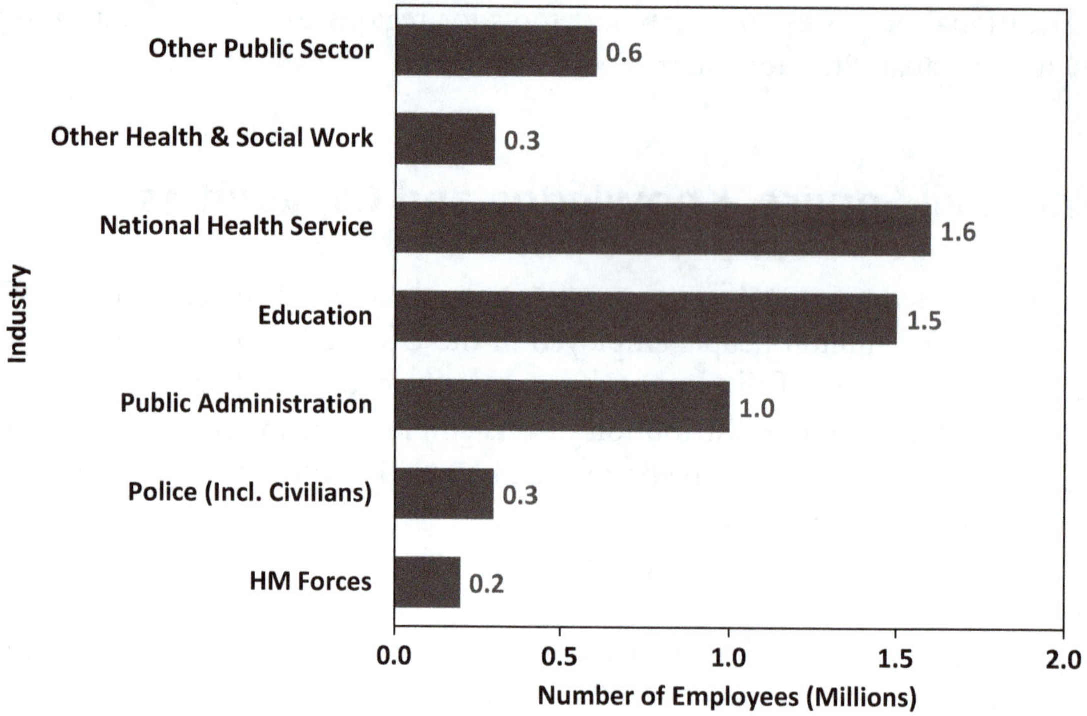


**Fig. 7.1** Number of people employed in the public sector by industry, seasonally adjusted, United Kingdom, September 2017. (Source: ONS 2017, Table 2)

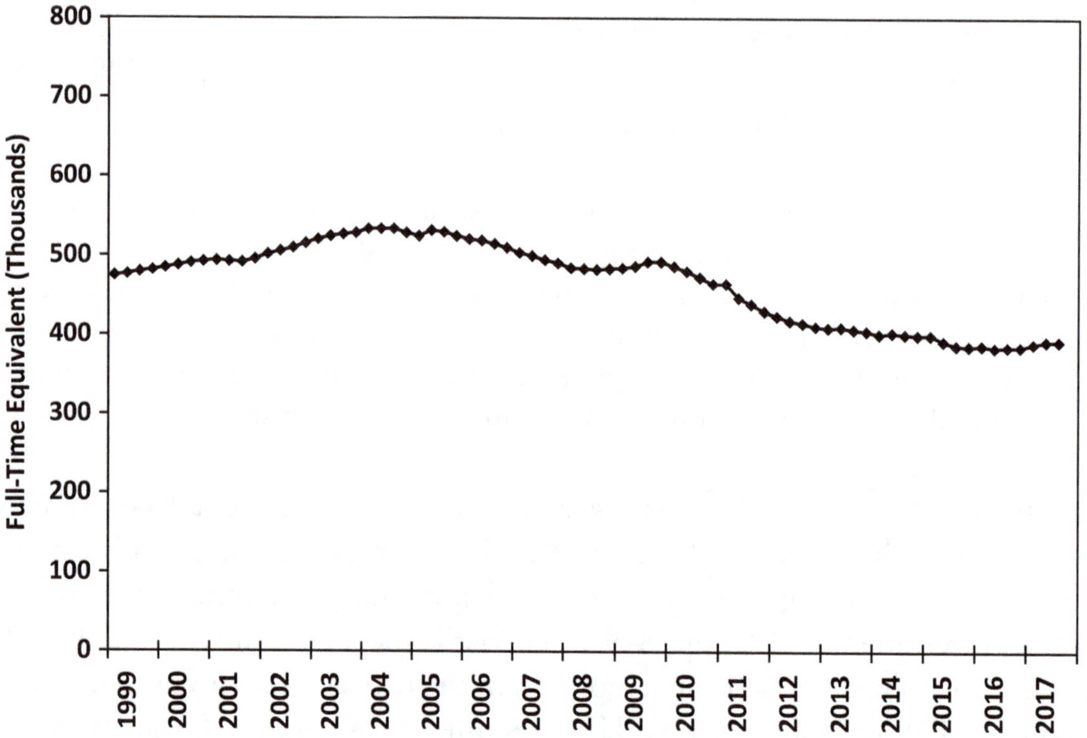


**Fig. 7.2** Number of people employed in the civil service, full-time equivalent seasonally adjusted, quarterly, United Kingdom, 1999(1)–2017(3). (Source: ONS 2017, Table 1)

The distinctive contribution of the civil service is its capability for working with knowledge as a public service on behalf of the Nation State. This is reflected in the final proposition of this chapter.

**Proposition 21** The civil service can offer a specialist capability for creating, collating, synthesising, utilising and disseminating knowledge capital for the common good.

Undertaking knowledge work for the public good requires certain values to be observed. The Constitutional Reform and Governance Act 2010 therefore requires civil servants to carry out their duties with integrity and honesty, and with objectivity and impartiality, which are defined in the Civil Service Code:[6]

- "integrity" is putting the obligations of public service above your own personal interests
- "honesty" is being truthful and open
- "objectivity" is basing your advice and decisions on rigorous analysis of the evidence
- "impartiality" is acting solely according to the merits of the case and serving equally well governments of different political persuasions

As the Code observes, these core values support good government. They are essential if citizens are to trust knowledge work undertaken by civil servants for the common good. The importance of this feature of good government has led to recent recommendations that public sector departments and agencies should adopt transparent practices so that people outside government can understand how evidence is used in policy decision, implementation and evaluation (Rutter and Gold 2015; Brown 2016).

## Conclusion

This chapter has focussed on the Nation State, beginning with its contribution to expanded capabilities by acting as wise custodian of the market economy and welfare state within its borders. This requires an integrated and balanced approach to all economic and welfare policies. Policy cannot be satisfied with promoting economic growth for its own sake; it must pay attention to *how* the economy is growing and the impacts this is having on the wellbeing of different parts of the national population. In particular, how is policy contributing to expanding the capabilities of persons to lead the kinds of lives they value, and have reason to value?

The second half of the chapter has been structured around the concept of knowledge capital. Discovery of new knowledge has long been recognised as a fundamental driver of economic and social wellbeing. Further, because existing knowledge does not depend on material resources and is non-rival in consumption, knowledge accumulation has great potential for contributing to enhanced wellbeing while respecting the material limits of the planet.

Knowledge, however, is often non-excludable, so that knowledge creation is an economic public good. This creates a distinctive opportunity for Nation States to contribute to enhanced wellbeing through policies that foster the growth and use of knowledge. At the same time, knowledge is essential to the operations of the Nation State, whose civil service can offer a specialist capability for creating, collating, synthesising, utilising and disseminating knowledge capital for the common good.

Some critical problems facing humanity clearly require actions that go beyond state borders. Pressing examples include persistent poverty in some of the world's regions and global climate change. Chap. 8 therefore analyses ways in which the global community can work together to enhance wellbeing on an international scale.

## Notes

1. As Chap. 4 observed, one of the horrors of institutional racism is that some citizens are unable to make this presumption because of the colour of their skin (Coates 2015; Eddo-Lodge 2017).
2. See Dalziel and Lavoie (2003) for a presentation of this theory in a labour market diagram. Note that Keynes does not imply that unemployment is *always* caused by inadequate demand; the classical theory has a place in explaining some episodes of high unemployment (Dalziel 1993). Boyer (2012) and Krugman (2012) are examples of analyses that drew on the theory of effective demand to critique the austerity policies implemented after the global financial crisis.
3. Pedersen (2018) observes that the welfare state was neither a British invention nor a British product.
4. Early uses of the phrase *knowledge capital* were by Griliches (1979) and Nelson (1982).
5. Recognising the exceptions, as well as the practice of creating legal mechanisms to make some forms of new knowledge a proprietary asset, economists observe that

knowledge is not necessarily a strict economic public good. Examples of alternative phrases to describe knowledge include "a partially excludable good" (Romer 1990, section II), having "spillover benefits" (World Bank 1998, p. 130) or "an impure public good" (Stiglitz 1999, p. 310). This does not affect this section's argument.

6. Accessed 23 January 2018 at https://www.gov.uk/government/publications/civil-service-code/the-civil-service-code.

## References

Abel-Smith, Brian. 1992. The Beveridge Report: Its Origins and Outcomes. *International Social Security Review* 45 (1–2): 5–16.

Aghion, Philippe, and Peter Howitt. 1992. A Model of Growth through Creative Destruction. *Econometrica* 60 (2): 323–351.

———. 1998. *Endogenous Growth Theory*. Cambridge, MA: MIT Press.

Ang, James, and Jakob Madsen. 2011. Can Second-Generation Endogenous Growth Models Explain the Productivity Trends and Knowledge Production in the Asian Miracle Economies? *Review of Economics and Statistics* 93 (4): 1360–1373.

Beenstock, Michael, and Peter Warburton. 1986. Wages and Unemployment in Interwar Britain. *Explorations in Economic History* 23 (2): 153–172.

Beveridge, William H. B. 1942. *Social Insurance and Allied Services: Report by Sir William Beveridge*. Report presented to Parliament by Command of His Majesty. London: His Majesty's Stationery Office.

Boyer, George R. 1990. *An Economic History of the English Poor Law, 1750–1850*. Cambridge: Cambridge University Press.

Boyer, Robert. 2012. The Four Fallacies of Contemporary Austerity Policies: The Lost Keynesian Legacy. *Cambridge Journal of Economics* 36 (1): 283–312.

Brown, Tracey. 2016. *Transparency of Evidence: An Assessment of Government Policy Proposals May 2015 to May 2016*. Report of a research project by Sense about Science, the Institute for Government and the Alliance for Useful Evidence, funded by the Nuffield Foundation. London: Sense about Science.

Cameron, Rt. Hon. David. 2010. PM Speech on Wellbeing A Transcript of a Speech Given by the Prime Minister on 25 November 2010. https://www.gov.uk/government/speeches/pm-speech-on-wellbeing.

Clark, Gregory. 2018. What Were the British Earnings and Prices Then? (New Series). Measuring Worth database accessed 26 January 2018 at www.measuringworth.com/ukearncpi/.

Coates, Ta-Neshi. 2015. *Between the World and Me*. Melbourne: Text Publishing.

Crafts, Nicholas F. R. 1989. Long-Term Unemployment and the Wage Equation in Britain, 1925–1939. *Economica* 56 (222): 247–254.

Cutler, Tony, Karel Williams, and John Williams. 1986. *Keynes, Beveridge and Beyond*. London: Routledge.

Dalziel, Paul. 1993. Classical and Keynesian Unemployment in a Simple Disequilibrium AS-AD Framework. *Australian Economic Papers* 32 (60): 40–52.

Dalziel, Paul, and Marc Lavoie. 2003. Teaching Keynes's Principle of Effective Demand Using the Aggregate Labour Market Diagram. *Journal of Economic Education* 34 (4): 333–340.

Davidson, Paul. 1998. Post Keynesian Employment Analysis and the Macroeconomics of OECD Unemployment. *Economic Journal* 108 (448): 817–831.

Eddo-Lodge, Reni. 2017. *Why I'm No Longer Talking to White People About Race*. London: Bloomsbury Circus.

Eichengreen, Barry, and Peter Temin. 2000. The Gold Standard and the Great Depression. *Contemporary European History* 9 (2): 183–207.

Feinstein, Charles H. 1972. *National Income, Expenditure and Output of the United Kingdom, 1855–1965*. Cambridge: Cambridge University Press.

Foray Dominique. 2006. Globalization of R&D: Linking Better the European Economy to "Foreign" Sources of Knowledge and Making EU a More Attractive Place for R&D Investment. Knowledge Economists Policy Brief No. 1. http://ec.europa.eu/invest-in-research/monitoring/knowledge_en.htm. Accessed 10 Jan 2018.

———. 2015. *Smart Specialisation: Opportunities and Challenges for Innovation Policy*. London: Routledge.

Foray Dominique, Paul A. David and Bronwyn Hall. 2009. Smart Specialisation – The Concept. Knowledge Economists Policy Brief No. 9. http://ec.europa.eu/invest-in-research/monitoring/knowledge_en.htm. Accessed 10 Jan 2018.

Fraser, Derek. 2017. *The Evolution of the British Welfare State: A History of Social Policy since the Industrial Revolution*. 5th ed. London: Palgrave Macmillan.

Glennerster, Howard. 2007. *British Social Policy: 1945 to the Present*. 3rd ed. Oxford: Blackwell.

Griliches, Zvi. 1979. Issues in Assessing the Contribution of Research and Development to Productivity. *Bell Journal of Economics* 10 (1): 92–116.

Ha, Joonkyung, and Peter Howitt. 2007. Accounting for Trends in Productivity and R&D: A Schumpeterian Critique of Semi-Endogenous Growth Theory. *Journal of Money, Credit and Banking* 39 (4): 733–744.

Hamilton, James D. 1988. Role of the International Gold Standard in Propagating the Great Depression. *Contemporary Economic Policy* 6 (2): 67–89.

Hart, Robert A. 2001. Hours and Wages in the Depression: British Engineering, 1926–1938. *Explorations in Economic History* 38 (4): 478–502.

Heckman, James J., Robert L. Nelson, and Lee Cabatingan, eds. 2010. *Global Perspectives on the Rule of Law*. Abingdon/New York: Routledge.

Hill, Michael. 1993. *The Welfare State in Britain: A Political History since 1945*. Cheltenham: Edward Elgar.

HM Government. 2012a. *The Civil Service Reform Plan*. London: Cabinet Office.

———. 2012b. *The Context for Civil Service Reform*. London: Cabinet Office.

Howitt, Peter. 1999. Steady Endogenous Growth with Population and R&D Inputs Growing. *Journal of Political Economy* 107 (4): 715–730.

Jones, Charles I. 1995a. R & D Models of Economic Growth. *Journal of Political Economy* 103 (4): 759–784.

———. 1995b. Time Series Tests of Endogenous Growth Models. *Quarterly Journal of Economics* 110 (2): 495–525.

Jones, Charles I., and Dietrich Vollrath. 2013. *Introduction to Economic Growth*. 3rd ed. New York: W. W. Norton.

Keynes, John Maynard. 1926. The End of Laissez-Faire. Pamphlet published by the Hogarth Press, reprinted in and cited from Chapter 2 in Donald Moggridge, Ed. *The Collected Writings of John Maynard Keynes, Volume IX: Essays in Persuasion*, pp. 272–294. London: Macmillan for the Royal Economic Society, 1972.

———. 1936. *The General Theory of Employment, Interest and Money*, reprinted in and cited from Donald Moggridge, Ed. *The Collected Writings of John Maynard Keynes, Volume VII: The General Theory*. London: Macmillan for the Royal Economic Society, 1973.

Krugman, Paul R. 2012. *End This Depression Now!* New York: W. W. Norton.

London Stock Exchange. 2018. *Rules of the London Stock Exchange*, Effective Date 3 January. www.londonstockexchange.com/traders-and-brokers/rules-regulations/rules-lse.pdf. Accessed 7 Feb 2018.

Lowe, Rodney. 2004. *The Welfare State in Britain since 1945*. 3rd ed. Basingstoke: Palgrave.

Maddison, Angus. 1962. Growth and Fluctuation in the World Economy, 1870-1960. *Banca Nazionale del. Lavoro Quarterly Review* 15 (61): 127–195.

McCann, Philip, and Raquel Ortega-Argilés. 2015. Smart Specialization, Regional Growth and Applications to European Union Cohesion Policy. *Regional Studies* 49 (8): 1291–1302.

Middleton, Roger. 2010. British Monetary and Fiscal Policy in the 1930s. *Oxford Review of Economic Policy* 26 (3): 414–441.

Ministry of Reconstruction. 1918. *Report of the Machinery of Government Committee*. Report presented to Parliament by Command of His Majesty. London: His Majesty's Stationery Office.

NAO. 2017. *Capability in the Civil Service*. Report by the Comptroller and Auditor General, HC 919, Session 2016–2017. London: National Audit Office.

Nelson, Richard R., and Edmund S. Phelps. 1966. Investment in Humans, Technological Diffusion, and Economic Growth. *American Economic Review* 56 (1/2): 69–75.

Nelson, Richard R. 1982. The Role of Knowledge in R&D Efficiency. *Quarterly Journal of Economics* 97 (3): 453–470.

Northcote, Stafford H., and Charles E. Trevelyan. 1854. *On the Organisation of the Permanent Civil Service*. Report presented to both Houses of Parliament by Command of Her Majesty. London: Her Majesty's Stationery Office.

OECD. 2013. *Innovation-driven Growth in Regions: The Role of Smart Specialisation*. Paris: Organisation for Economic Cooperation and Development.

ONS. 2017. Public Sector Employment, UK: September 2017. Statistical Bulletin released 13 December, Office for National Statistics.

Pedersen, Susan. 2018. One-Man Ministry. *London Review of Books* 40 (3): 3–6.

Renwick, Chris. 2017. *Bread for All: The Origins of the Welfare State*. London: Allen Lane.

Romer, Paul M. 1986. Increasing Returns and Long-Run Growth. *Journal of Political Economy* 94 (5): 1002–1037.

———. 1990. Endogenous Technological Change. *Journal of Political Economy* 98 (5 Part 2): S71–S102.

———. 1994. The Origins of Endogenous Growth. *Journal of Economic Perspectives* 8 (1): 3–22.

Rutter, Jill and Jen Gold. 2015. *Show Your Workings: Assessing How Government Uses Evidence To Make Policy*. London: Institute for Government.

Schneider, Patricia Higino. 2005. International Trade, Economic Growth and Intellectual Property Rights: A Panel Data Study of Developed and Developing Countries. *Journal of Development Economics* 78 (2): 529–547.

Skidelsky, Robert. 1992. *John Maynard Keynes: The Economist as Saviour, 1920–1937*. London: Macmillan.

Solow, Robert M. 1956. A Contribution to the Theory of Economic Growth. *Quarterly Journal of Economics* 70 (1): 65–94.

———. 1962. Technical Progress, Capital Formation, and Economic Growth. *American Economic Review* 52 (2): 76–86.

Stiglitz, Joseph E. 1999. Knowledge as a Global Public Good. In *Global Public Goods: International Cooperation in the 21st Century*, ed. Inge Kaul, Isabelle Grunberg and Marc Stern, 308–326. Oxford: Oxford University Press.

Weber, Max. 1919. Politics as a Vocation. Lecture delivered in Munich on 28 January 1919. Translated and edited by Dagmar Waters, Benjamin Elbers and Tony Waters, published as chapter 7 in Tony Waters and Dagmar Waters, Eds. *Weber's Rationalism and Modern Society: New Translations on Politics, Bureaucracy, and Social Stratification*. New York: Palgrave Macmillan, pp. 129–198.

World Bank. 1998. *World Development Report 1998/1999: Knowledge for Development*. New York: Oxford University Press.

Xu, Guangdong. 2011. The Role of Law in Economic Growth: A Literature Review. *Journal of Economic Surveys* 25 (5): 833–871.

Young, Alwyn. 1998. Growth without Scale Effects. *Journal of Political Economy* 106 (1): 41–63.

# 8

# The Global Community and Diplomatic Capital

**Abstract** This chapter examines how persons can collaborate for the common good of the global community through participation in international non-governmental organisations, multinational corporations and intergovernmental organisations. It also explains the collaboration of researchers globally to develop knowledge by following well-established norms and protocols to build an interconnected corpus of publications that offer evidence for falsifiable propositions. An example of researchers contributing to global efforts for wellbeing is the Intergovernmental Panel on Climate Change. The chapter introduces the metaphor of diplomatic capital to represent institutions and norms designed to foster cross-cultural collaborations in order to strengthen capabilities of the global community to act together for the common good.

**Keywords** Diplomatic capital • International non-governmental organisations • Intergovernmental organisations • Collaborative research • Climate change

Some of the most pressing issues threatening wellbeing can be addressed only with coordinated global action. Obvious examples include promotion of sustainable development, regulation of international trade, protection of human



P. Dalziel et al., *Wellbeing Economics*, Wellbeing in Politics and Policy,
https://doi.org/10.1007/978-3-319-93194-4_8

rights, resettlement of refugees, prevention of pandemics, resolution of inter-country conflicts, global peacekeeping, counter-terrorism, emergency disaster relief and effective responses to the risks of climate change.

Nevertheless, there are domestic pressures for some nations to reduce their engagement with international collaborations. In June 2016, for example, a majority of voters in a UK referendum supported withdrawal from the European Union. Across the Atlantic one year later, President Trump gave notice that the United States will withdraw from the 2015 Paris Agreement on climate change mitigation, which it had signed with 194 other countries in 2016–2017, on the grounds that he could "put no other consideration before the wellbeing of American citizens" (Trump 2017).

These examples reflect a tension that is common in collaborations among countries. Similar to the street lighting example in Chap. 6, citizens may calculate that their country's share of the costs of an international project is greater than the *extra* benefits they receive from making that sacrifice, and so vote to withdraw from the project. If a majority of citizens in enough countries reason the same way, the collaboration may collapse with all benefits lost, even if *total* benefits clearly outweigh total costs.[1]

This chapter therefore examines how persons are able to engage with collaboration for the common good of the global community, focusing on climate change as a case study. It begins with a description of three avenues for collaboration that echo, at the international level, the analysis in previous chapters of civil society institutions, market firms and government agencies. The second section then considers another significant collaboration on the world stage—the work of researchers engaged in creating and testing new knowledge. This human institution of collaborative research provides foundations for fostering many other types of international co-operation.

The remainder of the chapter then explores these ideas further using the example of global climate change. The Intergovernmental Panel on Climate Change (IPCC) illustrates how new organisations are being developed for the creation and communication of reliable knowledge. The consensus of the research community on climate change, for example, is very strong: "Warming of the climate system is unequivocal, and since the 1950s, many of the observed changes are unprecedented over decades to millennia" (IPCC 2014, p. 2). The final section of the chapter, before a brief conclusion, addresses the challenge of achieving effective responses to that scientific knowledge. It introduces the metaphor of *diplomatic capital* to represent institutions and norms that foster cross-cultural collaborations for the common good.

## Collaboration in the Global Community

The world population in 2017 was 7.6 billion persons and might reach 11.2 billion by 2100 (United Nations 2017, Table 1, p. 1). Such large numbers mean that effective actions at a global level require international institutions. Previous chapters have analysed how persons within a Nation State can collaborate through civil society institutions, market firms and different levels of government. Similarly, people can participate in three types of global institutions: international non-governmental organisations (INGOs), multinational corporations (MNCs)[2] and intergovernmental organisations (IGOs). Based on that classification, this section provides evidence in support of the following proposition.

**Proposition 22** International non-governmental organisations, multinational corporations and intergovernmental organisations can increase opportunities for global collaboration.

The number of active international non-governmental organisations increased sharply after World War II. Boli and Thomas (1997), for example, analysed INGOs going back to 1875. They found records for about 200 INGOs in 1900, rising to around 800 in 1930. This figure jumped to more than 2000 active INGOs in 1960, and to more than 4000 by 1980 (idem, p. 172; see also Clark 1995).

Although 20 years old, the data analysed by Boli and Thomas (1997) illustrate a broad range of INGO activities (see Fig. 8.1). They include associations promoting business and economic development, organisations supporting scientific knowledge and technique, international bodies managing sports, hobbies or other leisure activities, and groups advocating for protection of individual rights and other world causes such as environmental preservation (idem, pp. 182–184).

An example of an INGO that attracts support from millions of persons is the International Red Cross and Red Crescent Movement (ICRC 2014). This is one of the oldest INGOs still in operation. It began after publication of a book in 1862 by Swiss businessman Henry Dunant, in which he reported his witness of the suffering of combatants left to die after the Battle of Solferino. He appealed for organised humanitarian responses beyond ad hoc charity, which led to the creation of the International Committee of the Red Cross in October 1863 and the adoption of the first Geneva Convention concerning war conduct on 22 August 1864 (Bernard 2012, pp. 1198–1199).

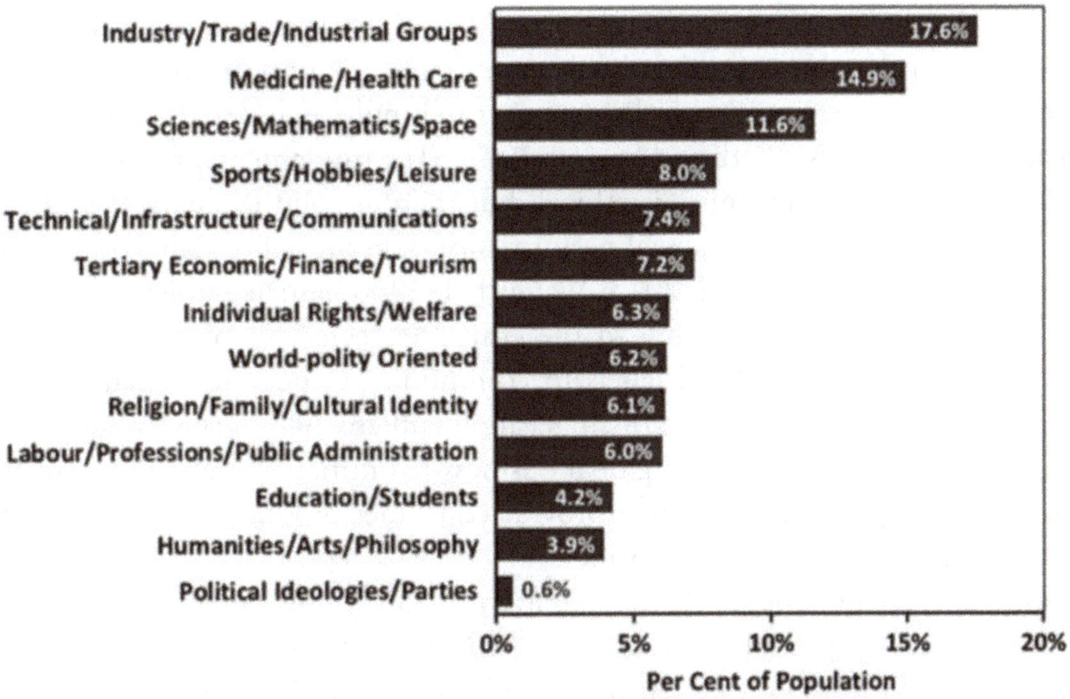


**Fig. 8.1** Percentage distribution of active international non-governmental organisations by sector, 1988. (Source: Boli and Thomas (1997, Fig. 2, using UIA (1988) data, p. 183))

More than 150 years later, there are 189 Red Cross and Red Crescent Societies around the world, united by seven fundamental principles: humanity, impartiality, neutrality, independence, voluntary service, unity and universality (ICRC 2014). Donors and volunteers support the Movement's mission of alleviating human suffering, protecting life and health, and upholding human dignity, especially during armed conflicts, natural disasters and other emergencies. Similarly, the Geneva Convention, extended over the decades, is now supported by 196 state parties (ICRC 2018).

MNCs play dominant roles in the global economy (Narula and Dunning 2000; Mudambi and Santangelo 2016; Forsgren 2017). Their number has also greatly increased in recent decades. Gabel and Henry (2003, p. 3) estimate that there were around 7000 MNCs in 1970, which jumped to around 30,000 in 1990 and 63,000 in 2000. This growth was part of the deeper process of *economic globalisation* that created an integrated global economy (IMF 2008, p. 2). In 2016, the 100 largest MNCs (excluding financial corporations) employed 16.3 million persons and owned assets valued above US$13 trillion (UNCTAD 2017, Table 1.5, p. 29).

Some MNCs are criticised for pursuing shareholder wealth at the expense of awful damage to the wellbeing of partners, workers and other stakeholders, especially in developing countries (Banks et al. 2015; Omoteso and Yusuf 2017). As a counter to that behaviour, individuals are able to support corporate social responsibility by acting as ethical consumers (Chipulu et al. 2018) or as socially responsible investors (Riedl and Smeets 2017). The fundamental motivation for corporate social responsibility is ethical, but there is solid evidence that it can also contribute to better financial performance (Chernev and Blair 2015; Crifo and Forget 2015; Saeidi et al. 2015; Wang et al. 2016; Jamali and Karam 2018).

Some MNCs are responding to the ethical expectations of customers and shareholders by using ethical labels to communicate their performance standards (Hartlieb and Jones 2009; Bissinger and Leufkens 2017). The Sustainability Consortium is an example of a global business-led initiative that is using scientific knowledge to help companies provide consumer products while respecting the environmental limits of the planet.[3]

The third category of global collaborations involves IGOs established for specific purposes by treaty or charter ratified by Nation States. These include prominent agencies focused on aspects of the global economy, including the Bank for International Settlements (established in 1930), the World Bank (1944), the International Monetary Fund (1945) and the World Trade Organisation (1995). Like INGOs and MNCs, the number of IGOs grew strongly after World War II. Held and McGrew (2007, p. 22) note that just 36 were recorded at the beginning of the twentieth century, but the number had reached 7350 by 2000, with most of that increase occurring after 1978 (see also UIA 2001).

The European Union is an IGO. The United Kingdom acceded to the European Economic Community (EEC) on 1 January 1973, and hence was a founding member of the European Union when it replaced the EEC in the Maastricht Treaty 20 years later. Article B of the Treaty records that the Union's five objectives are based on economic and social progress, international identity, the rights and interests of citizens, co-operation on justice and home affairs, and building on the Union's legal order. A majority of voters in the UK 2016 referendum were in favour of leaving the Union, so that Britain gave notice of its withdrawal by 29 March 2019.

The United Nations is another prominent IGO, created after World War II by a Charter that is currently ratified by 193 Member States.[4] The Charter sets out the organisation's purposes, which translate into five areas of activity undertaken with the global community:

- Maintain international peace and security
- Protect human rights

- Deliver humanitarian aid
- Promote sustainable development
- Uphold international law

United Nations' programmes for sustainable development are particularly relevant to the themes of this book. Indeed, the description of this aspect of its mission resonates strongly with the wellbeing economics framework (United Nations 2018):

> Improving people's well-being continues to be one of the main focuses of the UN. The global understanding of development has changed over the years, and countries now have agreed that sustainable development – development that promotes prosperity and economic opportunity, greater social well-being, and protection of the environment – offers the best path forward for improving the lives of people everywhere.

To mark the beginning of third millennium, the United Nations General Assembly adopted eight Millennium Development Goals (MDGs), accompanied by specific targets for progress by 2015 (United Nations 2001). That initiative mobilised global efforts that "helped to lift more than one billion people out of extreme poverty, to make inroads against hunger, to enable more girls to attend school than ever before and to protect our planet" (United Nations 2015a, p. 3). This illustrates the potential of global collaboration to enhance wellbeing, although there remain powerful interests working against global social justice. Following the achievements of the MDGs programme, the General Assembly adopted the *2030 Agenda for Sustainable Development*, which sets out 17 Sustainable Development Goals and 169 targets (United Nations 2015b).

## The Global Community of Researchers

Chap. 7 highlighted the contribution that knowledge can make to wellbeing, also observing that the creation of new knowledge is a global activity. The scale of collaboration required for discovering and testing new knowledge is demanding. It is made possible by developing norms and protocols that build confidence in scientific knowledge, despite researchers working in diverse institutions, cultures and countries. Widespread trust that the global research community is producing reliable knowledge is necessary for other forms of international collaborations.

Like the three groups considered in the previous section, there was a large expansion in organisations contributing to new knowledge during the latter half of the twentieth century. This was the result of increasing access to tertiary education, accompanied by the creation of a greater number and wider range of non-university research groups (Gibbons et al. 1994, p. 11):

> The massification of higher education and the appropriation, after the Second World War, by the universities of a distinct research function have produced increasing numbers of people familiar with the methods of research, many of whom are equipped with specialised knowledge and skills of various kinds. … Scientific and technological knowledge production are now pursued not only in universities but also in industry and government laboratories, in think-tanks, research institutions and consultancies, etc.

Universities continue to be a key source of new knowledge. In the United Kingdom, 154 universities were included in the 2014 assessment of the Research Excellence Framework. That assessment covered 52,061 academic staff, 191,150 research outputs published between 2008 and 2013, and 6975 case studies of impacts beyond academia (REF 2014). Another indicator of global scale comes from the QS World University Rankings in 2018, which featured 959 universities from 84 countries.[5]

An important issue is that researchers generally accept that there is no method for demonstrating with certainty that any scientific hypothesis is true (Nola and Sankey 2000). Progress in developing a body of scientific knowledge is nevertheless possible, achieved through the practice of publishing research results in journals and books. Karl Popper (1983, p. xxxv) famously suggested that this is a distinctive feature of human knowledge:

> The special thing about *human* knowledge is that it may be formulated in language, in propositions. This makes it possible for knowledge to become conscious and to be objectively criticisable by arguments and by tests. In this way we arrive at science.

Knowledge develops through the publication of results that are open to testing, refutation and further development by any researcher (Popper 1959, p. 41). There are strong norms and protocols for research publications. The research question must be clearly stated, for example, and its importance explained. Relevant publications that previously addressed the issue must be cited. The research method used to test the new knowledge claim must be described, so that the evidence is replicable by other researchers. Conclusions must not reach beyond what the evidence justifies.

The best research outputs are peer reviewed, meaning that manuscripts are assessed by qualified researchers before acceptance for publication. Further, the practice of citing relevant research means the corpus of scientific knowledge is strongly interconnected as it expands. Clarivate Analytics, for example, maintains an important citations database (the Web of Science Core Collection; see http://clarivate.libguides.com/home) as a curated collection of more than 18,000 peer-reviewed, high-quality scholarly journals representing more than 250 research disciplines. This database has tracked well over one billion cited references going back to 1900.

**Proposition 23** The global research community can develop knowledge by following well-established norms and protocols to build an interconnected corpus of publications that offer evidence for falsifiable propositions.

Popper (1959, p. 13) observed that researchers approach problems within "a structure of scientific doctrines [that] is already in existence; and with it, a generally accepted problem-situation". Thomas Kuhn (1962) introduced the word *paradigm* to describe this feature of what he termed "normal science". Researchers address problems within their adopted paradigm, recognising that occasionally a crisis may produce a scientific revolution. Imre Lakatos (1970) went further, arguing that normal science typically involves a hard core of theories accepted by adherents, defended by a "protective belt of auxiliary hypotheses" that is the focus of research effort.[6]

In this tradition, the economics discipline has a strong theoretical core. Its central paradigm has been fruitful in creating knowledge, but is also challenged by feminist scholars (among others) for being founded on gender-blind methodological individualism and for emphasising questions affecting the market economy at the expense of other important problems of wellbeing, such as those related to household economies.[7] The economics community recognises feminist economics as a valid field of research, but categorises it under the heading of "Current Heterodox Approaches" (American Economic Association 2017, category B54). Thus, feminist economics is explicitly labelled as outside the discipline's orthodox paradigm. This example illustrates that a research community does not operate in a vacuum. Like other global collaborations, research is influenced by the political, economic, social, cultural and technological forces of the times.

## The Science of Global Climate Change

Researchers have recognised that knowledge production has been extending from its traditional context of individual research disciplines into a new mode where "knowledge is created in broader, transdisciplinary social and economic contexts" (Gibbons et al. 1994, p. 1; see also Ledford 2015). This is resulting in new institutions for creating, synthesising and communicating knowledge. An outstanding example concerns the science of global climate change, where the IPCC has been created to support collaboration across research disciplines and among researchers from different cultures and countries.

The World Meteorological Organization and the United Nations Environmental Programme jointly established the IPCC in 1988 (Agrawala 1998a, p. 606). It followed the signing of the Montreal Protocol in 1987, in which countries had agreed to phase out the production of substances that scientists had demonstrated were responsible for ozone depletion in the atmosphere (see Murdoch and Sandler 1997; Douglass et al. 2014). The IPCC is currently supported by 195 countries.[8]

The United Nations General Assembly of 1998 endorsed the IPCC initiative, and commissioned it to produce a comprehensive review on five matters which continue to frame its mission (IPCC 2010, p. 4):

(a) The state of knowledge of the science of climate and climatic change;
(b) Programmes and studies on the social and economic impact of climate change, including global warming;
(c) Possible response strategies to delay, limit or mitigate the impact of adverse climate change;
(d) The identification and possible strengthening of relevant existing international legal instruments having a bearing on climate;
(e) Elements for inclusion in a possible future international convention on climate.

The IPCC published five assessment reports between 1990 and 2014. It is working on a sixth, and also produces technical papers and special reports. These outputs rely on the co-operation of thousands of experts from all regions of the world (IPCC 2010, p. 1). Following accepted norms for research publications, peer review is an essential element of its work programme, as observed by Agrawala (1998b, p. 623–624, emphasis in the original):

> However, the IPCC peer review is more comprehensive, *by many orders of magnitude*, than that in an average journal. For example, draft chapters of the 1995 Working Group II Second Assessment report went through two full scale reviews: the first involving anywhere from twenty to sixty expert reviewers per chapter (a total of 700 experts from 58 countries were involved), and the second involving all IPCC member governments and the experts who had sent their reviews in the first round.

The IPCC is bound by the standard principles of scientific integrity, objectivity, openness and transparency. Another key principle is "to be policy relevant, but not policy prescriptive" (IPCC 2010, p. 1). The IPCC therefore places strong emphasis on communication. Major reports begin with a summary for policymakers and include key graphics to illustrate the science.

The Fifth Assessment Report was based on a synthesis of physical science research relevant to climate change (IPCC 2013). It brought together ten indicators of a changing global climate (idem, Fig. TS.1, p. 38), including five going back to the beginning of the nineteenth century: land surface air temperature; sea surface temperature; marine air temperature; sea level; and summer arctic sea-ice extent. The scientific conclusion was clear (idem, p. 4):

> Warming of the climate system is unequivocal, and since the 1950s, many of the observed changes are unprecedented over decades to millennia. The atmosphere and ocean have warmed, the amounts of snow and ice have diminished, sea level has risen, and the concentrations of greenhouse gases have increased.

The higher concentration of greenhouse gases is significant because it is a major driver of surface warming and global climate change through radiative forcing (see IPCC 2013, pp.13–14). The largest contribution comes from carbon dioxide ($CO_2$) emissions. The IPCC has therefore collated data on the increased concentration of $CO_2$ in the atmosphere since 1958.[9] Again, the scientific conclusion is clear (idem, p. 11):

> The atmospheric concentrations of carbon dioxide, methane, and nitrous oxide have increased to levels unprecedented in at least the last 800,000 years. Carbon dioxide concentrations have increased by 40% since pre-industrial times, primarily from fossil fuel emissions and secondarily from net land use change emissions. The ocean has absorbed about 30% of the emitted anthropogenic carbon dioxide, causing ocean acidification.

Five specific reasons for concern guide the IPCC's risk analysis of climate change (IPCC 2014, Box 2.4, p. 72). A higher mean temperature of the globe produces: (1) greater risks of severe consequence for certain ecosystems and cultures; (2) a greater likelihood of extreme weather events such as droughts and storms; (3) greater risks of unevenly distributed impacts on disadvantaged people and communities; (4) a greater likelihood of adverse aggregate impacts globally; and (5) a greater likelihood that some physical and ecological systems will experience abrupt or irreversible changes.

In one of its most important graphics (see IPCC 2014, Fig. 3.1, p. 78), the IPCC links each of these five risks to the range of plausible changes in the earth's global mean temperature by 2050, relative to its value at the beginning of the industrial revolution. This is affected by cumulative anthropogenic $CO_2$ emissions, which depend in turn on annual greenhouse gas emissions over the next decades.

The analysis indicates that if greenhouse gas emissions are kept to their 2010 level, the cumulative anthropogenic $CO_2$ emissions in 2050 are likely to be in the order of 4000 to 5000 Gigatonnes of carbon dioxide, which is associated with a likely temperature rise of about 2.5 °C relative to pre-industrial levels. The first decade of this century saw an increase of between 0.5 °C and 1.0 °C, so the scientific analysis implies that human-induced climate change will create substantially increased risks for future generations of adverse impacts in all of the five reasons for concern.

This evidence provides compelling reasons for responses by actors in the global community, but the situation is more urgent than the previous paragraph might suggest. This is because greenhouse gas emissions are unlikely to remain at their 2010 level without deliberate action, since governments around the world are committed to economic growth. If nothing else changes, growth can be expected to increase greenhouse gas emissions.

Consequently, the baseline scenario in the IPPC risk analysis reveals that on current growth paths, the global mean temperature by 2050 may be 4 °C higher than pre-industrial levels. The IPCC (2014, p. 17) therefore concludes with high confidence:

> Without additional mitigation efforts beyond those in place today, and even with adaptation, warming by the end of the 21st century will lead to high to very high risk of severe, widespread and irreversible impacts globally.

Philosophers have argued that it is unethical for humanity to change the climate of the planet to this extent (Palmer 2011). In any case, the risks identified by the IPCC represent a major threat to future human wellbeing on a global scale, which raises its own ethical challenges (Gardiner 2004; Nordhaus 2007;

Weitzman 2007; Stern 2008). What is clear is that effective responses to mitigate climate change will require coordinated action around the world. The final section of this chapter addresses how this might be achieved.

## Diplomatic Capital

A useful starting point for considering globally coordinated responses to the threats of climate change is the Paris Agreement that came into force on 4 November 2016.[10] The Agreement is comprised of a preamble and 29 articles. Building on the United Nations Framework Convention on Climate Change adopted in 1992, its specific aim recorded in Article 2 is "to strengthen the global response to the threat of climate change, in the context of sustainable development and efforts to eradicate poverty", including by:

> Holding the increase in the global average temperature to well below 2°C above pre-industrial levels and pursuing efforts to limit the temperature increase to 1.5°C above pre-industrial levels, recognizing that this would significantly reduce the risks and impacts of climate change.

Based on the IPCC analysis discussed above, these targets are necessary to keep the risks from a higher global temperature to moderate levels, but they also require greenhouse gas emissions to return below their 1990 levels. The Agreement does not state how this will be achieved, leaving this for Nation States to decide (Article 3, emphasis added):

> As nationally determined contributions to the global response to climate change, all Parties are to undertake and communicate *ambitious efforts* as defined in Articles 4, 7, 9, 10, 11 and 13 with the view to achieving the purpose of this Agreement as set out in Article 2.

Note the reference to *ambitious efforts*. The task of reducing greenhouse gas emissions is indeed challenging, especially in the context of national aspirations for economic growth (Jackson 2017). A further challenge is that damage from emissions is an example of "the tragedy of the commons" (Hardin 1968; Ostrom 1990; Paavola 2008). A commons is a resource where no effective mechanism had been created for preventing anyone from freely consuming the resource. A classic example of a commons is an ocean fishery, where economic analysis and numerous case studies demonstrate that the incentives in the market economy for conserving fish stocks are very weak (Gordon 1954; McWhinnie 2009).

The earth's atmosphere is another example of a commons. Consequently, any nation agreeing to implement costly policies to reduce its share of damaging greenhouse gas emissions may reasonably worry about what will prevent other nations from taking advantage by increasing their own emissions. This is an example of the Prisoner's Dilemma (see this chapter's footnote 1). A solution requires effective mechanisms for ensuring universal compliance to agreements made about management of the resource (Ostrom 1990). In the case of global climate change, this may require new systems of "earth system governance" (Biermann 2012 and 2018; Dryzek 2016; Galaz et al. 2012).

Effective collaboration will involve new IGOs, but civil society organisations will also have important roles (Iati 2008). This was reflected, for example, in the International NGO Forum on Climate Change hosted by UNESCO in December 2017, involving more than 300 representatives of civil society.[11] Similarly, as discussed above, at least some MNCs are recognising that they must reduce their environment impacts for economic activities to be sustainable.

Chap. 4 introduced the metaphor of social capital to represent the idea that social collaboration is easier when residents in a nation are connected to each other through social networks and sharing social norms. Similarly, global collaboration is easier when relevant institutions and norms strengthen capabilities for cross-cultural common action. Echoing previous uses of the term "environmental diplomacy" in this context (see, e.g., Carroll 1988; Broadhurst and Ledgerwood 1998; Susskind and Ali 2015), Proposition 24 offers the phrase *diplomatic capital* as a metaphor to describe this concept.

**Proposition 24** Investment in diplomatic capital (i.e., in institutions and norms designed to foster cross-cultural collaborations) can strengthen the capabilities of the global community to act together for the common good.

Institutions and norms of state diplomacy have been developed over centuries to support co-operation between countries (Anderson 1993). This is an example of investment in diplomatic capital, but all international organisations must similarly develop norms and protocols to be effective. The seven fundamental principles accepted by members of the International Red Cross and Red Crescent Movement, discussed earlier in this chapter, is an obvious example. Similarly, the difficulties and rewards of drawing on cultural differences business enterprises is well recognised (Shenkar 2001). In short, any initiative that brings together diverse actors to address a global issue requires diplomatic capital to succeed.

## Conclusion

Persons engage with global issues through specialist institutions that aim to foster collaboration on the world stage. These institutions include INGOs, MNCs and IGOs. Some institutions have undertaken activities that damage wellbeing, particularly in developing countries. Nevertheless, it is clear that some issues affecting the common good of the global community cannot be solved without coordinated efforts from diverse countries, large corporations and representatives of civil society.

The capability to foster global collaboration must not be taken for granted. In the language of this chapter, it requires conscious investment in diplomatic capital, defined as institutions and norms designed to foster cross-cultural collaborations. This applies not only to diplomatic relations among countries but to all initiatives that bring together diverse actors to address global issues.

An important example is the work of the global research community. Researchers have developed norms and protocols that build confidence in the quality of the new knowledge created by research. New institutions are being created to engage in transdisciplinary research on issues affecting the wellbeing of billions of people. The work of the IPCC is an outstanding example.

Nevertheless, there are stresses evident in global collaborations. This chapter began by noting the withdrawal of the United Kingdom from the European Union and the withdrawal of the United States from the Paris Agreement. These events suggest that the current stock of diplomatic capital has been inadequate for meeting some urgent global challenges connected to sustainable development and climate change. Stronger institutions and norms will be needed in the future.

## Notes

1. In the language of economists, this is the Prisoner's Dilemma problem, in which isolated and self-interested individuals are unable to achieve a collaborative solution that would make each better off. Soroos (1994) warned that this could be a good representation of international negotiations to address climate change, and suggested reasons why the United States might not collaborate (idem, p. 329).

2. There are subtle and contested differences in the usage of terms such as multinational, transnational, stateless or global corporations (Hu 1992). This is not important for this chapter; the analysis could have used any of these terms.
3. See https://www.sustainabilityconsortium.org/, accessed 26 February 2018.
4. The material in these paragraphs is sourced from the United Nations website, www.un.org/, accessed 26 February 2018.
5. Data accessed from https://www.topuniversities.com/university-rankings-articles/world-university-rankings/out-now-qs-world-university-rankings-2018, 28 February 2018.
6. Maxwell (1998, 2005) has argued that the insights of Popper, Kuhn and Lakatos can be synthesised into a theory of science he terms *aim-oriented empiricism.* This suggestion is noted but not pursued here.
7. See, for example, Boserup (1970), Folbre and Hartmann (1988), Waring (1988), Ferber and Nelson (1993, 2003), MacDonald (1995), Bjørnholt and McKay (2014), Gammage et al. (2016) and Saunders and Dalziel (2017). One woman has received the Nobel Prize in Economics (Elinor Ostrom 2010).
8. See www.ipcc.ch/organization/organization.shtml, accessed 25 February 2018.
9. It also publishes data on the increased partial pressure of dissolved $CO_2$ at the ocean surface and increased acidity of ocean water (reduced pH levels) since 1988 (see, e.g., IPCC 2014, Fig. SPM.4, p. 12).
10. See http://unfccc.int/paris_agreement/items/9444.php, accessed 25 February 2018.
11. See https://en.unesco.org/news/unesco-hosts-international-ngo-forum-climate-change, accessed 26 February 2018.

## References


Agrawala, Shardul. 1998a. Context and Early Origins of the Intergovernmental Panel on Climate Change. *Climate Change* 39 (4): 605–620.

———. 1998b. Structural and Process History of the Intergovernmental Panel on Climate Change. *Climate Change* 39 (4): 621–642.

American Economic Association. 2017. JEL Classification System / EconLit Subject Descriptors. https://www.aeaweb.org/econlit/jelCodes.php. Webpage Accessed 23 Feb 2018.

Anderson, Matthew S. 1993. *The Rise of Modern Diplomacy 1450–1919.* London: Longman.

Banks, Nicola, David Hulme, and Michael Edwards. 2015. NGOs, States, and Donors Revisited: Still Too Close for Comfort? *World Development* 66 (February): 707–718.

Bernard, Vincent. 2012. Editorial: The Quest for Humanity 150 Years of International Humanitarian Law and Action. *International Review of the Red Cross* 94 (888): 1195–1207.

Biermann, Frank. 2012. Planetary Boundaries and Earth System Governance: Exploring the Links. *Ecological Economics* 81: 4–9.

———. 2018. Global Governance in the "Anthropocene". In *The Oxford Handbook of International Political Theory*, ed. Chris Brown and Robyn Eckersley, 467–478. Oxford: Oxford University Press.

Bissinger, Katharina, and Daniel Leufkens. 2017. Ethical Food Labels in Consumer Preferences. *British Food Journal* 119 (8): 1801–1814.

Bjørnholt, Margunn, and Ailsa McKay, eds. 2014. *Counting on Marilyn Waring: New Advances in Feminist Economics*. Bradford: Demeter Press.

Boli, John, and George M. Thomas. 1997. World Culture in the World Polity: A Century of International Non-Governmental Organization. *American Sociological Review* 62 (2): 171–190.

Boserup, Ester. 1970. *Woman's Role in Economic Development*. New York: St. Martin's Press.

Broadhurst, Arlene I., and Grant Ledgerwood. 1998. Environmental Diplomacy of States, Corporations and Non-Governmental Organisations: The Worldwide Web of Influence. *International Relations* 14 (2): 1–19.

Carroll, John E. 1988. *International Environmental Diplomacy: The Management and Resolution of Transfrontier Environmental Problems*. Cambridge: Cambridge University Press.

Chernev, Alexander, and Sean Blair. 2015. Doing Well by Doing Good: The Benevolent Halo of Corporate Social Responsibility. *Journal of Consumer Research* 41 (6): 1412–1425.

Chipulu, Maxwell, Alasdair Marshall, Udechukwu Ojiako, and Caroline Mota. 2018. Reasoned Ethical Engagement: Ethical Values of Consumers as Primary Antecedents of Instrumental Actions Towards Multinationals. *Journal of Business Ethics* 147 (1): 221–238.

Clark, Ann Marie. 1995. Non-Governmental Organizations and their Influence on International Society. *Journal of International Affairs* 48 (2): 507–525.

Crifo, Patricia, and Vanina D. Forget. 2015. The Responsibility of Corporate Social Responsibility: A Firm-Level Perspective Survey. *Journal of Economic Surveys* 29 (1): 112–130.

Douglass, Anne R., Paul A. Newman, and Susan Solomon. 2014. The Antarctic Ozone Hole: An Update. *Physics Today* 67 (7): 42–47.

Dryzek, John S. 2016. Institutions for the Anthropocene: Governance in a Changing Earth System. *British Journal of Political Science* 46 (4): 937–956.

Dunant, Henry. 1862. *Un Souvenir de Solférino*. Genève: Jules-Guillaume Fick. Trans. and Published as *A Memory of Solferino* by the American Red Cross, 1939.

Ferber, Marianne A., and Julie A. Nelson, eds. 1993. *Beyond Economic Man: Feminist Theory and Economics*. Chicago: University of Chicago Press.

———, eds. 2003. *Feminist Economics Today: Beyond Economic Man*. Chicago: University of Chicago Press.

Folbre, Nancy, and Heidi Hartmann. 1988. The Rhetoric of Self-interest: Ideology and Gender in Economic Theory. In *The Consequences of Economic Rhetoric*, ed. Arjo Klamer, Deirdre N. McCloskey, and Robert M. Solow, 184–203. Cambridge: Cambridge University Press.

Forsgren, Mats. 2017. *Theories of the Multinational Firm: A Multidimensional Creature in the Global Economy*. Third ed. Cheltenham: Edward Elgar.

Gabel, Medard, and Henry Bruner. 2003. *Global Inc. An Atlas of the Multinational Corporation*. New York: The New Press.

Galaz, Victor, Beatrice Crona, Henrik Österblom, Per Olsson, and Carl Folke. 2012. Polycentric Systems and Interacting Planetary Boundaries – Emerging Governance of Climate Change–Ocean Acidification–Marine Biodiversity. *Ecological Economics* 81: 21–32.

Gammage, Sarah, Naila Kabeer, and Yana van der Meulen Rodgers. 2016. Voice and Agency: Where Are We Now? *Feminist Economics* 22 (1): 1–29.

Gardiner, Stephen M. 2004. Ethics and Global Climate Change. *Ethics* 114 (3): 555–600.

Gordon, H. Scott. 1954. The Economic Theory of a Common-Property Resource: The Fishery. *Journal of Political Economy* 62 (2): 124–142.

Gibbons, Michael, Camille Limoges, Helga Nowotny, Simon Schwartzman, Peter Scott, and Martin Trow. 1994. *The New Production of Knowledge: The Dynamics of Science and Research in Contemporary Societies*. London: SAGE Publications.

Hardin, Garrett. 1968. The Tragedy of the Commons. *Science* 162 (3859): 1243–1248.

Hartlieb, Susanne, and Bryn Jones. 2009. Humanising Business through Ethical Labelling: Progress and Paradoxes in the UK. *Journal of Business Ethics* 88 (3): 583–600.

Held, David, and Anthony McGrew. 2007. *Globalization/Anti-Globalization: Beyond the Great Divide*. Second ed. Cambridge: Polity Press.

Hu, Yao-Su. 1992. Global or Stateless Corporations are National Firms with International Operations. *California Management Review* 34 (2): 107–126.

Iati, Iati. 2008. The Potential of Civil Society in Climate Change Adaptation Strategies. *Political Science* 60 (1): 19–30.

ICRC. 2014. The Fundamental Principles of the International Red Cross and Red Crescent Movement. Pamphlet published by ICRC. Geneva: International Committee of the Red Cross.

———. 2018. State Parties to the Following International Humanitarian Law and Other Related Treaties as of 2-Feb-2018. Geneva: International Committee of the Red Cross. https://ihl-databases.icrc.org/applic/ihl/ihl.nsf/vwTreaties1949.xsp. Accessed 12 Feb 2018.

IMF. 2008. Globalization: A Brief Overview. *International Monetary Fund Issues Brief* 02/08, May: 1–8.

IPCC. 2010. Understanding Climate Change: 22 Years of IPCC Assessment. Pamphlet published by the IPCC. Geneva: Intergovernmental Panel on Climate Change.

———. 2013. *Climate Change 2013: The Physical Science Basis. Contribution of Working Group I to the Fifth Assessment Report of the Intergovernmental Panel on Climate Change*. Cambridge/New York: Cambridge University Press.

———. 2014. *Climate Change 2014: Synthesis Report*. Contribution of Working Groups I, II and III to the Fifth Assessment Report of the IPCC. Geneva: Intergovernmental Panel on Climate Change.

Jackson, Tim. 2017. *Prosperity without Growth: Foundations for the Economy of Tomorrow*. 2nd ed. Abingdon/New York: Routledge.

Jamali, Dima, and Charlotte Karam. 2018. Corporate Social Responsibility in Developing Countries as an Emerging Field of Study. *International Journal of Management Reviews* 20 (1): 32–61.

Kuhn, Thomas S. 1962. *The Structure of Scientific Revolutions*. Chicago: University of Chicago Press.

Lakatos, Imre. 1970. Falsification and the Methodology of Scientific Research Programmes. In Imre Lakatos and Alan Musgrave, Eds. *Criticism and the Growth of Knowledge*. Cambridge: Cambridge University Press, pp. 91–196. Reproduced as, and cited from, *The Methodology of Scientific Research Programmes: Philosophical Papers*, ed. John Worrall and Gregory Currie, Vol. 1, 205–259. Cambridge: Cambridge University Press, 1978.

Ledford, Heidi. 2015. How to Solve the World's Biggest Problems. *Nature* 525 (7569): 308–311.

MacDonald, Martha. 1995. Feminist Economics – From Theory to Research. *Canadian Journal of Economics* 28 (1): 159–176.

Maxwell, Nicholas. 1998. *The Comprehensibility of the Universe: A New Conception of Science*. Oxford: Oxford University Press.

———. 2005. Popper, Kuhn, Lakatos and Aim-Oriented Empiricism. *Philosophia* 32 (1–4): 181–239.

McWhinnie, Stephanie F. 2009. The Tragedy of the Commons in International Fisheries: An Empirical Examination. *Journal of Environmental Economics and Management* 57 (3): 321–333.

Mudambi, Ram, and Grazia D. Santangelo. 2016. From Shallow Resource Pools to Emerging Clusters: The Role of Multinational Enterprise Subsidiaries in Peripheral Areas. *Regional Studies* 50 (12): 1965–1979.

Murdoch, James C., and Todd Sandler. 1997. The Voluntary Provision of a Pure Public Good: The Case of Reduced CFC Emissions and the Montreal Protocol. *Journal of Public Economics* 63 (3): 331–349.

Narula, Rajneesh, and John H. Dunning. 2000. Industrial Development, Globalization and Multinational Enterprises: New Realities for Developing Countries. *Oxford Development Studies* 28 (2): 141–167.

Nola, Robert, and Howard Sankey. 2000. A Selective Survey of Theories of Scientific Method. In *After Popper, Kuhn and Feyerabend: Recent Issues in Theories of Scientific Method*, ed. Robert Nola and Howard Sankey, 1–65. Dordrecht: Kluwer Academic Publishers.

Nordhaus, William D. 2007. A Review of the *Stern Review on the Economics of Climate Change*. *Journal of Economic Literature* 45 (3): 686–702.

Omoteso, Kamil, and Hakeem Yusuf. 2017. Accountability of Transnational Corporations in the Developing World: The Case for an Enforceable International Mechanism. *Critical Perspectives on International Business* 13 (1): 54–71.

Ostrom, Elinor. 1990. *Governing the Commons: The Evolution of Institutions for Collective Action*. Cambridge: Cambridge University Press.

———. 2010. Beyond Markets and States: Polycentric Governance of Complex Economic Systems. *American Economic Review* 100 (3): 641–672.

Paavola, Jouni. 2008. Governing Atmospheric Sinks: The Architecture of Entitlements in the Global Commons. *International Journal of the Commons* 2 (2): 313–336.

Palmer, Clare. 2011. Does Nature Matter? The Place of the Nonhuman in the Ethics of Climate Change. In *The Ethics of Global Climate Change*, ed. Denis G. Arnold, 272–291. Cambridge: Cambridge University Press.

Popper, Karl R. 1959. *The Logic of Scientific Discovery*. A translation of *Logik der Forschung* published in 1934. New York: Basic Books.

———. 1983. *Realism and the Aim of Science: From the Postscript to the Logic of Scientific Discovery*, ed. W. W. Bartley, III. Oxon: Routledge.

REF. 2014. Key Facts, December 2014. Leaflet Published by the Research Excellence Framework. www.ref.ac.uk/2014/pubs/keyfacts/. Accessed 22 Feb 2018.

Riedl, A., and P. Smeets. 2017. Why Do Investors Hold Socially Responsible Mutual Funds? *Journal of Finance* 72 (6): 2505–2550.

Saeidi, Sayedeh Parastoo, Saudah Sofian, Parvaneh Saeidi, Sayyedeh Parisa Saeidi, and Seyyed Alireza Saaeidi. 2015. How Does Corporate Social Responsibility Contribute to Firm Financial Performance? The Mediating Role of Competitive Advantage, Reputation, and Customer Satisfaction. *Journal of Business Research* 68 (2): 341–350.

Saunders, Caroline, and Paul Dalziel. 2017. 25 Years of *Counting for Nothing*: Waring's Critique of National Accounts. *Feminist Economics* 23 (2): 200–218.

Shenkar, Oded. 2001. Cultural Distance Revisited: Towards a More Rigorous Conceptualization and Measurement of Cultural Differences. *Journal of International Business Studies* 32 (3): 519–535.

Soroos, Marvin S. 1994. Global Change, Environmental Security, and the Prisoner's Dilemma. *Journal of Peace Research* 31 (3): 317–322.

Stern, Nicholas. 2008. The Economics of Climate Change. *American Economic Review* 98 (2): 1–37.

Susskind, Lawrence, and Saleem H. Ali. 2015. *Environmental Diplomacy: Negotiating More Effective Global Agreements*. 2nd ed. Oxford: Oxford University Press.

Trump, Donald. 2017. Statement by President Trump on the Paris Climate Accord. Issued 1 June. https://www.whitehouse.gov/briefings-statements/statement-president-trump-paris-climate-accord/. Accessed 8 Feb 2018.

UIA. 1988. *Yearbook of International Organizations*, Volume 25, 1988–89. Munich: K. G. Saur for Union of International Associations.

———. 2001. *Yearbook of International Organizations*, Volume 38, 2001–02. Munich: K. G. Saur for Union of International Associations.

UNCTAD. 2017. *World Investment Report 2017: Investment and the Digital Economy*. New York: United Nations Conference on Trade and Development.

United Nations. 2001. Road Map towards the Implementation of the United Nations Millennium Declaration. Report of the Secretary General to the 56th Session of the General Assembly. www.un.org/documents/ga/docs/56/a56326.pdf. Accessed 28 Feb 2018.

———. 2015a. *The Millennium Development Goals Report 2015*. New York: United Nations.

———. 2015b. Resolution Adopted by the General Assembly on 25 September 2015. 70th Session of the General Assembly. www.un.org/en/ga/search/view_doc.asp?symbol=A/RES/70/1&Lang=E. Accessed 28 Feb 2018.

———. 2017. *World Population Prospects: The 2015 Revision, Key Findings and Advance Tables*. Working Paper No. ESA/P/WP.248, Department of Economic and Social Affairs, Population Division.

———. 2018. Promote Sustainable Development. www.un.org/en/sections/what-we-do/promote-sustainable-development/index.html. Webpage Accessed 28 Feb 2018.

Wang, Qian, Junsheng Dou, and Shenghua Jia. 2016. A Meta-Analytic Review of Corporate Social Responsibility and Corporate Financial Performance: The Moderating Effect of Contextual Factors. *Business & Society* 55 (8): 1083–1121.

Waring, Marilyn. 1988. *If Women Counted: A New Feminist Economics*. San Francisco: Harper & Row. Also Published as *Counting for Nothing: What Men Value and What Women Are Worth*. Wellington: Allen & Unwin in association with the Port Nicholson Press.

Weitzman, Martin L. 2007. A Review of the *Stern Review on the Economics of Climate Change*. *Journal of Economic Literature* 45 (3): 703–724.

# 9

# The Wellbeing Economics Framework

**Abstract** This chapter summarises key points in the wellbeing economics framework and illustrates how it can be used to guide decision-making. The first section lists the 24 propositions that emerged as key points in the analysis of the preceding eight chapters. The second section introduces a diagram that integrates inputs into wellbeing capabilities (7 types of capital stock) with outputs of wellbeing capabilities (11 wellbeing indicators developed by the Organisation for Economic Co-operation and Development). The diagram is called the wellbeing fabric. The remainder of the chapter illustrates how the wellbeing fabric can be applied at different levels of human choices, before a brief conclusion.

**Keywords** Wellbeing economics • Wellbeing fabric • Economic policy • Capabilities • Skills

Despite international initiatives "to shift emphasis from measuring economic production to measuring people's well-being" (Stiglitz et al. 2009, p. 12), policy decisions in many nations continue to prioritise high economic growth over other objectives. In the United Kingdom, for example, this priority was emphasised by former Prime Minister David Cameron's (2010), even as he launched the country's Measuring National Wellbeing Programme, when he insisted that "growth is the essential foundation of all our aspirations".



P. Dalziel et al., *Wellbeing Economics*, Wellbeing in Politics and Policy,
https://doi.org/10.1007/978-3-319-93194-4_9

That statement holds that growth is a necessary, although perhaps not sufficient, condition for wellbeing. This understanding leaves policy advisors free to focus on growth in the first instance, while allowing for supplementary policies to address other aspects of wellbeing. A sharp distinction is made between economic policy, which is required to focus primarily on growth, and social policy, which is permitted to have a wider focus on welfare. Where there is conflict, priority is always given to economic policy, as demonstrated in the United Kingdom's austerity measures after the global financial crisis.

This book rejects that two-tier approach. It has argued that *how* economies grow can have large impacts on wellbeing, for better or for worse. Economic growth over decades, for example, has not solved major wellbeing problems such as affordable housing, living wages and the end of child poverty. There is clear scientific evidence of severe risks to future wellbeing on a global scale as a result of climate change caused by greenhouse gas emissions that are "driven largely by economic and population growth" (IPCC 2015, p. 4; see also Jackson 2017). This book has argued that the current approach to the design of economic policy must change, to directly address the wellbeing of persons.

The book has therefore developed a wellbeing economics framework built on the capabilities approach introduced by Amartya Sen (1983, 1999) and Martha Nussbaum (2000, 2011). Important foundations for the framework were set out in the first chapter, which explained that the objective is to contribute to enhanced wellbeing of persons by expanding the capabilities of persons to lead the kinds of lives they value, and have reason to value, through different types of capital investment at different levels of human choice.

Chapters 2, 3, 4, 5, 6, 7 and 8 then addressed seven levels of human choices, reproduced in Fig. 9.1. The analysis began in Chap. 2 with persons making time-use choices about activities they anticipate will contribute to the kinds of life they value, and have reason to value. Successive chapters analysed how expanding levels of collaboration can increase capabilities for wellbeing.

This final chapter summarises key points in the wellbeing economics framework and illustrates how the framework can be used to guide decision-making at the different levels shown in Fig. 9.1. The first section lists the 24 propositions that emerged as key points in the preceding eight chapters. The second section then brings together capabilities and capital stocks into a single diagram, which we call the wellbeing fabric. It is designed to assist decision-makers think about influences on wellbeing in an integrated manner.

The subsequent three sections illustrate how the wellbeing fabric can be applied at the different levels of human choice shown in Fig. 9.1. The first sec-

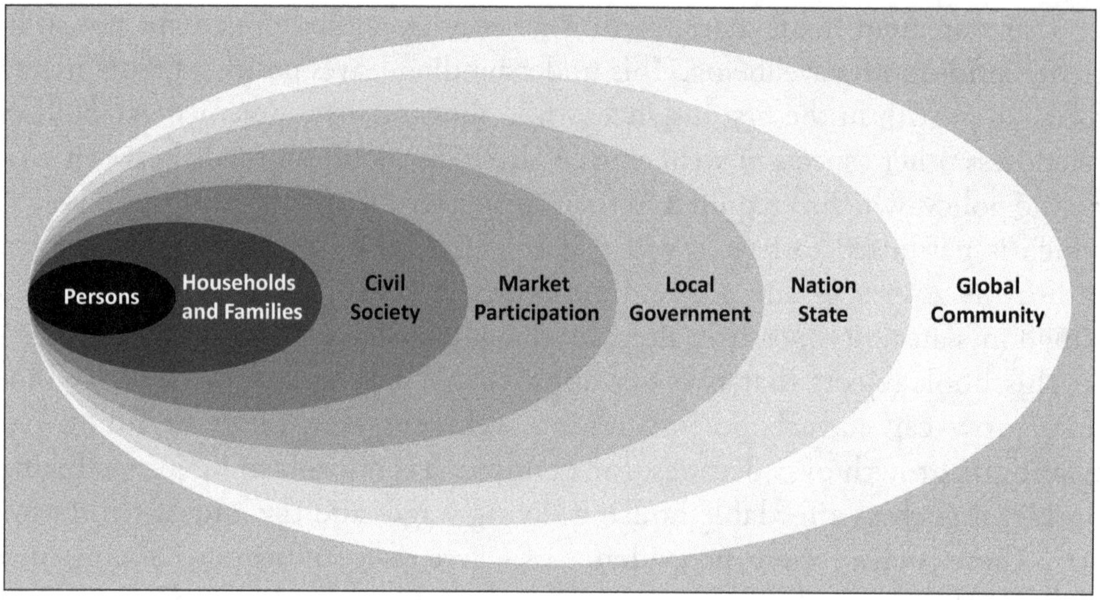


**Fig. 9.1** Levels of human choice in the wellbeing economics framework. (Source: Fig. 1.1 in Chap. 1)

tion discusses the wellbeing of individuals, households and families, taken together. The second section illustrates how institutions of civil society, firms in the market economy and initiatives of local government combine capital stocks in distinctive ways to create greater capabilities for wellbeing than households and families can achieve in isolation. This is followed by a section on the Nation State, discussing how the wellbeing fabric can be used to guide national and international collaborations to promote wellbeing. The chapter concludes with some final comments.

## The Propositions of Wellbeing Economics

Each chapter in this book has recorded three propositions that note key points in the analysis. The resulting 24 propositions offer a structured summary of the wellbeing economics framework, and are presented here in a single list for the convenience of the reader.

### Foundations of the Framework

**Proposition 1** The primary purpose of economics is to contribute to enhanced wellbeing of persons.

**Proposition 2** Wellbeing can be enhanced by expanding the capabilities of persons to lead the kinds of lives they value, and have reason to value.

**Proposition 3** The capabilities of persons can be expanded by different types of capital investment at different levels of human choice.

## Persons and Human Capital

**Proposition 4** Persons can make time-use choices they reason will promote wellbeing, influenced by their cultural values, personal abilities and social capabilities.

**Proposition 5** Investment in human capital through education can provide persons, in all their diversity, with opportunities to discover, discipline and display skills that contribute to wellbeing.

**Proposition 6** Personal wellbeing can be monitored using a set of indicators that include measures of subjective and objective wellbeing, supplemented by measured trends in different types of capital.

## Households, Families and Cultural Capital

**Proposition 7** Investment in cultural capital can enhance the wellbeing of households and families by expanding opportunities to express, develop, transform and pass on to the next generation their cultural inheritance.

**Proposition 8** Men and women can have equal capabilities for wellbeing.

**Proposition 9** Present and future wellbeing can be enhanced if children grow up in households that are able to access adequate economic resources.

## Civil Society and Social Capital

**Proposition 10** Persons can access enhanced capabilities for wellbeing by participating in institutions of civil society to collaborate with others in the pursuit of common interests and shared values.

**Proposition 11** Investment in social capital can occur through mechanisms that include: learning in schools; participation in networks; enforcement of norms; development of societal aspirations; and efforts for social inclusion.

**Proposition 12** Policy can enhance capabilities for wellbeing by ensuring persons are not disadvantaged in their equitable access to services from the country's capital stocks because of ethnicity or other personal characteristics.

## Market Participation and Economic Capital

**Proposition 13** Persons can enhance wellbeing by participating as sellers and as buyers in the market economy; but markets need rules, customs and institutions to work well.

**Proposition 14** Firms operating in the market economy can combine different types of capital to maintain specialist capabilities for supplying goods and services valued by their customers.

**Proposition 15** Investment in physical capital and the growth of financial capital can contribute to enhanced wellbeing, but recent patterns of economic development are also associated with cumulative environmental damage, episodes of financial instability and greater concentration of wealth.

## Local Government and Natural Capital

**Proposition 16** Good government can develop distinctive capabilities for managing the provision of certain types of goods and services, especially those with externalities or the characteristics of an economic public good.

**Proposition 17** Local government, sharing leadership with other actors in their communities, can develop and sustain regional capabilities for wellbeing through integrated investment in different types of capital.

**Proposition 18** Human activity can diminish ecosystem services provided by the natural environment, and so investment in natural capital is required to maintain and enhance wellbeing.

### The Nation State and Knowledge Capital

**Proposition 19** The Nation State can contribute to expanded capabilities for wellbeing by acting on behalf of citizens as wise custodian of the market economy and welfare state within its borders.

**Proposition 20** Knowledge capital has the properties of an economic public good, so that Nation States can contribute to enhanced wellbeing by fostering the growth and use of knowledge.

**Proposition 21** The civil service can offer a specialist capability for creating, collating, synthesising, utilising and disseminating knowledge capital for the common good.

### The Global Community and Diplomatic Capital

**Proposition 22** International non-governmental organisations, multinational corporations and intergovernmental organisations can increase opportunities for global collaboration.

**Proposition 23** The global research community can develop knowledge by following well-established norms and protocols to build an interconnected corpus of publications that offer evidence for falsifiable propositions.

**Proposition 24** Investment in diplomatic capital (that is, in institutions and norms designed to foster cross-cultural collaborations) can strengthen the capabilities of the global community to act together for the common good.

## The Wellbeing Fabric

Recall from the opening chapter that our approach to wellbeing capabilities is inspired by Solow's (1956) neoclassical growth model. Solow demonstrated how increasing the share of production devoted to physical capital investment can increase material living standards. Physical capital is *one* type of capital contributing to capabilities, and average material living standards is *one* measure of wellbeing outcomes. The wellbeing economics framework covers a wider range of capitals and wellbeing outcomes, but the fundamental insight is the same as Solow's: capabilities for wellbeing are expanded by investment in capital stocks.

Chapter 2 discussed an important debate about how a list of capabilities should be determined. Sen (2004) argues this determination should be made by members of each community exercising their own agency. Nussbaum (2003) argues that a list of central human capabilities can be developed to reflect the fundamental dignity of the human person, while being sensitive to cultural difference and open to change. Our approach avoids determining capabilities directly, but recognises *inputs* into capabilities (the different types of capital stock) and *outputs* of capabilities (wellbeing outcomes). This creates a matrix diagram that we term the wellbeing fabric, depicted in Fig. 9.2.[1]

| *Capital stocks expand the capabilities of persons to increase outcomes for wellbeing.* | | **Measures of Capital Stocks** | | | | | | |
|---|---|---|---|---|---|---|---|---|
| | | Human | Cultural | Social | Economic | Natural | Knowledge | Diplomatic |
| **Measures of Outcomes for Wellbeing** | Income and Wealth | | | | | | | |
| | Jobs and Earnings | | | | | | | |
| | Housing | | | | | | | |
| | Health Status | | | | | | | |
| | Work-Life Balance | | | | | | | |
| | Education and Skills | | | | | | | |
| | Social Connections | | | | | | | |
| | Civic Engagement and Governance | | | | | | | |
| | Environmental Quality | | | | | | | |
| | Personal Security | | | | | | | |
| | Subjective Wellbeing | | | | | | | |

**Fig. 9.2** Wellbeing fabric of capital stocks and outcomes for wellbeing. (Source: Constructed from OECD (2013, Fig. 1.2, p. 21, reproduced in Fig. 2.3 of this book) and from Table 1.1)

The rows in the diagram contain measures of outcomes for wellbeing taken from the OECD's (2013) wellbeing conceptual framework, which was designed to reflect elements of Sen's capabilities approach (OECD 2017, p. 23). That list identifies 10 measures of objective wellbeing and adds subjective wellbeing as an 11th measure (see Fig. 2.3 of Chap. 2). These measures provide a reasonable structure for monitoring the changes over time in wellbeing outcomes from capabilities. Capabilities are developed by drawing on capital investment. The columns of Fig. 9.2 therefore measure each of the seven types of capital stock identified in the framework, originally listed in Table 1.1.

The following three sections illustrate how this wellbeing fabric can be used.

## Individuals, Households and Families

The emphasis throughout this book has been on "persons leading the kinds of lives they value, and have reason to value" (Sen 1999, p. 18). Persons are members of households and families, and critical choices at key moments are often made with wider family involvement, influenced by cultural norms that are transformed and passed down through the generations (see, e.g., Buunk et al. 2010; Shockley et al. 2017). This section therefore considers individuals, households and families taken together.

The process of determining the kinds of lives we value, and have reason to value, is dynamic and conflicted. Values are continuously negotiated in a person's relations with others (White 2017). This is experienced most intensely within households and families, although influenced by wider social and cultural connections. The wellbeing economics framework has little to say about that process, but the wellbeing fabric is a tool for considering the range of inputs into, and outcomes from, the capabilities that people need to live their chosen lives.

The connection between the warp and weft of the wellbeing fabric is recorded in its first cell: capital stocks expand the capabilities of persons to increase outcomes for wellbeing. To illustrate, consider *Education and Skills*, which is a wellbeing outcome from capabilities that develop over a person's lifetime from an early age. During the person's school years, that development depends on the quality of seven types of capital that schools provide:

- Human capital, in the form of diversely skilled teachers and the school managers
- Cultural capital, in the form of education experiences that respect and support expression of cultural values and practices

- Social capital, in the form of norms and networks within the school that support collaboration and develop skills for future collaborations in wider society
- Economic capital, in the form of purpose built buildings, classrooms and equipment that support effective learning
- Natural capital, in the form of sports grounds, field trips and a safe environment at school (e.g., clean air)
- Knowledge capital, in the form of world-class best-practices for learning that are embedded in the school's teaching
- Diplomatic capital, in the form of opportunities to learn skills (including foreign languages) needed to engage in global initiatives to improve wellbeing

It is easy to write similar bullet points describing how each of the outcomes in the wellbeing fabric depends on access to the seven types of capital stock. The result is a tool for understanding causes of low wellbeing and for identifying potential solutions.

Using the rows of Fig. 9.2, for example, it is possible to determine which of the measures reflect low levels of outcomes for wellbeing in a group relative to the rest of the population. There is likely to be more than one. Poor housing, for example, typically leads to poor health. Poor health typically leads to poor education and skills, which typically lead to poor jobs and earnings. Poor jobs and earnings typically lead back to poor housing, creating a negative spiral of reduced wellbeing.

Using the columns of Fig. 9.2, it is then possible to investigate both the extent and the quality of each type of the seven capital stocks made available to a group with low wellbeing. Poor outcomes for education and skills, for example, may be due to the low quality of one or more of the capital stocks. Similarly, a region might be struggling with high levels of unemployment compared to the national average. The analysis might conclude that a contributing factor is reduced access to quality economic capital due to deindustrialisation (Tregenna 2009; van Neuss 2018).

To give another important illustration, recall the personal security data in Chap. 3. Figure 3.3 showed that UK women are much more likely than men to report intimate violence since the age of 16, with the likelihood being greater than two to one for partner abuse, and greater than five to one for sexual assault. The wellbeing fabric invites an analysis of how this female vulnerability might be affected by gender inequality in access to the seven capital stocks, resulting in women, on average, having fewer economic opportunities than male peers (Aizer 2010).

To address this, action is required to ensure women have equal access to quality human capital from an early age through to adulthood, to be able to attain the same level of education and skills as men. Action is required to ensure women have equal access to social capital, and so can make social connections with dominant networks. Action is required to ensure women have equal access to economic capital in firms, and so can access the same quality jobs and earnings. Action is required to ensure women have equal access to diplomatic capital, and so are able to participate equally with men in civic engagement and governance.

These examples illustrate that individuals or households acting in isolation may have little power for improving access to capital stocks in the face of powerful economic and social trends. Progress often requires collaboration on a wider and larger scale, as discussed in the following section.

## Civil Society, Market Firms and Local Government

Wellbeing is enhanced by bringing together different types of capital to create capabilities. An individual, household or family may be able to do this on a small scale, but capabilities are usually expanded by specialist organisations, including institutions of civil society (Proposition 10), firms in the market economy (Proposition 14) and initiatives of local and central government (Propositions 16, 17, 19 and 21). Persons and households then use the goods and services provided by these organisations to enhance wellbeing outcomes according to their own values.

Consider again the example of developing education and skills during a person's school years. Some families provide home schooling within their own households (Kraftl 2012), but more typically the work of bringing together human, cultural, social, economic, natural, knowledge and diplomatic capital for education is the responsibility of specialist institutions—that is, schools—created for this purpose.

That example can be generalised into a description of how organisations contribute to wellbeing. An organisation identifies goods or services it can provide to increase the capabilities for wellbeing of individuals, households and families. The organisation then brings together the different types of capital needed to create the capability to produce and deliver those goods or services. The nature of the organisation—whether it is an institution of civil society, a firm in the market economy or an initiative of local government—depends largely on the characteristics of the goods or services.

Civil society institutions thrive when goods or services rely on the time and financial donations of volunteers who are motivated by the pursuit of common interests and shared values (see Chap. 4). As stated in Proposition 10, members of these institutions access enhanced capabilities *through participation*. This includes collective action in solidarity with social peers. Throughout history, for example, women have come together in organised campaigns for equality with men in the private and public sphere.

Another example of collective action reliant on member participation is the trade union movement. This civil society institution has a long tradition in the United Kingdom (Thompson 1963; Oswald 1985; Aldcroft and Oliver 2017), but has declined over the last three decades. Figure 9.3 shows UK trade union membership as a percentage of employed and working-age populations since 1960. These series peaked around 1980 and have fallen steadily since then. This is likely to have had consequences for pay and conditions in some industries, including rewards for skilled work and the protection of living wages.

Many goods and services are provided by firms in the market economy, at least to those who can afford to purchase them. As discussed in Chap. 5, there

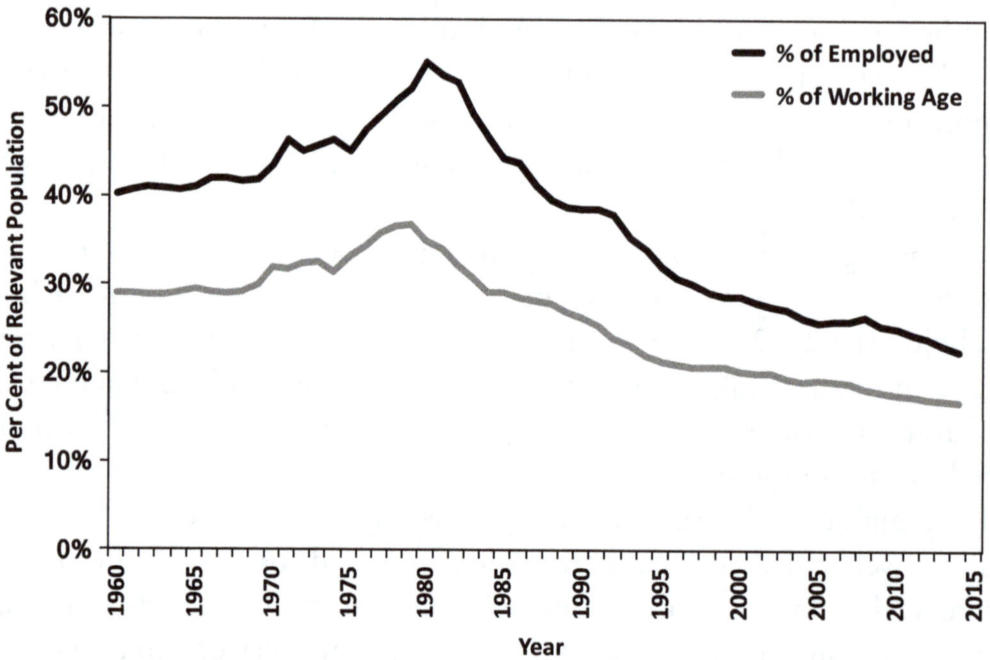


**Fig. 9.3** Trade union membership, percentage of employed and working-age populations, United Kingdom, 1960–2014. (Source: Department for Business, Energy & Industrial Strategy, Trade Union Statistics, and OECD, Employment and Labour Market Statistics)

is a well-established *capability theory of firms* in the economics literature (Teece 2017a, b). Proposition 14 summarises the key insight: Firms operating in the market economy combine different types of capital to maintain specialist capabilities for supplying goods and services valued by their customers. As discussed in Chap. 2, the value of a good or service in the market economy is founded on the contribution it makes to the benefits from time-use choices of persons creating the kinds of lives they value. Hence, firms are rewarded for delivering value.

Some types of goods and services are not supplied efficiently in the market economy. Proposition 16 elaborates that good government has distinctive capabilities to ensure goods and services that involve externalities, as well as economic public goods, are provided for wellbeing. Discussion around that proposition explained that if a public sector initiative can be greatly improved by local residents actively participating in its design or implementation, then this is a reason for the initiative to be overseen by local rather than central government (Lyons 2007, par. 2.8).

A second way in which local government contributes to enhanced capabilities is through co-production of regional development. This is summarised in Proposition 17: local government, sharing leadership with other actors in their communities, can develop and sustain regional capabilities for wellbeing through integrated investment in different types of capital. This role is distinctive because it does not involve the local government supplying goods and services; rather, the aim is to co-produce integrated strategies with other actors (including central government agencies) in which coordinated actions by various stakeholders can enhance capabilities for wellbeing (Ostrom 2010). Figure 9.4 presents a flowchart of how this can be achieved in practice. It comes from a diagram first presented in Saunders and Dalziel (2004), but developed further using the ideas behind the columns and rows of the wellbeing fabric in Fig. 9.2.

On the left-hand side of Fig. 9.4, an analysis is made of the available stocks of different forms of capital in the region and trends over time. On the right-hand side, processes are implemented to obtain the views of residents on what outcomes are valued for wellbeing (including consultation with institutions of civil society), alongside a dialogue with the business sector for insights on how to relax key constraints on promoting wellbeing. A third stream of work reviews the provision of public services to identify gaps and opportunities for enhancing capabilities.

This allows gaps and opportunities in regional capabilities to be identified, which provides a foundation for co-produced strategies to fill the gaps and take

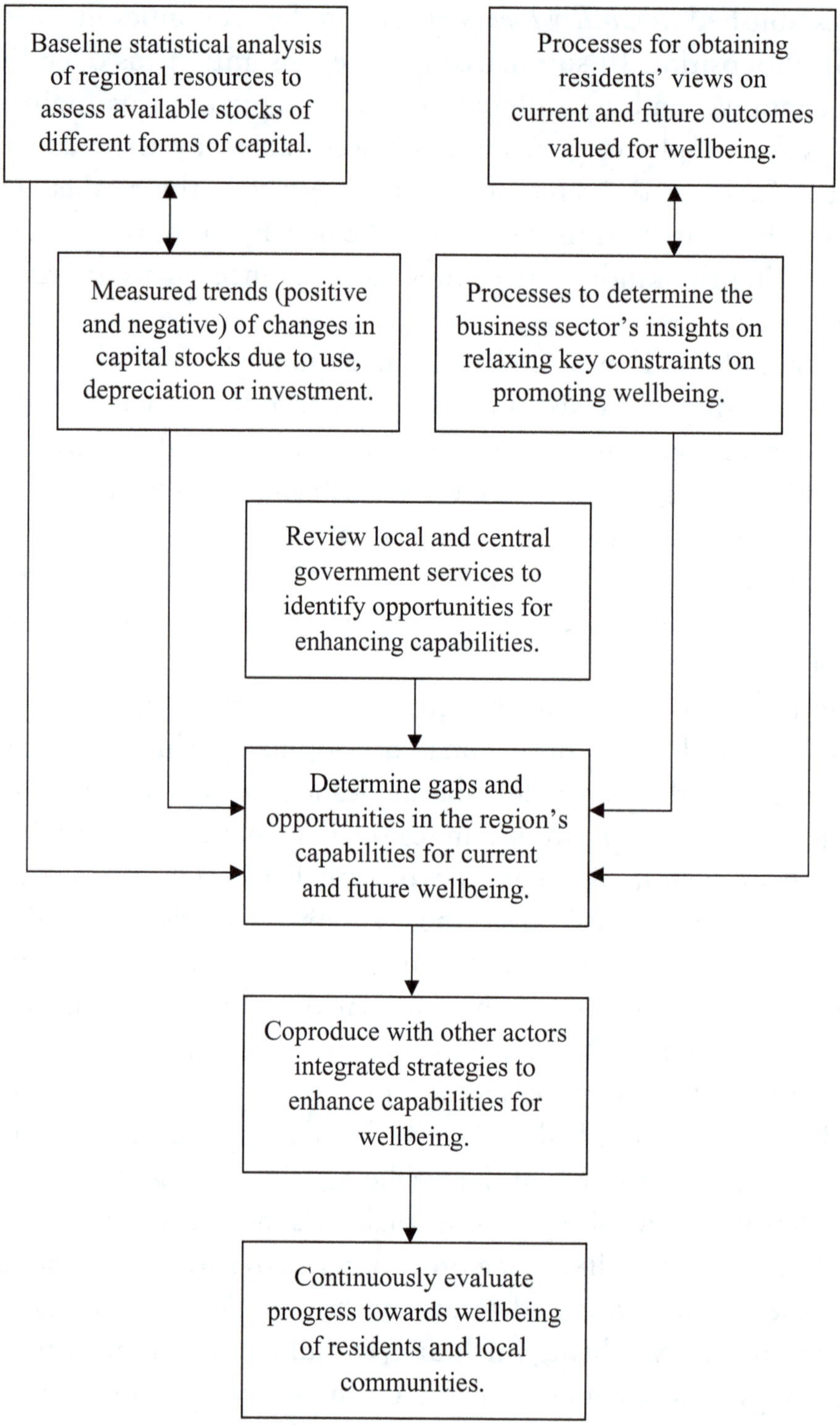


**Fig. 9.4** Framework for local government action. (Source: Developed from Saunders and Dalziel (2004, Fig. 1, p. 364))

advantage of the opportunities. The final step is to evaluate progress towards the strategy's goals.

## The Nation State

In many respects, the Nation State is simply a higher level of government operating at a larger scale than local government. Proposition 16 applies: the state has distinctive capabilities at the national level in ensuring access to goods and services that involve externalities, as well as economic public goods. Chap. 7 emphasised the state's role, including through its civil service, in contributing to enhanced wellbeing by fostering the growth and use of knowledge (Propositions 20 and 21).

The role of the state in addressing market failures such as externalities, economic public goods, monopolies and imperfect information is an important function. Another is to act as wise custodian of the market economy and welfare state within its borders (Proposition 19).

Recall from Chap. 7 that for most of the nineteenth and early twentieth centuries, public policy was disposed towards "individualism and laissez-faire" (Keynes 1926, p. 272). That disposition was overturned when Keynes (1936) demonstrated that an economy will move to an equilibrium level of production that, under certain circumstances, can be influenced by the level of government spending. More than 80 years later, it is perhaps difficult to appreciate the radical shift represented by this insight. It implies a world of multiple equilibria, creating the possibility that the Nation State, acting as custodian of the market economy and welfare state, can aim to coordinate actions that will move the country towards an equilibrium that supports better wellbeing outcomes.[2]

This possibility can be illustrated by combining analyses in Chaps. 2 and 5. Chap. 2 explained how personal skills are developed through a person discovering individual abilities, disciplining those abilities through education and displaying the disciplined abilities in contributions to wellbeing, including in employment (see Proposition 5). That model of personal skills is reproduced here in the upper diagram of Fig. 9.5.

In Chap. 5, Proposition 14 drew on the capability theory of the firm to state that firms combine different types of capital to maintain specialist capabilities for supplying goods and services valued by their customers. This was represented in Fig. 5.1, highlighting knowledge capital because of its centrality in the dynamic capabilities of an enterprise. That representation is reproduced in the lower diagram of Fig. 9.5.

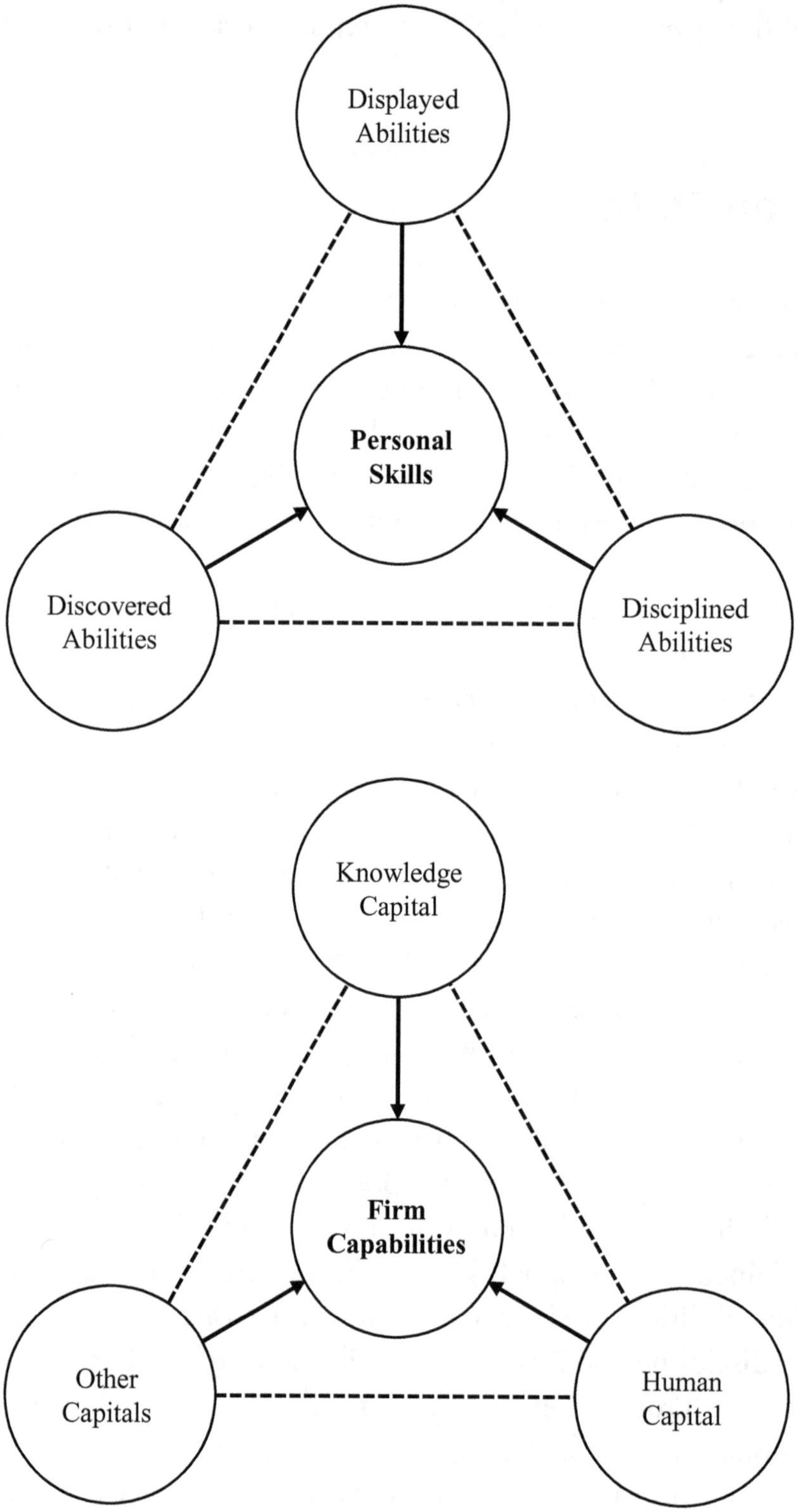


**Fig. 9.5** Personal skills and firm capabilities. (Source: Figs. 2.2 and 5.1)

Links between the upper and lower diagrams in Fig. 9.5 lead to two observations. First, the human capital drawn upon by a firm to contribute to its specialist capabilities (in the lower diagram) is the personal skills depicted at the centre of the upper diagram. Second, in this context of employment, the person's displayed abilities (in the upper diagram) contribute to the firm's capabilities at the centre of the lower diagram.

Figure 9.6 demonstrates these linkages, integrating the two parts of the previous figure into a single diagram.[3] It shows pictorially that firms need skilled persons to sustain capabilities, and persons need to contribute to firm capabili-

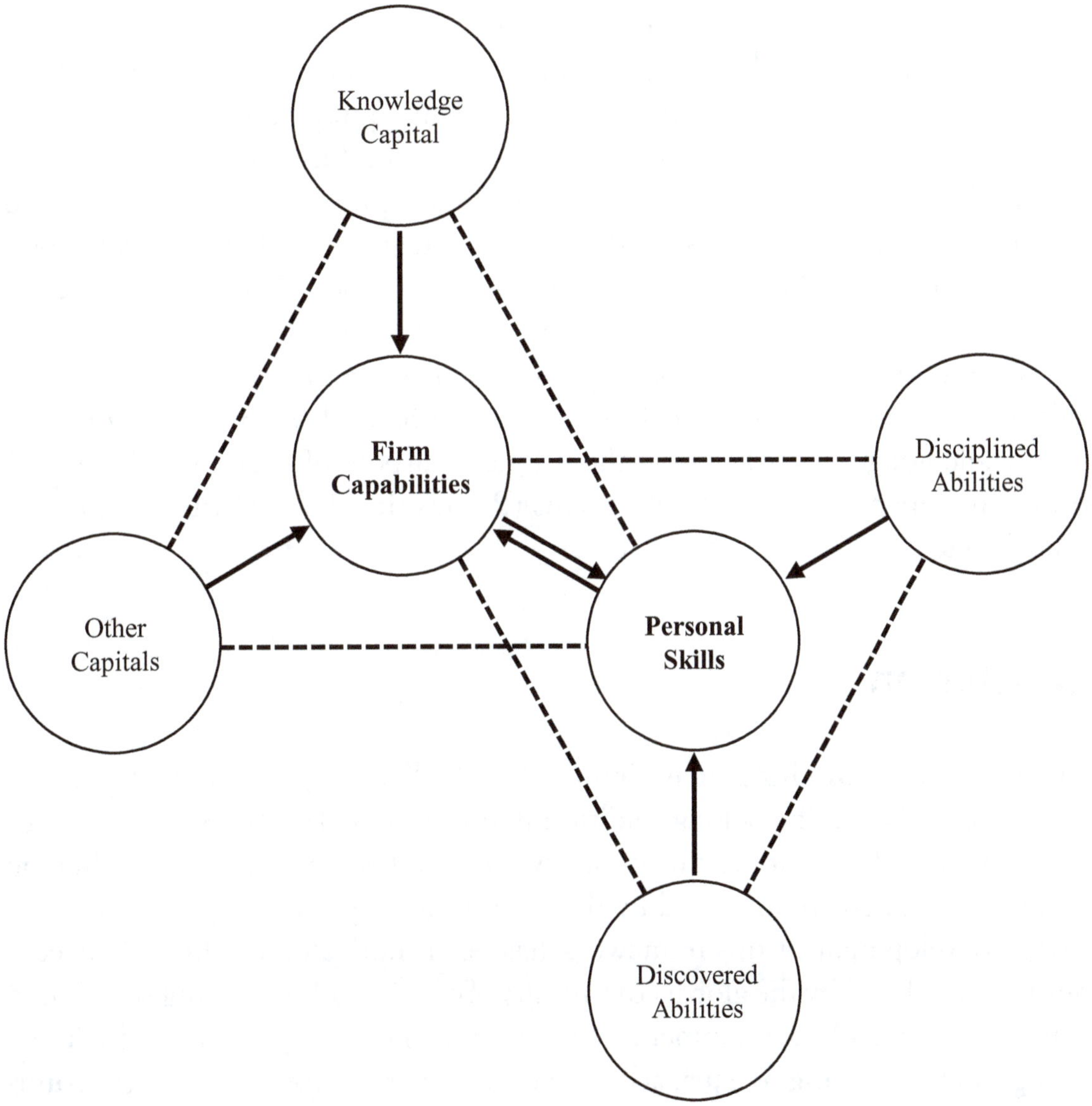


**Fig. 9.6** Integration of personal skills and firm capabilities. (Source: Integration of the two diagrams in Fig. 9.5)

ties to earn an economic reward for their investment in human capital. Personal skills and firm capabilities are reliant on each other. Thus, it is possible to imagine scenarios in which an industry settles on an equilibrium that involves low skills with weak capabilities, and other scenarios in which the equilibrium involves high skills and strong capabilities.

Public policy might therefore aim to move industry towards the high skill and strong capabilities equilibrium. The coordination problem revealed in Fig. 9.6 is that there is no direct link between the *knowledge capital* contributing to firm capabilities and the *disciplined abilities* contributing to personal skills. Consequently, to achieve an equilibrium characterised by firms with strong capabilities and employees with high skills, the state can construct a *skill ecosystem* that aims to match the evolving knowledge capital of firms with the evolving human capital developed in education institutions.[4] As stated by UKCES (2009, p. 8): "There is little that is more important than equipping ourselves with the skills we need, for the jobs we need, for the successful businesses of tomorrow."

The above example considers just two types of capital (knowledge capital and human capital), but illustrates the difficulty of integrating policies to deliver better outcomes for wellbeing. The wellbeing fabric in Fig. 9.2 includes 7 types of capital and lists 11 outcomes for wellbeing. The task of integrating public policies to support investment in each type of capital, and ensuring that residents are able to access quality capital stocks to produce enhanced wellbeing outcomes, is very challenging. Nevertheless, if the primary purpose of economics is to contribute to enhanced wellbeing of persons (Proposition 1), then these challenges must be faced.

## Conclusion

Chapter 1 began by citing Adam Smith's (1776) *Wealth of Nations* to argue that a focus on wellbeing has a long tradition in economics. This book is a contribution to that tradition. It has drawn on a wide literature to construct a wellbeing economics framework informed by the capabilities approach to prosperity.

The development of this framework has been motivated by the serious economic issues faced by the global community. These include achieving the United Nations' sustainable development goals, mitigating the urgent risks of climate change and addressing unequal access to economic resources within every country and between countries. It is no longer credible to presume that economic growth is the answer; indeed, current patterns of production growth have contributed to all of these problems.

The wellbeing economics framework is a tool not only for decision-makers in local and national governments, but also for individuals, households and families, institutions of civil society and firms in the market economy. It provides an integrated approach for actions to expand the capabilities of persons to lead the kinds of lives they value, and have reason to value.

## Notes

1. This term "wellbeing fabric" was first used in Dalziel et al. (2006, Table 2, p. 277) and Dalziel et al. (2009, Fig. 3, p. 15).
2. A recent discussion of the modelling difficulties created by multiple equilibria in a New Keynesian context is provided by Cochrane (2017).
3. Similar figures can be found in Dalziel (2015, 2017). The novel feature of this version is that it incorporates the capability theory of the firm.
4. See, for example, Crouch et al. (1999), Finegold (1999), Buchanan and Jakubauskas (2010), Buchanan et al. (2017) and Dalziel (2017).

## References

Aizer, Anna. 2010. The Gender Wage Gap and Domestic Violence. *American Economic Review* 100 (4): 1847–1859.

Aldcroft, Derek H., and Michael J. Oliver. 2017. *Trade Unions and the Economy: 1870–2000*. London: Routledge.

Buchanan, John, and Michelle Jakubauskas. 2010. The Political Economy of Work and Skill in Australia: Insights from Recent Applied Research. In *Beyond Skill*, ed. Jane Bryson, 32–57. London: Palgrave Macmillan.

Buchanan, John, David Finegold, Ken Mayhew, and Chris Warhurst. 2017. Skills and Training: Multiple Targets, Shifting Terrain. In *The Oxford Handbook of Skills and Training*, ed. John Buchanan, David Finegold, Ken Mayhew, and Chris Warhurst, 1–14. Oxford: Oxford University Press.

Buunk, Abraham P., Justin H. Park, and Lesley A. Duncan. 2010. Cultural Variation in Parental Influence on Mate Choice. *Cross-Cultural Research* 44 (1): 23–40.

Cameron, Rt. Hon. David. 2010. PM Speech on Wellbeing. A Transcript of a Speech Given by the Prime Minister on 25 November 2010. https://www.gov.uk/ government/speeches/pm-speech-on-wellbeing.

Cochrane, John H. 2017. The New-Keynesian Liquidity Trap. *Journal of Monetary Economics* 92 (December): 47–63.

Crouch, Colin, David Finegold, and Mari Sako. 1999. *Are Skills the Answer?* Oxford: Oxford University Press.

Dalziel, Paul. 2015. Regional Skill Ecosystems to Assist Young People Making Education Employment Linkages in Transition from School to Work. *Local Economy* 30 (1): 53–66.

———. 2017. Education and Qualifications as Skills. In *The Oxford Handbook of Skills and Training*, ed. John Buchanan, David Finegold, Ken Mayhew, and Chris Warhurst, 143–160. Oxford: Oxford University Press.

Dalziel, Paul, Hirini Matunga, and Caroline Saunders. 2006. Cultural Well-Being and Local Government: Lessons from New Zealand. *Australasian Journal of Regional Studies* 12 (3): 267–280.

Dalziel, Paul and Caroline Saunders with Rosie Fyfe and Bronwyn Newton. 2009. Sustainable Development and Cultural Capital. *Official Statistics Research Series* 5. Available at http://hdl.handle.net/10182/2427.

Finegold, David. 1999. Creating Self-sustaining, Highskill Ecosystems. *Oxford Review of Economic Policy* 15 (1): 60–81.

IPCC. 2015. *Climate Change 2014: Synthesis Report*. Contribution of Working Groups I, II and III to the Fifth Assessment Report of the Intergovernmental Panel on Climate Change. Geneva: Intergovernmental Panel on Climate Change.

Jackson, Tim. 2017. *Prosperity without Growth: Foundations for the Economy of Tomorrow*. 2nd ed. Abingdon/New York: Routledge.

Keynes, John Maynard. 1926. The End of Laissez-Faire. Pamphlet Published by the Hogarth Press, Reprinted in and Cited from Donald Moggridge, Ed. *The Collected Writings of John Maynard Keynes, Volume IX: Essays in Persuasion*. London: Macmillan for the Royal Economic Society, 1972, pp. 272–294.

———. 1936. *The General Theory of Employment, Interest and Money*, Reprinted in and Cited from Donald Moggridge, Ed. *The Collected Writings of John Maynard Keynes, Volume VII: The General Theory*. London: Macmillan for the Royal Economic Society, 1973.

Kraftl, Peter. 2012. Towards Geographies of 'Alternative' Education: A Case Study of UK Home Schooling Families. *Transactions of the Institute of British Geographers* 38 (3): 436–450.

Lyons, Sir Michael. 2007. *Place-shaping: A Shared Ambition for the Future of Local Government*. London: The Stationery Office.

Nussbaum, Martha C. 2000. *Women and Human Development: The Capabilities Approach*. Cambridge: Cambridge University Press.

———. 2003. Capabilities as Fundamental Entitlements: Sen and Social Justice. *Feminist Economics* 9 (2–3): 33–59.

———. 2011. *Creating Capabilities: The Human Development Approach*. Cambridge, MA: Belknap Press.

OECD. 2013. *How's Life? 2013: Measuring Well-being*. Paris: OECD Publishing https://doi.org/10.1787/9789264201392-en.

———. 2017. *How's Life? 2017: Measuring Well-being*. Paris: OECD Publishing https://doi.org/10.1787/how_life-2017-en.

Ostrom, Elinor. 2010. Beyond Markets and States: Polycentric Governance of Complex Economic Systems. *American Economic Review* 100 (3): 641–672.

Oswald, Andrew J. 1985. The Economic Theory of Trade Unions: An Introductory Survey. *Scandinavian Journal of Economics* 87 (2): 160–193.

Saunders, Caroline, and Paul Dalziel. 2004. Economic Well-being in Regional Economic Development. *Australasian Journal of Regional Studies* 10 (3): 355–366.

Sen, Amartya. 1983. Development: Which Way Now? Presidential Address of the Development Studies Association. *Economic Journal* 93 (December): 745–762.

———. 1999. *Development as Freedom*. Oxford: Oxford University Press.

———. 2004. Capabilities, Lists, and Public Reason: Continuing the Conversation. *Feminist Economics* 10 (3): 77–80.

Shockley, Kristen M., Jill Douek, Christine R. Smith, P. Yu Peter, Soner Dumani, and Kimberly A. French. 2017. Cross-cultural Work and Family Research: A Review of the Literature. *Journal of Vocational Behavior* 101: 1–20.

Smith, Adam. 1776. *An Enquiry into the Nature and Causes of the Wealth of Nations*, 2 volumes, University Paperbacks edition, ed. Edwin Cannan. London: Methuen.

Solow, Robert M. 1956. A Contribution to the Theory of Economic Growth. *Quarterly Journal of Economics* 70 (1): 65–94.

Stiglitz, Joseph, Amartya Sen, and Jean-Paul Fitoussi. 2009. *Report by the Commission on the Measurement of Economic Performance and Social Progress*. https://www.insee.fr/en/information/2662494. Accessed 16 July 2017.

Teece, David J. 2017a. Towards a Capability Theory of (Innovating) Firms: Implications for Management and Policy. *Cambridge. Journal of Economics* 41 (3): 693–720.

———. 2017b. A Capability Theory of the Firm: An Economics and (Strategic) Management Perspective. *New Zealand Economic Papers,* forthcoming, https://doi.org/10.1080/00779954.2017.1371208.

Thompson, E.P. 1963. *The Making of the English Working Class*. London: Victor Gollancz.

Tregenna, Fiona. 2009. Characterising Deindustrialisation: An Analysis of Changes in Manufacturing Employment and Output Internationally. *Cambridge Journal of Economics* 33 (3): 433–466.

UKCES. 2009. *Towards Ambition 2020: Skills, Jobs, Growth*. London: UK Commission for Employment and Skills.

van Neuss, Leif. 2018. Globalization and Deindustrialization in Advanced Countries. *Structural Change and Economic Dynamics*. Forthcoming, Available Online at https://doi.org/10.1016/j.strueco.2018.02.002.

White, Sarah C. 2017. Relational Wellbeing: Re-centring the Politics of Happiness, Policy and the Self. *Policy & Politics* 45 (2): 121–136.

# Index[1]



[1] Note: Page numbers followed by 'n' refer to notes.


P. Dalziel et al., *Wellbeing Economics*, Wellbeing in Politics and Policy,
https://doi.org/10.1007/978-3-319-93194-4

www.ingramcontent.com/pod-product-compliance
Lightning Source LLC
LaVergne TN
LVHW082232200926
848484LV00008B/2343